COLIN THUBRON

Journey into Cyprus

VINTAGE BOOKS
London

Published by Vintage 2012

4 6 8 10 9 7 5 3

First published in Great Britain in 1975 by
William Heinemann
First published in paperback in 1986 by Penguin Books

Vintage
Random House, 20 Vauxhall Bridge Road,
London SW1V 2SA

www.vintage-books.co.uk

Addresses for companies within The Random House Group
Limited can be found at: www.randomhouse.co.uk/offices.htm

The Random House Group Limited Reg. No. 954009

A CIP catalogue record for this book
is available from the British Library

ISBN 9780099570257

Printed and bound in Great Britain by Clays Ltd, St Ives plc

This journey, dear Noo-Noo, is dedicated to you,
remembering your love.

Contents

Preface

This six-hundred-mile walk through Cyprus in the spring and summer of 1972 traversed an island which is now no longer recognizable. The world which it depicts – a mosaic of Greek and Turkish villages interknit – has seemingly gone for ever, and such a journey, wandering at will among the two communities, is now impossible.

Since the Turkish invasion of 1974, the population has drastically polarized. The Greek Cypriots – some eighty per cent of the inhabitants – have crowded into the southern part of the island, while the Turkish Cypriots occupy the north. The line which divides them runs west from old Famagusta through Nicosia to the Bay of Morphou, reserving to the Turks the rich Mesaoria plain and the long spine of coastal mountains, while leaving the Greeks their ancient stronghold of the Troodos Mountains and the southern cities of Limassol, Larnaca and Paphos.

It is an unhappy and unequal division, but after the atrocities of recent years these two peoples, whatever their political agreement, will live apart. Already the two halves of the island are stamped with their personalities.

The north has fallen into neglect, the south into over-exploitation.

The nervous cohabitation which I witnessed in 1972 was, I now realize, the island's halcyon time – and this is the record of a country which will not return.

C.G.D.T.
London, 1985

Acknowledgments

Once again I am indebted to Rae Sebley for her help with the manuscript.

I gratefully acknowledge assistance from the Arts Council of Great Britain. I also wish to thank Mr T. G. Ionides of the Cyprus High Commission; and Cyprus Airways for generously allowing me the use of their flights between London and Nicosia.

Like many writers on Cyprus, I am in debt to the great compendiary of Claude Delaval Cobham, *Excerpta Cypria*, and to the standard history of Sir George Hill.

Not least I am grateful to the people of Cyprus themselves – the farmers, monks and shepherds who will not read this book: for their kindness to the stranger.

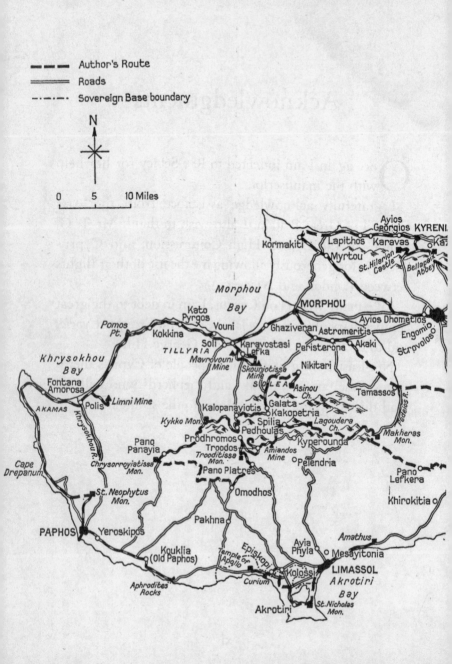

CHAPTER ONE
·········
The Goddess from the Sea

As the seas flow eastward into one another – Adriatic, Ionian, Aegean – and Europe merges with Asia, the past leaves itself visibly on the landscape. The soil of the Levant is eroded to its shoreline where forests were felled for ancient fleets, and villages remain on inland hilltops where they were driven by pirates. These half Asiatic lands, dazzled into harshness, elicit awe and a strange excitement. Their beauty is of contour and light. The olive, the rock, an arc of blue – their effect is made with magic economy, and to them a man is always, inexplicably, returning, as if their very starkness were a lure.

A March evening brought back this hard affection, on a Cyprus hillside where no colour intimated spring. Below me the land lay in calm. Half the ridges were eroded to glittering bones, and the tracks showed white and perman-ent in its valleys. Above the grain- and fruit-bearing plains this toughness becomes the country's core – an earth durable rather than resilient, whose rock is the despair of farmers. Too much coveted, trodden by generations of peasants and soldiers, its dust is thick enough with stones to break the back of any plough or man.

Over the hill where we stood, the remains of the

1

Neolithic town of Khirokitia lay in and out of scrub. The paling light lent the walls a variegated softness which was not their own.

'You see, it's like I told you.' The man sank his grizzled head on his hands. 'Nothing. Just stones.' And it is true, these ruins are little more than the foundations of walls built with rocks carried from the winter stream eight thousand years before. But they mark a beginning. Laid down unhewn for streets and houses, they once enclosed the island's earliest men, and my own journey, which is to be a voyage through time as well as space, begins in this archaic twilight.

The old man had attached himself to me out of curiosity. 'You should go to Salamis,' he muttered. 'There are bigger stones there. Or try the castles round Kyrenia. Now there's something! They grow out of the mountains like horns.'

I promised I would see them, Salamis too and all those coasts, and to walk along the mountains.

'Walk!' he shouted – among the country people it is not rude to shout – 'You can't walk here!' His bloodshot eyes bulged in dismay. 'Do you know anything about this country? You won't last a minute! The Turks will think you a spy. Any sentry could skewer you on the spot!' Then he lowered his voice and said in a tone almost of comfort: 'In fact I expect they'll just throw you into prison. But of course nobody will know where you've gone. You'll just stay there for years . . .' He made a chewing motion with his mouth and revolved his hands. 'Years and years and years . . .'

I grinned into this stubborn face, which looked back

teasingly out of its whiskers. He was genuinely concerned for me and had clapped a horny hand on my knee to prevent my leaving him. But at this time, when there was hostility between Greek Cypriot factions as well as against the Turkish minority, I considered myself safer than him. And in a year, after Turkish invasion and civil war, I was proved right.

'But there are things more fearful than the Turks,' he said. 'Grivas is training guerrillas in the Troodos Mountains. Did you know that?'

Yes, I had heard that. In these last months of his life, Grivas was still trying to impose his ideal of ENOSIS, Cypriot union with Greece. But if Grivas could escape a hundred thousand British soldiers in the mountains for six years, he would surely elude me?

'But what if *you* can't elude *him*? He eats Englishmen for dinner. He *kebabs* them. They just vanish.' For all the man's moustache and furious eyes, something was winking under the face. He touched my elbow and added in a whisper, as if the ghosts of Neolithic men might overhear him: 'Seriously, the Greeks are all right. We are a hospitable, civilized people. But the Turks – may the Devil wipe his nose on them! – never trust a Moslem.'

I looked back at him with the lethargy of someone who has found no nation much crueller than the rest. To experience a land as varied as Cyprus, I wanted to walk. To go through a country which transforms itself valley by valley, from whose mountains the land on one side may throw up a commotion of limestone hills, on the other spread a corn-softened plain, an island which threads between centuries in a perpetual astonishment of architecture – to walk here is only reasonable, if a person has time. And I had four months of spring and early summer. To go on foot was to entrust myself to the people, a gesture of confidence, and to approach the land as all earlier generations had known it, returning it to its old proportions.

'But in four months you could walk to America!' the man grumbled. 'Or somewhere proper. You could earn . . .' And while I told him where I intended to go, he smiled at me with a mocking sympathy. I did not know, and nor did he, that the land would soon have grown too dangerous for such journeys and that mine would be the last, perhaps for decades.

By coast and mountain it would cover six hundred miles. Where I would sleep I did not know, but trusted to peasant hospitality and the mildness of spring nights, preferring to lie under the stars rather than be burdened all day by carrying a tent on my back.

My first objective was the north-west shores, straddled by beleagured Turkish villages which made walking precarious. Beyond, I planned to skirt the foot of the Troodos Mountains, where the copper mines of Phoenicians and Romans can be traced in their workers' graves and in mineshafts driven to terrible depths, and from here I would circle into the ranges above, which lift more than six thousand feet and nurture tiny Byzantine churches whose frescoes are among the most perfect which remain. These mountain tracks, if one chooses well, go wild and empty. The valley-heads are crowned by monasteries where the monks are so few that they can scarcely muster voices enough for the

4

Liturgy. Even in spring the heights freeze at night and I would have to rely for shelter on the farmers and goatherds with whom my way of travelling would link me.

After Easter spent among the mountain Christians, I would descend to Limassol and explore ancient Amathus under the sea. On either side the coasts are resonant with classical names – Paphos and Curium, which passed in mediaeval times to the Knights Templar and Hospitaller, Salamis whose chariot-burials are like an epic from Homer; with biblical Chittim and Hala Sultan by the salt lakes. Northward, I would reach the Maronite villages and tramp along the Kyrenia Mountains through Bellapaix abbey and the eyries of Crusader kings, and at last cross south again to the ruined jewel of Famagusta and up the Karpas peninsula, where the land ends.

By this time the old man had lost interest in my fairy tale, and had sat down sleepily on a rock; so I wandered about the ruins alone. Out of the cleft of the river the town's street ascended in rubble, surrounded by the foundations of beehive dwellings. All the way along it the circles and broken arcs of these tholoi showed traces of steps and doorways, or the curve of a passage. In them their excavators found obsidian arrow-heads, amulets of mother-of-pearl, and violin-shaped figurines so faintly carved that they seem to be no more than expressions in the stone. Obsidian speaks of trade with Asia Minor, which may have been the first home of these men, and flint sickle blades tell that they were farmers as well as hunters. Under their beehive roofs they sat on stone seats or reclined along mud platforms, lit by a single shaft of sunlight falling through a niche window. Beneath the floors the dead lay with their knees drawn up to their chins like foetuses, sometimes one upon another in a succession of burials, all facing the East – the source of light; and although they were interred with gifts, boulders were sometimes found crushed upon their chests to prevent them haunting.

But now the indecipherable corridors seemed to place these people infinitely far away. In their few brick walls only a faded line showed the clay between the brick, the one as soft as the other – a darker on a lighter grey. What they had thought or believed, squatting in those pools of light, was barely imaginable. The women whose primitive vanity put on necklaces of shells and carnelian – had they conceived anything beyond their walls? Perhaps the most potent answers are the conical stones and the female idol which were found buried with them – fertility symbols, perhaps, betraying a simple concern for the continuance of life, the mystery of a returning spring and the child-bearing powers of their own transient bodies.

'Have you discovered anything?' the old man shouted.

'No,' I said. 'Nothing.'

Yet all cultures have arisen out of this nothing, and the squat, broad-headed people who were found huddled beneath these floors are the infant Cyprus. So rich and complex is the island's history, so various the blood which it has mingled, that it is impossible accurately to trace its maturing. The country's pageant is that of other races: of western powers travelling eastward – Mycenaeans, Romans, Crusaders; and of eastern powers west – Egyptians, Phoenicians, Turks. So it is true that only these Neolithic stones can tell what was original to the people. No other culture absolutely expresses them, for afterwards they were absorbed or silenced by alien civilizations.

Yet it is precisely through such civilizations that the Cypriots were formed, and my own journey was in part to be a burrowing upwards through these alien strata, as through the layers of a rich and gigantic cake. In so short a time I would have to sacrifice balance to my own ideas of what was significant. Yet one of these – the recurrence in legend and belief of a goddess, a many-faced Aphrodite – would keep the link unbroken between Neolithic embryo and modern man.

But for such a journey – six hundred miles through one of the most fascinating islands in the world – a destination was partly an excuse. Travel is one of the most complex forms of self-indulgence, and ideally is undertaken for its own sake. At its goal it dies. Or that at least was how it seemed to me, wading up the river of Neolithic stone. The wall of one dwelling was so complete that an are of its ceiling survived, and on one of its steps it was possible to see, polished by hardened skin, the curve worn by the feet of those earliest men. I reached the summit of the ruins. Southward the slope eased into tree-softened inclines. Beyond the Nicosia–Limassol road grew the hard coastal ranges, with a calm sea between them, and to the north – in a strange, contrasting smoothness – volcanic hills folded on the sky.

The old man had stood up now and he too was picking among the ruins, although what he hoped to find I did not ask. The earliest settlement at Khirokitia came to an unexplained end about 5250 B.C. Either earthquake or abandonment left the dead still plunged in their mud graves and their house foundations undisturbed in overlapping rings, so that after almost eight thousand years archaeologists discovered with awe these first stone ripples broken on the pool of time.

I could not tell what had woken me, but lay shivering as if my sleeping-bag was made of paper, and staring at the silhouetted rocks: chunks of limestone cliff fallen into the waves. Then I saw the lights of the Paphos fishing boats in the dark, and heard the men's faint cries over the calm. Towards sunrise they passed near, pulling in nets floated by clumps of gourds tied together, then vanished westwards, the lamps still lit at their prows.

The day was breaking with a great stillness over the sea. The rocks rose on a hushed sky. Here, said the ancients, in this green-blue bay, Aphrodite was born from the foam. The child of Zeus by the nymph Dione, daughter of Air and Earth, she stepped out of the rock-encircled waters where the Graces covered her nakedness.

> *I will sing of stately Aphrodite*
>   *gold-crowned and beautiful,*
> *Whose dominion is the walled cities*
>   *of all sea-set Cyprus.*
> *There the moist breath of the Western wind*
>   *wafted her over the waves*
>   *of the loud-moaning sea . . .*[*]

But myth, of course, is never so simple as would seem, and from its earliest telling an ugly crack shows in this

[*] Homeric Hymn.

8

fantasy. It was common knowledge among the Greeks that before the Olympian gods ruled the world there had lived an older race of cosmic divinities. Of these the sky-god Uranus was the son of Mother Earth herself, and his son, the Titan Cronus, usurped his rule by castrating him.

Around these genitals, thrown into the sea, there spread a white foam, and from this grew up the goddess Aphrodite.

The rocks on the Paphos shore are sometimes surrounded by seaweed mingled with the bodies of minute crustaceans, which produce a brilliant foam. On days of storm, people have even imagined that the high waves contained some shape which they carried in to shore and which vanished on the headland. But the sea was now so still that I could not make out whether it contained the dead crustaceans, let alone a hint of this imagined Aphrodite. The sun had not yet risen, but its premonition picked out every fissure in the rocks. The water slopped and gurgled beneath them. I climbed the largest, and disturbed rock-pigeons which circled and moaned in surprise. The crevices showed flowering cistus, and weeds swayed to an invisible current below them.

For a while the sea retained its grey-blue shadow. It lay not uniform, but in faintly ruffled slopes and glassy plains. In just such a twilight calm perhaps, some priest or poet of an unknown time, watching with the eye of faith, saw the goddess in the crystal of the dawn, and touched this bay with his belief for ever.

Yet divinities, of course, are not born so simply. They stir in a dark of the mind, swelling like the rings of a tree-trunk, generation by generation. As far back as Neolithic

Khirokitia a female idol was found among the offerings to the dead, and it may not be haphazard that the graves of women, whose functions were so mysterious and vital, contained more gifts than those of men. By 3000 B.C. the prodigious breasts and child-bearing hips of the fertility goddess form figurines in many Cypriot tombs, and later the Mycenaeans carried their own idols from the west – bird-faced creatures with flared ears, who finger their breasts and suckle babies. Finally the Phoenicians brought their great earth-mother, whose cult absorbed all others. She was Aphrodite's closest ancestor. But her origins stretched back to Babylon and she did not come gracefully on the foam; instead she was cast up rude and barbaric on a tide of Phoenician immigration, with swollen nipples and nubile hips, and her rites were licentious.

Perhaps the birth of Aphrodite was not so much a myth as an explanation. Here, where Asia touched on Europe, she first began to be transformed – as in sculpture, so in thought – from a shapeless cosmic power to the creation of an imagining mind. It was not divinity which was being born, but man.

'Good morning, English! Sleeping in the sea?' Fishermen, clambering down to the coast with rods and sun-hats, bellowed their cheerful greetings, shattering the dawn. Already its glimmer had congealed into practical daylight. I got up and shook the sand from my hair. Westward, in the direction of Paphos, the pebbles and sand gave poor purchase for walking. Behind me the rocks had turned harsh, and lunged towards Egypt.

It was now, starting out, that I felt a vague apprehension. In eastern Mediterranean lands nobody goes on foot unless he must. To walk out of pleasure or curiosity is unimaginable. A man walks only because he is poor. The fishermen watched me, puzzled, and a shepherd on an inland ridge turned among his flock to shade his eyes. There was no hostility, and no understanding. They mentally shrugged their shoulders. In this deeply conservative land, I was an anomaly. Why should a man trudge between Limassol and Paphos when he can share a taxi for seven shillings? And what is so interesting about the land? The soil is a wrecker of hearts and bodies. It is for those who cannot escape it. Beauty is merely for tourists. Ruins are only stones. All life, all comfort, is in cities. So the countryman reasons, and bends to his work without singing.

After an hour's walking I was wryly sympathizing with this view. Unused to the weight of the rucksack, I stooped like a charcoalburner under his load. Somewhere in front of me was Old Paphos, once the greatest of Aphrodite's shrines, now shrivelled – if my map was to be believed – to a village called Kouklia. On my left the sea ran in a waveless flow before the wind. The maquis-covered slopes came down unimportantly to the shore, flattened here and there by winter rain. Only an easy promontary or a low ridge ever occupied the distance, so that my gaze dropped to the ground and discovered tiny flowers: orange vetchling and violets, with fretted blue anemones shining in grass among the trees. That afternoon I passed a farmhouse filled with the sound of lute and violin – a wedding party beginning. Hoopoes fluttered before me up the track to Kouklia.

For more than a thousand years the shrine of Aphrodite rose here in the grandeur and mystery of an aged cult, a temple-city of glowing limestone, its bloodless altars bathed in incense and flowers. Some said that Paphos was founded by Pygmalion the island king, who fell in love with a statue of the goddess and took it to his bed. Others claimed that the hero Cinyras sailed here from Asia Minor and himself became king of Cyprus and lover of Aphrodite. But the goddess grew jealous of his daughter Myrrha, more beautiful than she, and turned her into a myrrh tree – and from her trunk was born the infant Adonis who, in a new cycle of myth, himself courted Aphrodite and died an untimely death.

These legends – three generations in love with the Great Goddess – reveal a family of priest-kings, the Cinyrids, who were gods to their people and were the consorts of Aphrodite through temple prostitutes. On the death of their wives the kings married their own daughters, for the royal line descended through the queens, and their offspring, themselves gods and goddesses, would later ascend the throne and renew the pattern of worship and incest.

The goddess, of course, was older and more durable than these lover-kings, and in earlier times they were sacrificed to her. She was even identified with Queen Semiramis, and the tumuli scattered over Western Asia were said to be the graves of her lovers, buried alive.

The rites of Paphos involved sacred prostitution far into classical times. Herodotus records that parts of Cyprus maintained customs by which every woman had to give herself once to the service of Aphrodite by waiting in the temple until a stranger came to lie with her. 'Many of the rich women, who are too proud to mix with the rest, drive to the temple in covered carriages with a whole host of servants following behind, and there wait . . . Tall, handsome women soon manage to get home again, but the ugly ones stay a long time before they can fulfil the conditions which the law demands, some of them, indeed, as much as three or four years.'*

The Cypriot rites lacked both the harshness of the Asiatics and the austerity of the northern Greeks. Then as now, there are signs of mellowness in this island moored between Europe and Asia. The Semitic passions are tempered, the Greek pride blunted. It was said that no rain ever fell on the altars, although they stood in the open air. Flowers and fruit were the temple gifts, and blood sacrifice was accepted only once a year, when a flock of doves was thrown through the pyre's smoke, ascended, then fell suffocated into the flames: a minor barbarism for its day. Every spring, at the festival of Aphrodite and her lover Adonis, pilgrims landed from all parts of the ancient world and took the processional way to Paphos through groves whose lushness symbolized the fruitfulness of the goddess. The nearby village of Yeroskipos keeps this memory in its name, which means 'holy gardens', and many streams still tumble into its valley before wending seawards through reedy and desecrated pools.

But the mysteries of the *Aphrodisia* remain enigmatic. All that is left to us is a knowledge of some of the tokens used:

---

* Herodotus, *The Histories*. Trs. Aubrey de Sélincourt.

a miniature phallus, a gift of salt which symbolized the rising of Aphrodite from the waves, and a bearded figure of the goddess as deity of the moon, which was considered to be hermaphrodite and was worshipped by men and women in the dress of their opposite sex.

Over the centuries the numbers of votaries to the Great Goddess must have mounted into millions, and their statues – terracotta throngs of bearded men and jewelled women – stood in the sanctuaries as a perpetual prayer. In the temple's twilight their starved faces must have set up a barrage of supplication; but their eyes were soulless, shaped in shallow almonds, whose paint has worn away.

Almost all the pieces found at Paphos are broken; their fragments are like syllables from a forgotten sentence. Who, for instance, were the string-belted youths, the girl or goddess whose hair fell in three locks against her shoulders? What deity did the fragile face portray, whose coiffure rises like the crown of a Siamese Buddha?

The temple too was shattered to its roots. Now, even in twilight, it lay unenchanted. The earth thrust up fluted stumps where columns had been, and no wall stood higher than a half-rotted carob tree, which knocked its branches drily together. The courts and chambers described no coherent plan; Semitic or Mycenaean, even their style is in dispute. They evoked only a distant enigma, a feminine barbarism. I wandered back and forth under the diseased-looking tree, like a deaf man who can see the instruments playing but hears nothing.

As for the history of Paphos, it was strewn on all sides. The tombs dug in these mild valleys have been pilfered by robbers or archaeologists. But to the north, against the city walls, a Persian assault-mound was thrown up by the armies of Cyrus in 498 B.C. The tunnels which the Greeks drove beneath it are still there, with the niches for their lamps, and the timbers, which were fired to undermine the siege-engines, collapsed in heaps of carbonized wood and lime.

Paphos itself declined in the Roman age. A series of earthquakes shook the land over several centuries. After an earthquake in the reign of Theodosius, the temple was not rebuilt, and Paphos passed out of classical literature in the verse of Claudian, the last Roman poet, who described a palace of Venus built in precious stones on a hill sown with balsam – the vulgar mansion of a late Roman imagination.

The château of La Covocle, which stood on the outskirts of Kouklia, had once been a centre for the royal sugar estates of the Crusaders. The caretaker was a sad-faced man whose conversation was broken by the silences characteristic of those who, like himself, had suffered as prisoners-of-war. Men, perhaps, had forfeited his respect; but he spoke of the antiquities with devotion.

'A curious thing – a Roman villa was discovered almost on the temple area. Now what business had it there? I don't know.' He screwed up his eyes as we left the dusk of the castle for the light of the ruins. All the lines in his face ran together at these eyes. 'As for the temple, half the village – walls, streets, churches – is built of its stones.'

We walked between banks of crown daisies. Among them the Roman villa spread its mosaic pinks and blues, crackling with sunlight, and a church, long since decayed, traced a pygmy apse among the weeds.

'You see,' said the caretaker, whose name was Giorgos (if a Cypriot is not Andreas, he will probably be Giorgos), 'they found the plaster of the chapel vault fallen in a heap, and a little graveyard, and underneath it all were Roman walls, broken glass, lamps, terracottas . . . The altar to the church was supported – you can still see it – on the drum of a pagan column.'

He spoke without surprise that the stones dedicated to an Asiatic fertility goddess had bolstered an altar of Christendom. All over the eastern Mediterranean the blocks from overturned temples have been incorporated into the body of the incoming faith. The gods usurp one another in gentle ways, stealing an attribute here, a custom there. The new, in fact, is not new at all, but a reconstitution of numberless divinities who inherit one another's sanctity and proffer the old consolations under a new name. When archaeologists removed a sacred conical stone from the temple ruins and took it to the Cyprus Museum, they found it shiny with olive oil; for the young mothers of Kouklia village, when the milk was running dry at their breasts, had for centuries anointed it as a petition to 'the Lady of the place'. Even now, in a perforation of one of the temple cornerstones, I noticed a nest of expired candles.

'They're offered to the Virgin,' said Giorgos. 'The village women bring them as gifts, even the Moslems . . .'

'They place them in the temple of Aphrodite?'

'Yes.'

The centuries were peeling back at his voice. It is

16

impossible to drive out a god. All over the Levant the ruins of Aphrodite's temples are betrayed by trees hung with the clothing of diseased petitioners, by candles and figurines which are offered to 'the Lady'. In uninterrupted worship, Aphrodite has become the Virgin Mary. The temple itself falls, the deity remains.

'They call her the *Panayia Galaktariotissa*,' said Giorgos, 'the Virgin who gives milk to mothers.'

I nodded, still peering into that cavity resonant with its centuries. These few candles held unbroken the thread of worship between the present and the distant past. They were the last human link, a link of vaguest memory, with three thousand years of reverence: with the restored Augustan glories of the temple's Roman age, even – unimaginably far – with the myth-laden kings of the Phoenician rite, at a time when the immortals mingled with men.

I fingered the yellowing candles. How fragile and inci-dental they seemed! The customs of a few women. And in a generation at most, so quickly was life changing, the thread would be snapped. I gingerly replaced the thin stone slab which protected them.

The village of Kouklia, as we walked through it, seemed almost asleep. But it was an optimistic community, in which Greek and Turk still lived together. The Turkish quarter, as always, was poorer than the Greek, but its poverty was of a clean, rural kind, and the whole village, as Giorgos had said, was knit with the stones of Aphrodite's temple. These streets, bounded by houses pleasantly shabby, with tile roofs, converged on a tiny square where a church and the coffee-shops were. On the outskirts they petered into tracks, and the courtyards were littered with ploughs, cattle troughs beaten out of petrol cans, turkeys, bread ovens and a hundred improvised odds and ends. Donkeys stood patiently in this dowdy surrealism, and the women, dressed in headscarves and dour European clothes, stooped over their washing to show thick stockings pulled unalluringly above the knee.

Giorgos lived in a house whose ceilings were built of beams and matted reeds. 'I prefer old things,' he said, wrinkling his eyes. 'Old things are more comfortable. But my wife would like something new.'

She was one of those vivid, capable women who are the natural partners of quiet men. She spread a meal of stuffed artichokes and yoghourt in front of us, and I found myself surrounded by a family which was the echo of countless others I had known – in Greece, in southern Italy, in Arab countries. Not that Mediterranean people vary less than those farther north, simply their sensuous character is more explicit.

How beautiful these daughters, who move with the ease of sun-softened lands! Their bloom has a firework brilliance. The schoolgirl becomes a woman overnight. '*É!*' exclaims her mother, 'she is lovely as a nereid!' (But exclaims this softly lest one of these jealous ones overhears.) And it is true. The girl's heyday is sudden, and cruelly brief. An enriched complexion, a transient firmness of flesh, create the moment's harmony. She moves with a new self-awareness. She will shortly marry. But in a few years all has collapsed into a ruin of middle age; the flesh curdles about the bones and the lissom shape has become a heavy maternal presence working with a stamina of which her husband is incapable.

Despite their patron goddess, the women of Cyprus are not especially beautiful, and the emigration of young men leaves a flotsam of spinsters in most villages. But Giorgos' eldest daughter, Andreoula, already had a fiancé, a big, handsome man from Limassol who sat and ate with us. At first he affected not to notice her, but engaged in the masculine conversation of politics and sport. Giorgos spoke about the misery of the Greek and Turkish friction. In Kouklia they had always lived pleasantly side by side. Their houses and their land abutted – he rubbed his fingers in a gesture of concord – but when trouble began, 'It was as if the whole village had been picked up and shaken!' – he brandished an imaginary cluster of hovels – 'And now we live together, in fear . . .'

Andreoula grew attractive with her smile and seemed to know this, nuzzling at her man and smiling at whatever he said, or at nothing. Soon he began finding chances to touch her. What was that on her eyebrow? He smoothed it over, like a tiny wing. He took her wrist – could the time be right? Wasn't there a thread loose in her cardigan at the back, just under her neck? His hand stayed there.

Giorgos' aged mother, watching these veiled endearments in silence, inhabited her corner as preordained as furniture. She never smiled nor spoke. It was impossible to guess what she was thinking. I remember her only as one of many widows, swathed in compulsory black, who sit with every other household sewing like the Fates in gloomy corners. Apart from their exclamations – '*É!*' or a

'*Panayia!*' – these frail women rarely speak when visitors are close, but sit staring with their hands in their laps. Old age brings a fearful emaciation. Cheeks are scooped away, eyes fill with water. When they cat-nap they look alarmingly dead. The mouth falls toothless and open, the eye-sockets darken; even in the slackness of sleep the skin is pitifully shrunk, and the skull seems to press through the very flesh, impatient to be free.

But Kouklia was a village of children: shaven-headed Turkish boys and the longer-haired Greeks. Even after I had left Giorgos and it was growing dark, a group of Turkish schoolgirls trailed after me, a crocodile of moist eyes.

I decided to find a secluded place to camp near the sea, and followed a track by moonlight. In the farm on the village outskirts, the wedding celebrations had reached their height. The music sounded clearly over the night-scented fields. I peered curiously through a chink in the shutters, but saw only the backs of two old men's heads, which nodded and wagged in speechless complicity. I slid half my face round the open doorway and looked down the passage, but could see nothing. A cat flew over my feet.

'You!' shouted a voice.

I stood still. I could see nobody.

'Come here!' A small, robust man jumped into the passage. He was holding a bone from which a flap of chicken skin dangled.

'Me?' I stood in the corridor, my rucksack bumping its walls.

The man stared back. 'God forgive me! I was calling the

cat. I wouldn't speak to a visitor . . . not in any such way.'

I could not turn in the passage with my rucksack. I tried to edge out backwards, like a courtier leaving a king. 'I'm afraid I'm not a visitor. I wasn't asked. I was just . . . looking.'

'Not asked!' he shouted almost angrily. 'Of course you were! I ask you. I ask you now.'

I made a futile, inhibited gesture to indicate my clothes, but he did not even understand. Instead he demanded suddenly: 'How much did you pay for those boots?'

The fascination for barter! I could not remember (I can never remember what I have paid for anything). The boots were Spanish and already old, but something about them was to attract continual curiosity during following months, and later I had to decide on an arbitrary cost for them. But this first time I remained glaring stupidly at my feet, as if they must yield an answer, and finally said: 'I've no idea. I've forgotten.'

'Ah,' said the man, in clear disbelief – no Cypriot ever forgets a price. 'But come in, all the same. Come in.'

So I became a part of a country wedding. The groom was a farmer and his bride a farmer's daughter, a buxom girl with sultana eyes and a voluptuous mouth. She was dressed in silk, even her hands gloved and her arms sparkling with tinselled muslin. Her hair erupted in glistening coils, twined with white roses, and her neck showed a double row of artificial pearls. The old customs are three-quarters gone.

But the bridal mattresses were still made by married women of the village, filled with wool and aromatic twigs, and a small child rolled in them as a charm for fertility.

During the wedding service, when the words 'to love and obey' are uttered, a Paphiot country groom will tread on his bride's toes to make sure she is listening.

Self-conscious in my dirty clothes, I was greeted warmly by this couple while a tiny bridesmaid – a pair of orphaned eyes in a cloud of white – offered me Turkish Delight from a basket. Inside the room a tremendous feast was going on. The house exploded in laughter and singing, and brandy was gurgling from bottles and glasses. The people sat at plastic-topped tables on chairs ransacked from a local cinema, and dug their forks into hillocks of cold mutton and potato.

On one side I was wedged against an aged woman who covered herself in her headscarf with embarrassment. On the other sat a sheep-farmer who kept picking the potatoes off my plate. The rest of the table was circled by a smiling pantheon of drooping whiskers and corrugated brows. Everywhere I looked, their merry eyes glittered above tilted glasses, and white moustaches hurtled over smacking lips. Opposite me the circular red face of my self-appointed host cried: 'Here's to you, John!' (All Englishmen are John.)

He clashed his glass against mine.

'Here's to Big Ben!'

We clashed again.

'Here's to the King!' (I did not discover which.)

'Here's to women!'

We were surrounded by women too – tiny, black-clad old ladies who sat before mounded plates of food with a look of contented impotence.

Only the food looked hostile. By now the potatoes had

disappeared from my plate, but I was faced by the mutton. The bride and groom were allowed a pair of roasted doves, symbols of marital concord, but the guests must battle with this mutton. It knocked my teeth defenceless, squirming into unexplored cavities and burrowing under my gums.

Ten minutes later, the people settled down to drinking, picking their enfiladed teeth and talking over tables strewn with bottles and bones. The man opposite me was still clashing his glass against mine, even when I was not holding it, and drinking to a medley of people and institutions which I could not unravel. The other tables looked more respect-able than ours, but everywhere the generations and classes were mingled. Women wearing short skirts chattered to grandmothers whose ankles had been a fiercely guarded mystery for half a century, and the older peasants sat with their baggy *vlaka* hitched in below the knee, leaving a gap above high boots, where their legs showed white and spindly.

The music came from a room which we could only reach by the back yard, scrambling through darkness along planks laid over rain-sodden mud. The women with their tight skirts and ample bodies went tripping and gasping through the mire. Chickens awoke in the courtyard and ran blindly in the dark, fanning their wings against our feet as we teetered along, so that the old woman who had sat next to me lost her delicacy and held onto the back of my pullover as if she was drowning.

On the flagstones of the farther room, under its high beams, the younger women were dancing. A violinist and two *laoutaris* played the old steps – simple tunes to which the girls responded in pairs, moving lightly on their heavy-soled feet. They held up coloured handkerchiefs, then grasped the end of their neighbour's, turned around her, joining, separating, dancing closer, all in a solemn, attentive way, as if it was a ceremony. And because the others watched without talk and scarcely smiled, they too preserved the feel of some ritual being enacted over those worn stones, while the lutists bent sleepily above their instruments, and the violinist closed his eyes.

'Hullo, John!' The russet face was staring into mine. 'Can you dance?'

'Not this.'

He clapped a grey-haired hand on my shoulder, while the other held the arm of his grown-up granddaughter. 'Something else will happen,' he promised. 'They won't go on like this. It's too dull . . .'

'Perhaps she will dance?' I asked. She was pretty in a quiet way, with modest, faintly drooping eyelids. She whispered something to him.

'No,' he said. 'She doesn't dance.'

She looked supple and very embarrassed. The old man was a little drunk. He swayed lightly between us. 'Something else will happen.'

But nothing else happened. We simply went on watching the dancing and listening to the music – eastern-tinted music, unvarying as the lives of eastern generations – until the guests began to filter into the night and I walked unsteadily back along the path, listening to their muffled departures.

The head man of Kouklia, a schoolmasterly person whose

hair crested his head in a black cockscomb, overtook me and proffered the hospitality of his village. He would secure me a bed. 'Sleep out? It's cold enough to freeze a Turk! Besides, there are snakes . . .' He would give me, he said proudly, the Kouklia clinic and library.

We passed the moon-whitened church and stopped in front of a corrugated iron door which he unlocked and jerked upwards. 'The Kouklia clinic,' he said formally. 'And library.' I crept underneath and thanked the darkness where he stood. 'You will find everything you want.'

Immediately his steps faded. I listened for other sounds, but heard only the mourning of dogs and the click of a woman's boots very close, now farther away, along the street. I pulled down the iron shutter and fumbled in my rucksack for a torch. The light travelled over white walls. A case of books confronted me: the Kouklia library. I peered behind it. There was a basin, a medicine cupboard and an operating table beside which stood canisters of oxygen and a pair of scales for weighing babies. I undressed and turned on the tap. The water came from a tin container overhead, flopped into the basin which had no plug, and reemerged from a crack in the wall, flooding the floor. I seized my sleeping-bag and splashed to the centre of the little room, wondering where to sleep. My torchlight revealed nothing new except a chart spread across one wall, giving directions on 'How to bath Baby'.

The operating table looked very white and clinical, but there was nowhere else to lie. I hoisted myself onto it, feeling unhygienic, and stretched out delicately. My intestines gurgled. I covered myself with my sleeping bag.

Outside, all over the village, the dogs were baying in requiem. The glow from some street-lamp, falling through a tiny skylight, glistened on the watery floor. I turned away from it, and slept.

The nights, it was true, were still cold, but there was no wind and the sea had fallen silent. I had walked six miles that day, which was little when six hundred awaited me, but enough to deepen sleep. I heard no tap or cry from the watchman, and country sounds – night shriekings and rustles – were kept away by the little village.

A long time later I woke with a start in total darkness. Where was I? I could not remember. The narrow hardness of the bed was extraordinary. I groped about, half in sleep. My fingers felt the torch. I flicked it on nervously and close against my eyes across the wall read: 'Put Baby into the bath, holding him firmly . . .'

CHAPTER TWO
· · · · · · · · · ·
Tombs and Twilight

The Troodos Mountains fall in easy hills to the island's south-western coast. This indeterminate littoral, a place of vegetable and pig farming, is spotted with vines as it was in Roman and Crusader years. Here and there the cliffs leave alluvial plains to lap at the sea, and the region of Akamas, where no road has yet been engineered, reaches to the island's westernmost point in a spiny and derelict peninsula.

In Roman times the shore was more busy and peopled than now; scores of bays and headlands have been abandoned and measure out this faded aquatint of a country in haunted pauses and voids. It was the Akamas that I was now approaching, tramping in a leisurely way towards a rain-filled horizon. The landscape seemed to be composed less of earth than of great translucent spaces carved from it – a vast caesura between mountains and sea – nothing but low, uncomplicated hills and the watery expanse of the sky itself, which left a sense of desolation and incompleteness. An old woman knelt alone in a field, planting young vines with an expression of abstract benignity. A mile away, two bullocks dragged a plough before the shadow of a man; while on another hill a United Nations lookout post showed a wireless aerial and blue-painted barracks among the rocks.

This Paphos area, say Cypriots, is not like any other; its people are more open and rural. 'Mere peasants,' declare some, adding darkly: 'But what can you expect? Their blood is mixed with the Turk . . .' But the Paphiots claim themselves both more honest and more intelligent than their compatriots. 'All Paphiots are clever,' they say. 'If you meet a stupid Paphiot, then he is not from Paphos.'

The town itself, ten miles west from Old Paphos, has a self-contained look. Its public buildings line the road in a style of wedding-cake Ionic, which gives it the feel of a petty capital. Trudging past these confections, with my pockets weighted by oranges, I reached the main square during its noon sleep. No hotelier bothered to hail my dust-clogged figure. I tramped down a street where sun-sodden men dozed on chairs, their coffee-cups empty on other chairs in front of them. Their grins or scowls were accidents of sleep.

Eventually I found a room above a restaurant whose owner, grown plump on his own cooking, served me *souvlakia* and later broke two bottles of sweet red St Hilarion, which sent me floating down towards the sea on a wisp of wind. Below me, around a tree-filled bay and headland, the ruins of Paphos shimmered in confusion.

Pausanias wrote that the city was founded by Agapenor of Arcadia returning from the Homeric war, and an Arcadian dialect may still be heard in the Paphos hills. But archaeology has not yet confirmed this early origin, and the new city seems to have been built instead by Nicocles, the last of the kings of Old Paphos, where the great temple stood. Soon afterwards, in 295 B.C., the whole island passed to the Ptolemies of Egypt, and from them to the Romans.

But what kind of people, I wondered, did the Romans discover here? Who were the Cypriots? What had happened since the Neolithic men of Khirokitia had died in their stone-encircled houses three thousand years before?

The answer emerging out of many complexities, concerns two races. Other nations – Egyptians, Assyrians, Persians – governed the land yet never touched its soul. But these two, the Mycenaean Greeks and the Semitic Phoenicians, colonized the country and absorbed its indigenous inhabitants. The Mycenaeans began to filter into the island in about 1400 B.C. during their expansion eastward after engulfing Minoan Crete. Dynastic lords and charioteers, builders of cyclopean walls and lion-guarded gates, their heartland was the Grecian Peloponnese, whose arid hills were parcelled among their kings; and because they form the very backbone of the Cypriot people, and their language and culture endured, we shall meet them again, in greater depth, at Salamis.

The Phoenicians, on the other hand, arrived as colonists in about 1000 B.C. at the dawn of the Iron Age, and eventually vanished under Rome. But the aura of an eastern people remained, and Semitic groups – whether Syrian traders or Arab pirates – trickled westward over many centuries.

So these two civilizations constituted, in unequal measure, the raw materials from which the Greek Cypriot race was hammered out. At first they had little in common. To the masculine Mycenaean world, the Phoenicians opposed a quicksilver people, born not to war but to merchandise. And their gods reflect them. Against the semi-human Mycenaean deities, ranked like a feudal caste, the Phoenicians set the master-gods of Asia, whose worshippers were slaves. The Mycenaeans, of course, were more numerous and eventually absorbed their rivals, but by then, exposed to the mellowing Mediterranean and to the conquerors and traders of half the developed world, they had acquired a softer and more flexible heart.

Ironically it was the Greek kings of Egypt, the Ptolemies, who put an end to the Greek city-states of Cyprus at the close of the fourth century. They found a mosaic of independent kingdoms in the island, and demolished them all. These petty states, whose jealousies and alliances had formed the warp and woof of Cypriot history over a thousand years, mostly succumbed with ease or vanished unrecorded.

Soon afterwards, the Ptolemies chose Paphos for their island capital, and something of the spirit of Alexandria – cruel, élitist, refined – blew over the sea to the new metropolis. Sculpture took on an unwonted sophistication. Paphos even produced a comic poet, Sopatros, but his works are lost. And superficially the Paphiots seem to have flourished in these times, serving a dynasty whose family tree, like that of their own past rulers, writhed with incestuous pedigrees.

The indulgence of the nobles became a byword. One of the governors, oppressed by the summer heat, had his hair anointed with a precious unguent to which pigeons were so attracted that they fluttered about his head and cooled him with their wings. The princesses entered and alighted from their litters by a flight of steps composed of the backs of women of good family who were specially trained to the duty. And even when these exotic nobles died, they were buried in tombs like palaces sunk in the earth.

A hint of luxury still hangs round their lonely necropolis by the sea. From a distance its sheaf of rock surges weightless into the light, and over a full square mile looks mysteriously complete. But as I approached, this clarity faded. The cliff walls split and the ground opened on the anterooms to family sepulchres. Local people call them the 'Tombs of the Kings' and although they cannot have been royal, their dimensions are often regal. I climbed down steps into porticoed courtyards, whose columns and entablatures held up the ground above in living rock. The Ptolemaic luxury hung faint on them in sand-eaten friezes whose gloss was gone. Their chambers, rifled centuries ago, plunged left and right in passageways and rooms where the dead had been laid along the walls or thrust deep into the rock face. Entering this dried darkness, fifty feet beneath the ground, the traveller suddenly feels insulated and alone. His presence is a violation. On all sides the shafts and corridors gape and beetle and echo, stagnant with bats' urine. The lips of long-since-crumbled doors succeed one another in suffocated repetition. The thickness of stone muffles all noise and light. Even the sea, as it chews off another piece from the wave-battered cemetery, can be heard only as a harmless and ubiquitous whisper. To the ancients these places must indeed have seemed the crossing-place to Styx, where the ferryman and the triple-headed dog would usher them away to the long halls of eternity.

The people's attitude to death at this time is eloquent of the Greek continuity. The spells and formulae of Syria and Egypt do not appear. In fact no relieving element appears at all. The attitude is heroic and undeluded. In the cult of Old Paphos Aphrodite still promised resurrection, but to what kind of afterlife it is hard to say. Her ritual was concerned more with earthly regeneration – with harvest, healing and childbirth – than with immortality. To regenerate she had to kill, just as she destroyed the sacred kings after first consorting with them. Only she, the continuity of life itself, persisted. The individual spirit, mind, body – all that is loved and valued – perished, and the soul went gibbering down to the twilight, into which only a handful of legendary heroes had ever gone and returned alive. The Greeks loved life. To them, death meant the end of everything meaningful, and the elysian fields were nothing more than a flutter of ghosts among the asphodel. Callimachus wrote the dialogue between a living man and Charides, a dead man, thus:

'Q. Charides, what is below?

A. Great darkness.

Q. What about resurrection?

A. A lie.

Q. And the God of the Dead?

A. A myth. We perish utterly.'*

It is this spirit, unique to the Greek world in its day, which pervades tombs of the period all over Cyprus. About their memorials there is the courage of hard reason and

* *The Greek Anthology*. Trs. Andrew Sinclair.

clear sight. Their epitaphs have the timelessness of total
sincerity. Sometimes they are desperately poignant and sad.
On funerary steles the figures stand or sit in the familiar
stillness of the Greek farewell. Yet they are shown encapsuled in the warmth of their families' affection. Hands
touch. Heads are bent in intimate and dignified union. A
son's arm rests on his father's shoulder. An old woman
cradles a bird before her grandchildren, and was evidently
loved as grandmothers are, who can afford to be indulgent.
'Good Artemo, daughter of Socrates, farewell.' The inscriptions are simple and final. 'Good Eudemonia, farewell.'
'Even Thou . . .' '. . . farewell.'

Yet the steles are not simply portraits of domestic
harmony, which was doubtless as precarious then as now,
but memorials to people seen at their best: the mother with
her children, the man as soldier or as a father. Besides the
courage of their intelligence, the answer which the Greeks
summoned against death was that in memory their glory
should survive them, whose

> . . . *valour lifts them yet*
> *Into the splendour from the night beneath.*[*]

Because these feelings belonged peculiarly to the Greeks,
it is significant how completely the Cypriots responded to
them. The islanders, then as now, were deeply conservative.
The movements which had stimulated the rest of Greece
had passed them by. There is scarcely a trace of Ionian

---

[*] Simonides, *The Spartan Monument at Plataea*.

culture in Cyprus, and the great Dorian invasion stopped short at Rhodes. The Cypriots remained chiefly of the ancient Mycenaean and Achaean stocks, and had so long been in contact with the orient that they scarcely experienced the excitement felt by a remoter Greece for eastern culture. There was no clash and inspiration of discovery, only a gentle fusion. In the fourth century B.C., as in the fourteenth, the Cypriots preserved their hoary monarchies, clung to the Minoan syllabary, and had only recently abandoned the use of chariots in war. Yet the pride and reticence in their funerary tableaux tell that they were Greeks, as surely as their long fight against Persian domination.

Climbing to level ground again, I could gauge the full size of the Paphos necropolis. The subterranean tombs were only part of a vaster complex, marked by outbursts of hewn cliff. But the earth had drifted against them, and the whole area was three-quarters submerged. Their doors opened like the gasps of swimmers suffocating beneath the earth, while above them the sandstone threw up a grotesque debris which dwindled on the shore into wave-tormented rocks. Only in milder clearings were caves whose grave-slabs lay complete. Here the slash of a chisel showed on the walls, there a pediment startled the stone into life.

The afternoon was waning. Within the harbour arm, whose Roman breakwater had sunk under the waves, fishing-boats were rising and dipping as if in answer to some deep-breathing god under the calm. To the west, beyond the Turkish fort, a cargo boat had foundered on the headland at the foot of the lighthouse. Along the quay an aroma of charcoal cooking mixed with the smell of tar, and two pelicans washed their plumage at the water's edge.

As for the great city which had stood here – the island capital of the Romans – it was heaped invisibly upon itself for four square miles. 'Augusta Claudia Flavia Paphos, Holy Metropolis of all the towns of Cyprus' – the pompous name has faded to that of 'Lower Paphos' and the Roman population of twenty-five thousand has shrivelled to a village in one corner of the walls. Still afloat on a sea of ruin, these stuccoed houses, with their washing and chickens, looked frail and transient. Since the troubles between Greek and Turk half of them had been abandoned, and one by one their walls were flopping into the dust.

But their rubble went to join a vaster turmoil, more deeply buried. I came upon the lines of Roman streets. Granite columns, sometimes grey, sometimes a beautiful, veined blue, showed above the soil a foot or two, or were strewn like lopped fingers among the corn. Clean through the houses and through cactus which tumbled everywhere in rotting confusion, these avenues drove their symmetry unseen, set down porticoes or dignified some orchard with the trace of a temple. Accident has softened them. Fig trees swarm over the stones; villagers use them for door-posts and foot-scrapers.

There is an acropolis too, and a ravaged little theatre carved from its flank. An oracle-cave to Apollo of the Woods lies under a ruined shrine, where the sibylline voice could be heard whispering in the earth. And many lesser ruins testify to the Roman grandeur.

These were peaceful years. After Cato's conquest of the

island and its shuffling between Cleopatra and Rome, Paphos settled to a history of happy uneventfulness. Cicero came as governor of Cilicia – he appears to have valued the Paphiots – and Augustus was quick to rebuild the city in his reign. In A. D. 46 St Paul, arriving with Barnabas on his first missionary journey, converted to Christianity the island's pro-consul, Sergius Paulus.

'But Elymas the sorcerer withstood them,' runs *The Acts of the Apostles*, 'seeking to turn away the deputy from the faith. Then Saul (who is also called Paul), filled with the Holy Ghost, set his eyes on him, and said, "O full of all subtlety and all mischief, thou child of the devil, wilt thou not cease to pervert the right ways of the Lord? And now, behold, the hand of the Lord is upon thee, and thou shalt be blind, not seeing the sun for a season." And immediately there fell on him a mist and a darkness; and he went about seeking some to lead him by the hand. Then the deputy, when he saw what was done believed, being astonished at the doctrine of the Lord.'

An old man living near the ruins pointed out a broken column to me. '*Na, paidi mou* – look, my child. That is where St Paul was tied to be scourged. You may still see the marks . . .' he squinted at the marble. '*É!*, perhaps they are faded now. But that is certainly where . . .' Over several centuries pilgrims reduced this column to a stub by hacking off pieces for talismans; but it merely belongs to the Byzantine cathedral close by, and the scriptures mention no such scourging.

Paphos declined in Christian years – Salamis replaced her as capital – but she was the seat of a bishopric and even in ruin her churches are impressive. All over this graveyard of a town they stand up as if in memory. Even the grottoes are sacred as the haunt of hermit-saints – St Agapiticos, St Misticos – but their names have been confounded with the Greek for love and hatred, *agape* and *misos*, and the cave of 'the love-saint' is choked with candles left by suitors as a plea for him to smite the hearts of their beloveds – precisely as the ancients once prayed to Aphrodite. And just as a little dust from its floor is a sure stimulant in the drink of laggard lovers, so the earth from the nearby grotto of St Xorinos the Exiler, if thrown into the sea, will ensure the banishment of a rival.

In this Aphrodite-haunted land the cave of the love-saint may once have been a pagan shrine, and in legend, certainly, it became the sanctuary of a mysterious Queen. This Queen reappears in every part of the island, whose people simply call her 'the Raegina'. She is, as far as I know, exclusive to Cyprus, and her stories fall in fading echoes down the Christian centuries, like a memory of the older goddess. Yet if she is related to Aphrodite, it is only as a rustic cousin. Nobody conjures or petitions her. She leads a robust, eccentric life of her own, battling with twin brothers, 'the Diene', who hurl rocks at her until she escapes them into caves. 'The Diene' in their turn have been confused with the folk-hero Dighenis, who repelled the Saracens in mythic battles celebrated by an epic poem now mostly lost. The offshore boulders scattered along the Cypriot coast were hurled there, say the country people, not by earthquake or the crumbling of cliffs, but by the arms of this warrior whose fingerprints are visible on many crags.

Dighenis fell in love with the Queen, who proved difficult to seduce, and he threw at her a gigantic rock which lies by the caves of the saints. The Queen, who was a lady of character, replied by heaving her spindle at him – and this is sprawled half a mile away in the shape of a granite column.

Such tales arose from the years when Cyprus was tormented by Arab invasion, and against these insecurities a Byzantine castle stands bastioned on the hill above the port. Its foundations are riddled by underground passages, and Roman columns poke from the walls where they have decayed, like the barrels of cannon. But inside the glacis the rooms are all but fallen, and on several sides the angle towers have sloughed their ramparts in heaps. I found stables, and pairs of latrines well preserved; their stone seats were comfortably worn down by successive Byzantine garrisons, and a Christian prudishness showed in their entrances, which were grooved for doors.

Walking beneath the gate-tower I noticed a small opening under the ramparts. I remembered stories of a Turkish bandit who had hidden in tunnels beneath this fortress and had emerged to surrender himself, gibbering about vaults filled with human bones. This was too much for my curiosity. Entering, I found myself under the fortress pavements in a tunnel whose walls were of jointed stone, sleek and warm on either side, but so low that I was forced to crawl on my belly, shining my torch ahead. On the floor the seeped earth came smooth from the darkness under my hands. Once or twice I struck my fist into a satin mound of it, filtered down from a crack.

But little by little the passage tightened, and I could only elbow myself along inch by inch. Where the way separated, I stopped to regain my breath and listen. For a second the silence was absolute. Then, distinct in front of me, came the noise of something writhing over stone. I threw a spray of dust in front of me, but heard nothing more. It was obvious that the tunnel could never have been intended for people. I felt the walls again, and realized with a start that their gloss had been formed by running water, and that I was crawling through the sewers.

I moved on and stopped again, but heard only my own breath quickening through dust-filled nostrils. The place suddenly seemed airless. The weight and darkness of stone were suffocating. I felt as if I was worming into the pith of a giant body, squeezing down the marrow of its bones. Its mildest contraction – if it so much as sighed – would snuff me out.

But it remained sterile and quiet. The walls thrust on. Once a grey light appeared where a pipe entered from the stables, and a little farther I was able to rest with my face turned upward to a thread of sky: a vision of paradise. I was staring through a deep crack in the pavement, and listening to a strange, regular drumming. The next moment a crêpe sole landed high above my face and I saw the billowing skirt of an elderly British tourist. She was staring down.

'Look there, Leslie.' The tone was brusque and capable. 'The standard of hygiene – isn't that astonishing?'

An obedient voice murmured its astonishment.

She peered down harder then suddenly, with a stifled

exclamation, stiffened and frowned. From the gloom of the Byzantine sewer an eye was staring back at her. Her face, haloed by a sun-hat over a sensible hairstyle, puckered in revulsion. Yes, a dark Cyclopean eye (my other one was closed) was gazing unwinking from phantom layers of excrement. The eye might even have been laughing. She jerked upright. Impossible, of course. There was no such thing as a sewage-demon. She refused to look any more. The next moment she had vanished from the slit of sky and I heard the exorcising click of her tongue and the march of practical shoes over the pavements.

I edged forward again. A minute later the sunlight splashed into the tunnel from an opening above me, the passage ended in a blank wall and I lay beneath the perfect ellipse of one of the seventh century latrines. A thousand years before I would have looked up at the threat of a Byzantine bottom. Now there was only the framed sky, an oval of deep and purest sapphire, and my own laughter.

By the time I left the castle the sun was setting. No lamps showed in the village, although twilight was gathering about the headlands and the almond blossom in the gardens had darkened to sepia. On the inland cliffs, a mile away, the upper city, now named Ktima, showed a chaplet of lights and a few cars were roving between town and port.

I started to walk back to my lodgings over desolate stretches where the cathedral of the mediaeval city had left the spring of an arch. Its most famous bishops rest in other towns: Francesco Contarini was slaughtered by the Turks at the fall of Nicosia, and Jacopo Pesaro was buried in Venice in the church of the Frari beside Titian's *Pala dei*

Pesari, the altarpiece which he commissioned. By the twelfth century the Arab raids had made their mark. The people were retreating to the clifftops of Ktima. The port remained a station for resting pilgrims, where many were buried; but Cyprus was plagued by a demon which dug up corpses and returned them to their homes at night, and only when King Eric the Good of Denmark was interred here did the curse lift.

Already by the fifteenth century the lower town was as shrivelled as it is today. 'The harbour too is abandoned,' wrote a Dominican monk in 1480, 'and ships only enter it when forced to do so, as was our fate. As the city was laid low by earthquake so it lies still, and no king nor bishop gives a hand to raise it up again.'

I could sense the artificial contortions of the grass-covered ground. They stubbled the whole darkening headland and I kept tripping over their hummocks. Already half the sky was perforated with stars, and an ailing moon lay on its back above the harbour. The only people I met were children gathering brushwood, who stared at me with the inquisitive yet melancholy eyes of all this region. For more than half a mile the city walls followed a scarp above the sea. Their stonework had almost disappeared, but the man-made smoothing of the cliffs and ramps embraced the entire city. In the north they had been hollowed out for a garrison's camp around a circular hall, the seat of an oracle, but dedicated to what god – Isis, Apollo, Mithras – I could not tell.

It was growing cold. Now the lighthouse showed its flame above the cargo boat ludicrously run aground at its foot. I brushed through a field of corn and came with surprise upon a small theatre, pale under the moon-flooded sky. Its proscenium was gone, but its seats rose gently in stubbled tiers, and traces of its galleries and of the road which circled it remained. A stairway led me to its uppermost tier, where I sat down, tired. The cold wind had dropped and I could hear the waves falling on the ruined headland with a lapidary thud.

In the orchestra below where the chorus had stood about the altar of Dionysus, spread a snow of wild garlic. I wondered what the plays of Sopatros of Paphos had been like, but the theatre was Roman and semi-circular, not built in the Greek horseshoe, and doubtless its entertainments were bawdy enough. Yet its seclusion and intimacy suggested something tragic or pastoral, as ruins do. Decay gives to many Roman remains, undistinguished in their day, this fraudulent solemnity. So an arena for vulgar farce may erode to something as simple and moving as this arc of faded stone, pervaded not by the voices of the actors trumpeting artificially through painted masks, but by the grandiloquence of the sea, beating at the shore with the pulse of eternity.

I returned to my lodgings to find the restaurant filled with people and Antis, the owner, sprawled grinning over two chairs. His belly was seeping under an old-fashioned waistcoat and his fist closed around a bottle of brandy, which he held like an idol on the table before him.

'*Kopiaste*. Welcome, welcome.' He fumbled to his feet and came towards me, using his hands as a seal manoeuvres its flippers, to part the air in front. He was not drunk, simply unwieldly with size. 'You see, I cook too well. There's nothing I can't cook. But I taste everything, and then I want to eat it, and then I want more – and in a moment' – he caressed the tumulus of his stomach – 'I am like this.' But now his condition distressed him. His eyes peered plaintively over colossal cheeks, as if they expected to vanish in a final cataclysm of flesh.

'What will you have to eat then? My cuisine is international. Chips?'

That is the legacy of the British occupation. Chips have slid into the recipes of ordinary families, and have conquered the remotest hamlets of the Troodos and Kyrenia mountains. So when Antis proposed these greasy invaders I shook my head.

'Ah then,' he suggested. '*Patcha*?'

'What's *patcha*?'

'Sheepshead.'

'Chips.'

After staying several days I realized that Antis believed genuinely in his cuisine, even though his 'beef' and 'lamb' were probably no more than different buttocks of the same goat. But he apologized for the people who patronized his restaurant. They were not those he would have chosen. Tourists did not seem to come, he said, in a tone of mystified hurt.

How could I tell him that I suffered the cooking for the sake of the people? His lodgings were the caravanserai for a dying race: travelling conjurors, country violinists, lute-players. A gypsy fortune-teller came, a mendicant strong-man, a lapsed priest; and three Syrian prostitutes slopped about the corridors in carefully disarrayed dressing-gowns. There also appeared a dealer in colocassia – a potato-like vegetable which I had tasted in the South Seas and had hoped not to see again; once, during lunch, his aged wife crept up behind me and emptied a bottle of water over my head. 'Holy water of St Napa!' she cried, as I wrang out my hair, 'Sovereign against arthritis!' and my irritation at being thought arthritic was dissipated by her crinkled smile.

Every morning I was greeted by the faintly unhappy figure of Antis, emerging from his kitchen splay-footed like an ageing ballet-dancer, and complaining of verrucas. Breakfast always found him unwell. The most perfunctory 'How are you this morning?' caused his eyes to screw up and his whole face to drip into his collar.

'Not good. No. I am sick. I work too much, too much. And what does it bring me?' He cast up an imaginary bubble to heaven. 'Nothing. And these *artistes* (he meant the prostitutes) they are rotten to the roots. They say whatever comes into their heads. What can you do with such girls? I mean, apart from . . .' In the desert of his face his mouth opened like a petulant bud. 'May they copulate in hell!'

Sometimes I tried feebly to defend these women, who had been cast out of puritanical Moslem homes after a night's naiveté had bequeathed illegitimate children. The strong-man was generally there to scowl at this, shaking his massive, globular head in denunciation. The idea of anything sexual nauseated him. He would absent-mindedly pick up the restaurant forks and twist them double in his fingers.

I met him first on the night of my arrival in Paphos. A furtive shuffling outside my room made me switch on the light and open the door sharply. The shape of the man in the entranceway was featureless as a mountain. In one hand he held up an absurdly delicate taper.

'I'm sorry, I'm sorry,' he mumbled. 'I can't find my room. Antis has changed my room and gone home and . . . well, I am not sure which to try.'

'Try them all,' I said sleepily.

He shifted his feet uncomfortably. 'I have tried several and all I hear is . . . is . . . women.' His tone turned querulous. 'But I'm a single man. I have nothing to do with that sort of thing . . . I assure you, a single man . . .' He stared at me through sheeplike eyes. He was afraid.

I tried to cheer him up. After all, I ventured, there was nothing very frightening about women. They were nearly as helpless as men. Why didn't he try the doors on the far side?

The taper jigged in his hand. He did not want to leave the island of light which his candle had cast round us. Yes, he said, he knew about women. He had even fallen in love. He started to shuffle his feet again. His watery eyes pleaded with me not to mock him. He had been in Germany doing his strong-man act, and he had met a woman for a few moments, a marvellous woman . . .

'You speak German?'

'No. Oh no. We never spoke. But I followed her home.'

'Yes?'

'Well, I stood outside her house for an hour and . . . and . . .' He gave a lost shrug. 'Nothing.'

45

He had stood under her window like a fairy-tale troubadour and waited, wringing his clumsy hands, not knowing what to do. For four nights he had returned and simply stood there, as if something must happen, staring at the curtained rectangle in dumb, child-like adoration. Then his visa had run out and he had been forced to find work elsewhere. And ever since then he had travelled over Europe, snapping metal bars and lifting dumb-bells, tearing up Larousse and the Greater London Telephone Directory.

The taper was guttering into his vast, hairless hand. I told him to go to the corridor on the other side before the light went out. There might be empty rooms there. The candle-flame flatered down the passageway, drawing an orange halo around his creeping shape. Then it vanished as he turned the corner, and I could only hear his voice, whispering, 'I'm a single man . . . a single man . . .'

At lunch the next day the restaurant was crowded. I was toying with a piece of Antis' 'lamb' when the strong-man sat down beside me. He seemed to have forgotten the misfortunes of the night. 'Here,' he mumbled. 'Try some of this.' He pulled an old bottle from his pocket. He had filled it with whisky which he tilted into my glass, while a cloud of tiny, embalmed flies rose from its bottom. I made a gesture at drinking.

'That's it,' he said. 'Makes you strong. When I was in Paris twenty years ago I got wonderfully drunk on this. The French police came to pick me up so I clung onto a tree, and what d' you think? They couldn't budge me! Not three of them!' He chortled into the bottle and imbibed another troupe of drowned flies. 'They had to telephone for more police, until there were *eight*. They formed a chain to pull me away and in the end – Holy Mother! – the tree came up by its roots! Yes, truly. A young chestnut on the Boulevard Saint-Michel. They took me away to prison still clutching it.' He pounded his thighs with delight, then sobered suddenly and said: 'But that was years ago. In those days I could balance a small fellow like that' – he pointed to an old man across the room – 'on my little finger!'

Sitting alone, the tiny old man sensed that we were talking about him. He half turned in our direction. His face – a boneless oval beneath his dust-covered trilby – wore an expression of faintly humorous regret.

'Who's that?' I asked.

'That?' grunted the strong-man. 'You don't know *him*?'

'No. Who is he?'

'He's . . . he's . . .' He frowned and rubbed his forehead. 'I've forgotten.'

The old man was wearing one of the saddest-looking suits I had ever seen – villagers often wear old-fashioned English dress – and down his lapels fell a miniature cascade of silver violins.

'I remember now,' said the strong-man. 'That's the violinist. He plays at country weddings, or used to.' Scowling, he added: 'He was a great one for the women, they say.'

After the restaurant had emptied and even my companion had gone, this old man continued to stare through pale, red-rimmed eyes at nothing in particular. When he at last stood up he remained a long time hunch-backed over his stick, as if he felt dizzy. His trousers stopped short six inches

47

above his ankles, which vanished into outsize shoes; he reminded me of those top-heavy toys which are thrown into the air but always land on their feet.

'Yes, a violinist,' he said, when I asked him. His voice wavered between hoarseness and fluting. 'Do you have violins in England?' He looked sad and grey, as though everything about him was cast in a faint shadow. 'Not much of a job any more, a wedding violinist. People still get married, you can't stop that, but they want different things now. And next year will be even worse. That's the Year of the Snake. People don't like marrying in the Year of the Snake. It isn't propitious.'

Besides, he said grudgingly, he was getting a little old.

How old was that, I asked?

He was not sure, but he thought he was about eighty. He remembered that his father had administered the wheat tax for the Ottoman sultans in the Troodos Mountains, and had become a forester when the British arrived in 1878. 'But my father,' he said, planting the nob of his stick between his exaggerated feet, 'had no music in him. He could not tell a *zeybeki* from a *syrtos*. I learned the violin from a man in our village who played like Apollo – Ah the sounds he made! – You could pour them down your throat!'

'And he gave you the idea of playing?'

'No, not him.' Under the squashed trilby the mouth smiled secretly. I wondered what he was remembering. Who else had inspired music in the twelve-year-old boy walking the Troodos forests in the last century?

'Women!' he piped in answer. 'I wanted to play love-songs to women! That was the way to attract them.' His eyes were watery with emotion. 'Imagine it, a young girl at a wedding . . . she is dreaming of marriage. And along comes this man. He is small, perhaps he is ugly – but he can sing and play and dance all at once! Almost a magician!'

I asked if he could still dance, but did so out of courtesy, for he scarcely seemed able to walk.

'Dance?' he cried. 'Why, yes!' He balanced tenderly on one foot. Then he raised his hands and tried to click their fingers, but they emitted only a damp tapping. 'I will find my violin. Would you like me to play my violin?'

I nodded with more enthusiasm than I felt. 'What sort of violin?'

He ran a finger along his lips. 'I bought it fifty years ago,' he said, 'from a merchant in Paphos. There was a certificate inside the instrument. Let me see . . . What did it say?' He tugged off his hat to rub his knit brows; his head was as smooth as a stone. Then his face cleared and he answered with a grave innocence: 'Yes, I remember. It said "Antonius Stradivarius. Number 17."'

A Stradivarius! Had a Venetian pilgrim, centuries ago, been robbed of this treasure on his way to the Holy Land? Or perhaps the master of violins had made a gift to an Ottoman pasha? Or did some musical Turkish corsair, raiding the coast of Liguria . . . ? My mind was still boggling with possibilities when the old man returned. For a moment I thought that he had arrived with a 'cello. He was so small that the violin looked enormous in his hands; but I saw at once that it was as rough and ill-made as a violin could be, almost without varnish and with its gut strings replaced by wire.

He tucked it affectionately under his chin and found a space in the passage where a few chairs traced a semicircle. Frailly he plucked a string, adjusted a knob and tried to straighten his shoulders. 'I dance to my own poetry,' he said. 'A few of us still do.' Then, with an inclination of his upper body as if bowing to a ghostly audience at some wedding feast long ago, he began to play. His feet started to tap on the worn tiles, his knees tentatively bent. And there arose out of his throat a strangely robust voice which seemed to have nothing to do with the elfin figure whose stiffened fingers touched the strings.

> *O cursed pair of breeches*
> *Which rustle like taca-taca,*
> *Who now is going to wash my breeches*
> *In the lake?*
> *And who will put them*
> *On a line to dry?*

> *O my lady from Yeroskipos,*
> *Where are your promises now?*

And suddenly he was dancing in an odd, rickety gait, his eyes closed and his hunched back almost straightened. He seemed less like a man than a figure which gambols for a moment on the lid of a musical box, tinkling in an attic – but a figure which might stop as abruptly as it began, because the Greek song, like the Arab, has no birth or end, but continues like human suffering, repeated and repeated through sameless years, days, centuries. Life, it seems to say, is an effervescence, a gesture to embroider Time.

> *O my lady from Ktima,*
> *Kissing is no sin.*

Now the cramped, tiny dance had become a creaking revel. His trousers flapped. His feet rattled in their giant's shoes. Stradivarius Number 17 mewed and squealed, while the blood climbed into his face. A dwarf in the big corridor, he appeared to be physically attached to the violin, which was dragging him hither and thither in the wake of its music. By the time he had finished, the metamorphosis was complete. His face, from his neck to his leaf-shaped ears, was a violent, sunset red, broken with smiles.

Such mendicant poets and musicians have almost vanished. A handful of rustic versifiers, the *poietarides*, can still be heard at festivals, but the names in Cypriot verse are few: Michaelides, an epic poet; the lyric Lipertis whom the old man had known as a youth, and who had written songs for him to sing. These men were of the popular tradition; they wrote in the island dialect. Cypriot too is the tenderness which informs their work, and the drift to an oriental richness and hyperbole. This flavour comes down from the earliest of the island's poetry, the *Cypria*. An epic known only in fragments, it is less spare and cohesive than its model *The Iliad*, but is sensual and melodramatic, and keeps a spasmodic beauty of its own.

The old violinist, now slumped in a chair, was fighting

a humble rearguard action. Any modern element in his verse was locked in a traditional frame, such as the almost untranslatable poem which he had written decades before, when the influence of Singer was creeping into the mountain villages.

> *My love, I shall buy you a sewing-machine*
> *To make embroidery and silken dresses,*
> *Then you will need no Greek nor Turkish seamstress,*
> *You will not have to tread the threshing-floor*
> *Nor work for others – but yourself grow rich,*
> *O my most polished lady.*

Until lately the old man had done well enough. The silver violins on his lapels had been won at the summer festivals, and among them hung a locket given him by President Makarios, which he opened to show a photograph of the archbishop ('There's a person for you!') but now he was reduced to penury. In the restaurant at evening the prostitutes took turns to pay for his meals.

The age of classical Greece, haloed in the reverence of post-Renaissance Europe, seems infinitely remote. But the remnants of Rome are intimate with everyday life. The faces of its portrait busts are familiar; you can see their prototypes any day, crowded into trains or sitting behind desks. With the coming of Rome, Aphrodite, the nymph-like and ambivalent goddess, becomes a matronly Venus, and the history of Cyprus is delivered over to graphs and commerce, the exploitation of her wood, cereals, wine and copper. Greece is spirit, Rome is matter. Such is the simplification of hindsight.

Fourteen years ago a farmer, ploughing his fields near the harbour of Paphos, heard the blade of his ploughshare grate over level stone. He had struck the most beautiful ancient mosaics in the eastern Mediterranean. They belonged to a Roman villa whose walls had been destroyed, but the layout of the rooms, luxurious or private, was preserved by the pattern of the floors. Those of the kitchen and workshops were of beaten earth, and the bedrooms paved in lime; but spreading along grander rooms and passages, a sea of mosaic portrayed legends and fantasies with an eerie delicacy.

Visitors walk along wooden platforms now, and gaze down astonished on these disinherited panoramas which pass into one another without door or wall to stop them: Meleager and Atalanta, Amymone and Poseidon, Apollo and Daphne. The whites, browns and greens of the tesserae are natural to the limestone, and have not faded. You wander above them in a bemused trance. Here Dionysus offers wine to a wreathed nymph seated with one casual knee bent under her; vine leaves sprout about her face, and her robe has fallen to reveal the erotic dimple of her navel. Beside them Icarios, the mortal to whom Dionysus taught the planting of vines, leads a pair of stumpy oxen and a cart-load of wineskins, while two peasants, the first wine-drinkers, loll nearby.

This part of the island was known for its wines in the Roman age, as it is today, and the villa may well have belonged to a rich wine merchant. The motif of wine constantly recurs, with the invocation 'Be Merry'; even the geometric decorations enclose cups. Archaeologists, lacking true identification, have called the villa 'the House of Dionysus', and the most astonishing of the mosaics portrays the god in triumphal procession.

His girlish figure straddles a leopard-drawn chariot, while one hand holds a thyrsus and the other points to his ivy-crowned brow in a gesture of flaccid self-applause. The robes which lap his thighs are corroded green; his wreath is a little torn. And on either side of him there gambols a suite of dissolute followers: nymphs and Indians, cymbalists and trumpeters. Between the leopards walks a Silenus, his face picked out in a handful of damaged tesserae which heighten its lecherous senility, and a satyr tries to climb the chariot from behind, clasping an empty wineskin, while the chariot-drawing leopardess (she has spotted teats) turns and snarls at him.

When the custodian sprinkles water over this pageant, the figures quicken out of the stone. The curve of the lymphatic god's limbs and torso, accented in variegated pink, suddenly becomes flesh; the wheels of his chariot seem about to turn. But the next moment the dry air covers them over, and the exquisiteness is lost. And now that I examined the procession, it looked oddly purposeless. I noticed that its members bore no true relation to one another. They had been envisaged singly. This gives them a look of futility, almost of sadness, as if the cavalcade existed simply for itself, urged by a hollow revelry. Its musical accompaniment, if it had one, would be that of a thin, toneless flute. Its cohesion, its very obscenity and robustness, are an artifice, and even the god is alone. He points an effeminate finger to his crown as if to proclaim his divinity, but his followers take no notice, and the leopards pull him away into oblivion.

The upper town of Paphos is charming without distinction. It covers the clifftops of Ktima in a medley of shops and churches, municipal Ionic and down-at-heel Ottoman. The old-fashioned mansions are slowly vanishing, as are the timber-roofed fishermen's houses. Already the suburbs going down to the sea have a look of bungaloid uniformity, whose saving grace is its evident impermanence, so poorly are the concrete cottages built.

Westward along the clifftop I went into the Turkish quarter, which saw bloodshed in 1964 when the animosity between Greek and Turk reached a new height. Sentries sauntered in a No-Man's-Land of abandoned houses, whose streets seemed as old and haunted as those of Pompeii, and echoed the quietest footstep. Already the roofs were falling in and the grass starting up through the pavements. The Turkish air of regulated, conservative living had been tainted by isolation and displacement. People had come from outlying villages where they felt unsafe, and there was nothing for them to do. The blue-painted shacks of the United Nations squatted on salient roof-tops, from which their bored soldiers, Scandinavians or Irish, examined each other through binoculars.

Sometimes the trouble between Greek and Turkish Cypriots is blamed on the British with unreasonable whole-heartedness. 'You used the Turks against us during the War of Liberation,' said Antis, pointing a finger at me over the restaurant table as if I had been personally responsible. 'Before that they were our friends. And now look. Look what you've done!'

I started to protest, but a voice at my elbow anticipated me. 'Whatever the British had done, the Turks would be at our throats now. They never wanted union with Greece.' I saw the heavy head and solid, comfortable features of Christos, a schoolmaster who had become a friend. He had carried his meal over to our table. 'All the same, England didn't help.' He looked at me without apology, because he spoke of my country as somewhere dissociated from human beings. 'England used the Turks as auxiliary police. And we have never been friendly with them since.'

Defensively I asked him about EOKA.

'That's right,' said Antis, leaving us. 'You ask *him*. *He* can tell you.'

What did Antis mean by that, I asked.

Christos was staring at the remains of his meal. His frank grey eyes appeared to be debating something. 'He means that I was in the resistance,' he said. 'In EOKA.'

'But everyone in Paphos was in EOKA,' I answered. 'Or so they say.' Christos went on spearing wisps of dry chicken with his fork, so I added: 'What was special about your role?'

'Oh,' he said casually, 'I was caught.'

'And tortured.' Antis grimaced melodramatically over his shoulder.

Christos looked up without a trace either of resentment or of guilt. 'I was head of the Gymnasium bomb group,' he said. 'Youths.'

I frowned slightly, and now he too started to frown. His

face was docile and transparently honest. But I sensed he was afraid that I did not believe him. 'I will show you the prison camp if you like,' he said. 'It's still there.'

It stood on the edge of a track with its back to the cliff-side: a large house and the remains of an enclosure behind. The tiles were sliding from its roof and the verandahs had slumped along the arcades in piles. In front of it a fountain pool was choked with earth.

We stepped through the compound wall, no more than rubble. A change had come over Christos. Before, he had been faintly embarrassed, but now he had become almost oblivious of me. He spoke fast and with a disconnected animation.

'They brought me in through this entrance. There was a sentry box there.' An iron door swung loose in the wall. 'And the English colonel was standing where those almond trees are. As I was led past him a dead man was carried out through the doors of the house. I saw his face, and I knew him. He was Giorgos Christoforou from Emba. And the colonel said "If you don't speak, you'll be like that by the end of the day." Then I was afraid.'

He might have been talking to himself, remembering aloud. When I spoke he stared at me a moment as if he had to recall me. 'The British kill many men? No, I don't think so. I think Christoforou was the only one they killed like that in Paphos. It must have been a mistake.' He gazed at the ground under the trees. 'The colonel was short and rather fat. He had strange eyes. He spoke very good Greek.' He stroked the grass with his foot. 'He was standing here. I remember exactly.'

Behind the house was a corrugated iron hut and the

floors of others whose walls were gone. Half the upper storeys had collapsed. The only sound was the groaning of timbers in the wind.

'A Turkish sergeant with black gloves stood at the top of the ramp. He bawled at me to put my hands up then hit me with his fist. I think I have seen that man in Paphos since . . .' He walked up and down the courtyard. 'So decayed now . . .' The doors gaped open. Windows showed their bars like pulled teeth. The almond trees were filled with birds singing. 'When I arrived I found many of my friends sitting here on the concrete, including my old school-teacher. I walked to what I thought was the washroom but the sergeant ran up behind me and clubbed me on the back of the head. I fell unconscious. Later they took me to that room there.'

'Where?' I could see no room where he pointed.

'It's gone now.'

I went over and saw perforations in the concrete floor where iron wall-struts had been fixed. Christos was still talking in his quick voice, but was walking there alone, a youth. I simply followed him in numb astonishment. The place itself, with its burst ceilings trickling light and dust, its faded military *graffiti*, its chill of organized violence, made us both speak softly. It turned us into ghosts.

'There was a room there all right,' said Christos suddenly. He cut an ample figure for a ghost, in his shiny suit and leather shoes. 'The Turkish auxiliaries did the torturing. The British officers cross-examined. I was tied down to a table. Then they blocked my nostrils and dripped water onto a scarf over my mouth. That way you have to take in water as well as air when you breathe. When my stomach was full, they started to punch it. They did it again and again, and day after day. The pain was like nothing I can explain. So that in the end I was glad when more of my friends were captured. When they were torturing them there was less time to torture me.'

I looked down at the concrete floor, knowing nothing to say. The faintest cracks were spreading over it, like the first lines in a young face.

'In between, a British captain questioned me. They knew all about our group. The first words he said to me were "Hullo, Dracos" – that was my secret name. Dragon. "Dragon," he said "I'm going to turn you into a sheep." And he laid his pistol on a table in front of him and said "I've seen your plans to kill me. Go ahead." The pistol, of course, was empty.'

'Had you planned to kill him?'

'Yes.'

I looked at Christos again, at the mild eyes and the face whose features blurred one into the next.

'Then the captain showed me a list of my friends and said "Is this your group?" They had every one of them. After that he wanted to know who had given us arms, but we all said the same: a man who came from the mountains. I'm not pretending we were brave. Plenty of us confessed things. And some were more afraid of EOKA than they were of the British, and so kept silent.' He paused, kicked at a fallen timber. 'A few even secretly wanted the British to stay.'

I asked: 'How many? One in twenty?'

He looked embarrassed. 'I'm afraid not so many.' (I do not know if this is true. How can anybody know?) Christos walked into the shadow of the house and stared at the flaking walls. 'If it was terrorism, it was the only way left to us. Talking had failed, so what were we meant to do? Every people has a right to be free . . .' He turned to me with a look of pinched concern. 'In those days we thought that freedom would solve our problems. It seemed simple.' He smiled faintly. 'We were young.'

A row of cells faced us. Their iron doors stood ajar in the grass. The grilled windows were still in place, but the bolts shattered. Swallows were dipping in and out. Christos pointed to the cell beneath the stair. It measured six feet wide and was filled with goat's dung. 'That was mine.' Some military joker had since scrawled over one wall: 'Abandon hope all ye who enter.'

'The captain used to rattle a stick over the corrugated iron to frighten us,' said Christos. With a cold pang I remembered how, at my own school, the prefects had done precisely that, had run their canes along the sides of the passages when summoning a boy to be beaten. I think only then was I certain that Christos was not lying, and that my own countrymen had done these things. It seemed now that I was naïve not to have believed it before. In every people, when angry or afraid, there is a quality which can be distorted into brutality. In my own, perhaps, it was a lack of sensitized imagination.

'Don't look so worried,' Christos said, touching my arm. 'I don't feel any bitterness against the British, or even the Turks.' How could I explain to him that this too disturbed me, that if a person condones violence in others, he may start to condone it in himself?

But Christos said: 'I couldn't kill a man now. Or even a chicken.' He folded his arms philosophically. 'And why should I blame anyone? It can't be helped. The captain was only doing what the colonel said, and the colonel was obeying a general, and the general had to do things for the government. And the government was miles away.' In an obscure, Asiatic way he saw himself as a part of history, of immutable forces; he was powerless against them.

Back in 1958, when these things had happened, I had narrowly missed being inducted for National Service before it was abolished. Otherwise I might have been posted to Cyprus, and hunted Christos as a criminal, and he might have planned my death. Instead we were walking together in the sun. When I told him this grotesquery, he only shrugged and laughed in his easy way.

'Life is like that.'

So one man's terrorist is another man's hero. Now there are streets and statues dedicated to those whom the British hanged as criminals.

We went back through the almond trees. The sky was drained of light. It hung dead over a mottled sea. A woman, squatting in the field nearby, was crushing something with a stone, and a boy was leading a calf over the low hills which separate Paphos from the world.

CHAPTER THREE

· · · · · · · · · · · ·

Wilderness

Next morning I set out for the Akamas peninsula and for the slopes which mark the westernmost reach of the Troodos. The way led through Emba village, then climbed among hills scarcely softened by trees. For centuries this region was rumoured to be filled with diamonds, although it merely contains rock crystal or analcime, and legend links it to the underground kingdom of Venus, the bewitcher of Tannhäuser. Here the demon-goddess kept a court of dwarfs and beautiful women, and waylaid wandering scholars.

But today nothing could have looked less enchanted than the eroded flanks of these hills. Their rocks gave out an igneous glitter which hurt the eyes, and the sea stood in the angle of each valley, deader than a lake. In the middle of the twelfth century the hermit St Neophytus fled to this area because of its barrenness, leaving a bewildered family and an insulted fiancée behind him. His eccentric piety attracted imitators, who invaded his seclusion, until today the monastery which occupies the site is the only large building to break the wilderness of this westernmost stretch of the island.

It came into sight suddenly. Built foursquare around its

church, it possessed a rude grandeur, faintly staled by an air of lucrative pilgrimage. The gaunt passages and rooms were inhabited by a bare handful of monks – one of those shrivelled fraternities which are common over all the Orthodox world. Only on holy days and summer weekends are these mountain monasteries filled with families who drive up from the cities on a sybaritic pilgrimage which is the pastime of almost every class. The people process around the icons, leave votive offerings of whatever miracle-working saint or Holy Mother is special to the place, then sit at rough-hewn tables in the sun while the men roast *kebab* and the women unwrap huge picnics.

But today, in March, Ayios Neophytus was almost empty. A monk showed me a cell where I might spend the night, and led me round the church in the glazed manner of a dragoman forbidden to beg a tip. Two peasants were kissing the painted saints along the iconostasis, their noses thumping the protective glass with each kiss.

'In the English church there are no saints,' said the monk, as if recounting a fact to himself. His stare either penetrated clean through me or failed to reach me at all, I could not tell.

'They are less important,' I said.

'Less important.' He shambled to a wooden chest and stared down at it. 'The bones of St Neophytus,' he said.

I remembered that the saint had painstakingly hollowed out his own sepulchre in the floor of his cave. Why, I asked, had his body been removed?

The monk's frozen eyes fixed me. 'It was more convenient.'

I wondered after what lapse of centuries it became permissible to steal the dead from their graves, and whether at some conscientious time bodies will not be restored to the places where their owners wished them to lie. But this was a useless question, in the case of holy necrolatry, since the consecrated limbs are often scattered in countless places, and when gathered might be found to have multiplied embarrassingly. As for the great saints, who could ever return their corpses to rest? And what monsters they would be, after all their controversial bones had been assembled, sprouting hydra heads and fraudulent sheafs of fingers.

The voice of the monk, itself dead, interrupted these puzzles. 'You may kiss it,' he said.

I stared stupidly in the candlelight. Kiss what?

Something blackened lay cupped in a silver reliquary.

'The head of St Neophytus. You may kiss it.'

The monk stood over me. Countless lips, I saw, had worn a shiny orange circle on the skull. So well-kissed was it that it had taken on a patinated, mineral look, like chrome or amber. I hovered, unwilling to kiss it or to offend the monk, but the next moment he had walked away in his pre-occupied fashion and had stepped out into the sun. I was left alone in the darkness with the orange skull. I offered it a weak smile and followed the monk into the day.

He was standing with folded arms, gazing out at a rougher, older place: a succession of caves in which the hermit had lived for over fifty years. 'That is the *Encleistra*,' he said. 'There is nothing like it in the world.'

At the age of twenty-five the hermit had scooped out these grottoes with his own hands, but quarter of a century later, in 1183, his followers were clustered like bees around him and his walls were being covered with frescoes. Annoyed beyond endurance, he escaped them by burrowing a cave still higher in the cliffside, reached only by a ladder which he could pull up after him.

I discovered the first of these grottoes to be the nave of a tiny sanctuary, on whose south wall the inscription was still legible: 'The most venerable church of the life-giving Cross was hewn out, built and painted by the contribution and great toil of our holy and divinely inspired father Neophytus, in the year 6704 from Adam (A.D. 1196) . . .'

The coarse walls and ceiling were smoothed by plaster to waves and bumps. But on them the frescoed saints erupted in sallow glory, frightening the worshipper to his knees. They ranked along its western face like an Inquisition: figures in shroud-like robes, whose faces held a look of time-worn grief. They clasped their crosses self-consciously before them, and rolled out parchments inscribed with the formulae for salvation. Products of a primitive Byzantine style, whose roots are in Cappadocia and Syria, they had been drawn with a naïve, linear strength, their beards bifurcated like icicles, and from beneath corrugated foreheads they all gazed on the world with the same occult misgiving.

Yet the sanctuary beyond, barely three paces wide, was a jewel-box from another age. It had been painted in the court style of Constantinople, whose sophistication marks the other pole of Byzantine art. Oriental force is replaced by Hellenic poise and calm. The lines are softer, subtler. They fade to one another, and gather light. The Syrian saints, in their famished hardness, look like men risen by willpower from hospital beds; but these other walls were peopled by serene and tapering enchanters. Above the door the angel of the Annunciation lifted his hand in a delicate sign, his pink and white robes surging about his feet. And a delightful composition showed St Neophytus himself, carried to heaven by angels and wishful thinking. He flew between them with his hands crossed on his chest while they, holding him each by an arm, were nothing less than transposed Greek gods, with golden, ringleted hair.

The saint's cell looked as small as his chapel. The emptied tomb was cut into one wall, and the room still contained a stone bench and table where he had written his *Ritual Ordinance* for monastic life and a piece *Concerning the Misfortunes of the Land of Cyprus*. This was a diatribe both against the island's last Byzantine ruler and the Crusader who dislodged him, Richard Coeur-de-Lion. For 'England is a country beyond Romania on the north, out of which a cloud of English with their sovereign, embarking together in large vessels called smacks, sailed towards Jerusalem . . . But the English king, the wretch, landed in Cyprus . . . The wicked wretch achieved nought against his fellow-wretch Saladin but achieved this only, that he sold our country to the Latines.'*

I sat down at the cold table where eight hundred years ago this anger was vented, and idly scribbled my own impressions of the frescoes in the cell. They too are in the Constantinople style, but are fragmented. Above the saint's

* Trs. C. D. Cobham, *Excerpta Cypria*.

sepulchre the Christ of the Anastasis breaks the gates of Hell underfoot and pulls the dead Adam back into the light, while David and Solomon stand in their tombs and raise their hands in small exclamations of wonder. This figure is beautiful, and seems to look down at the grave of St Neophytus with a severe compassion; for he is the resurrector of the body, and the bones of the saint, however kissed and dismembered, await his ministration.

At dawn, from a ridge near the monastery, I could see the day's journey spread in front of me. The near hills were green with carob trees, and went down softly to a sky-filled sea, to toy bays and dotted islands in the west. Even in the distance the shoreline kept this closely-worked brightness.

The Akamas, although small, is the most desolate region of Cyprus. No road crosses it. A few herdsmen graze their flocks and keep makeshift huts on the hillside. Then the mountains peter out in a spur which is the island's western limit. Beyond Paphos the shore immediately becomes so lonely that it was here General Grivas chose to land from Rhodes one November night in 1954 to initiate his guerrilla war against the British.

It was a hard descent from the monastery to the sea. My rucksack, full of luncheon meat and fish which are favourites in the villages, dragged on my shoulders, and there was no track to follow. I blundered down slopes planted with vines – the last cultivation in the waste – and tramped through maquis which was filled with partridge. All morning I encountered nobody but a shepherdess, who looked at me with the same curious, marbled eyes as her flock, then strode away with brushwood piled on her back and a twig in her hand.

The Paphiots used to train their horses and donkeys to a long-distance amble called *chapqun*, which they could maintain for six hours. In my effort to acquire this I arrived footsore at the sea by midday, and lapsed into a more cowardly gait. All afternoon I wandered westward along a shore whose rock the waves had worn to tiers and stairways. The loneliness in these shapely bays was faintly disturbing. The pale sand looked as if it had been prepared for a charabanc-load of holidaymakers. But instead the inlets were empty. The waves fluttered in without break of land between themselves and Libya. Northward the cliffs grew tall and threw off islands. Caves loomed in their flanks. The hills became stonier and supported only insults of trees, from whose shadow goatherds, watching me pass, raised their hands in a grave, mystified salute, while their flocks grazed on nothing. I was entering the wild.

Akamas takes its name from a Grecian hero whom Aphrodite loved, the son of Theseus by Phaedre. Legend tells of his courtship with the goddess on the remote peninsula, and until recently the Paphiots would point out a local rock as the petrified hag who had betrayed the lovers to the Olympian gods. The country people still treat Aphrodite matter-of-factly. 'She came and married here,' one will say, as of some prominent girl in the village, 'but that was before my grandfather's day . . .' This will be the signal for a wagging of heads and forefingers and the invoking of stories heard from village elders so diluvian as to seem contemporary with the goddess herself. 'She had an affair on the Akamas peninsula . . . everybody knows that, my child . . . Adonis found her there. They went to Lebanon . . .'

'Lebanon!' another will cry in outrage. 'Who'd go there for a honeymoon? No! She went north of Nicosia to Kythrea. It's a fact in that part. Beautiful country.'

Then an old man, wiser than the rest, demands: 'How can you believe such fairy tales?' He taps his stick authoritatively on the floor. 'It stands to reason that Aphrodite stayed at Paphos. After all, she was born there wasn't she? And they've dug up her temple, haven't they? Well then, what more do you want? Archaeology is a science . . .'

In ancient times the Akamas was richer than now. Its coast is still dusted with fragments of ruin – so faint that you might walk across them without noticing, but whose extent betrays a modest prosperity. The archaeologist David Hogarth, who came at the end of the nineteenth century, was, as far as I know, the first and last person properly to explore the peninsula. He discovered cisterns, graves and traces of houses, and I saw again a few of the tombs which he found, and the flotsam of a Roman city over Cape Drepanum.

The Aphrodite cult is perhaps remembered in the little church of St George which stands on the site. It is a lodestar for lovers among the goatherds. There they light a candle, repeat three times the name of their beloved, then turn the candle downwards. Only if the flame continues to burn is their love returned, and the church floor is littered with tapers dropped in misery or elation. St George is also friendly to those who have lost their animals, Moslem as well as Christian, and a Turk who prayed for the return of his vanished mule is reported to have looked up and seen it obediently swimming towards him over the ocean.

That evening, trekking southward, I glimpsed the deeper wilderness where I was going – a flow of hills into the sea, silken and empty. I searched for a place to sleep – a cave, a sheltering tree or merely some softening of the ground. But there was nothing. So I settled in the scrub and munched the kind of meal which is only good under hardship: local cheese, tinned fish and a slab of village bread. Night came harshly. The sun drowned like a molten coin. I huddled in the sleeping-bag with my knees to my chin, like the dead of Khirokitia.

For a while I was kept awake by a sad, mechanical double-note – an owl which I could not identify – and later awoke shivering with the dew thick on the grass. I shone my torch over its glistening. The waves were inaudibly calm. It was that time of early morning, still dark, which turns the heart as grey and thin as itself. I lay wondering how many more such nights were to come before the spring warmth turned them pleasant, and why I was here at all and not viewing the island from taxis and hotels. Might that not be truer in its way? Much of Cyprus is already composed of taxis and hotels. Cypriots themselves dream of them. I could not sleep again, but remained staring upwards at a sky immaculate with stars.

Morning revealed a country where nothing flowered. Between the sea and the hills spread a scentless waste, where the ghosts of last year's shrubs dragged their branches among stones, dying. Even the acacia scarcely grew; only cistus, whose petals look wrinkled and papery from birth, exploded fitfully in white and synthetic pink.

But the coast kept a desolate brilliance. The cliffs had collapsed in enfiladed boulders, which lay like the debris of some monolithic wall which had once crowned them, and the waves nagged at their wreckage now, or thundered in half-submerged caves. By midday I reached the point where the hills begin to drop to Cape Akamas, and I climbed inland. A disused track led to a British military training ground, abandoned a decade ago, where a rusted notice still read: 'Keep out when red flags are flying as firing is then in progress. Do not touch anything it may . . . and kill you.'

As I crossed into the watershed of northern hills, the western promontaries vanished and the great bowl of Khrysokhou bay rose into view – a hanging curtain of mountains where the valleys of Tillyria fed the sea. A wind was fretting the waves into foam below me. In tranquil weather this coast, with its neatly incised bays and headlands, must possess a miniature loveliness, but now the slopes had been stripped by fire. My boots left their prints in ash. A goat's skeleton gleamed on the rocks. Even the spiny violence of scrub was gone, and the trees where I walked were silver ghosts, whose stumps smote upward, broken. To the east the deadness of Mount Shirin descended into the waves. The only life was that of a five-foot snake squeezing into a fissure where for a minute afterwards I heard the rustle of its body reassembling.

The evening cold was intense as I reached the shore. Under my feet anemones and vetchling grew from the dust in an insane fragility. I reached Mount Shirin on feet which were by now very painful. I had walked some twenty-five miles over stone that day, and found my socks soaked with blood and the skin broken over my toes. Everything I had done to prevent this – plaster bandages, a buffer page of the *Cyprus Mail* wedged between boot and socks – had made no difference. I caught myself apologizing to these toes as if they were not a part of me. They were purple with insult.

As I was bathing them in the cold water I noticed Roman piping along the rocks. Such a thing is almost commonplace on this shore, but between my fingers the flowers reminded me that the Fontana Amorosa was nearby. Cypriots say that Aphrodite wedded Akamas here, and that whoever drinks from it will fall in love. Classical writers praised the place, although few could have seen it, and in mediaeval romance its site became a watered valley, the scent of whose shrubs and flowers was wafted out over the sea. 'And in truth', wrote Ariosto, 'every woman, every girl is more pleasing there than anywhere else in the world; and the goddess makes them all burn with love, old and young, until their last hours.'

Today most of that glade has become a jungled gully. Yet after the Akamas its flush of green was entrancing, and hosts of butterflies were tumbling about the trees. I threaded through the thicket – the bamboo grew as high as thirty feet – and heard running water. It sounded faintly above the hush of the sea, and looking down I saw it glimmer between the trunks of eucalyptus trees.

I followed it to where cliffs overhung a pool. Through

them, as if from nowhere, the water fell, piercing the quiet with an innuendo. This simplicity was the miracle which the ancients hailed – water wrung out of stone and flowing away to replenish the earth. There was nothing else but a trampled path, a reminder that the human world was close, and three or four fig trees which groaned from the rocks and sent their roots into the pool.

And what of the love-giving properties of the fountain? 'I had no curiosity to taste of the water,' wrote Alexander Drummond, the British consul from Aleppo in 1750, 'the effect of which upon old people like me, is said to be that of making the spirit willing while the flesh continues weak . . .'

As for the beauty of the Cypriot women, the goddess has abandoned them. The explorer Samuel Baker described their bodies as covered with ancient and modern fleabites, and in their deportment, as a Victorian lady put it, they 'all have a slovenly gait, and look as if they were tumbling to pieces.' Even today their virtues are the homely ones of physical sturdiness and fecundity, and their loveliness only that of extreme youth and of the astonishingly lustrous and innocent Greek eyes.

Yet over several centuries the Greeks themselves have attributed to Cypriot women a fascination which has less to do with beauty than with female politics. They appear softer and more sensual than northern Greeks, and certainly that is their reputation, which has never quite recovered since ancient times. Even the most famous Cypriot woman of antiquity, the Byzantine empress Theodora, began her life on the streets and ended it by setting up the first home for reformed prostitutes (some of whom preferred to throw themselves into the Bosphorus).

As late as Venetian and Turkish years Cypriot women were considered indecent in the Levant for their self-exposure, and their love of frippery was proverbial. 'After dinner we heard a crying and a singing,' wrote Le Saige in 1518. 'They were carrying a young woman to her grave . . . They had put a mask on the corpse, painted like the face of the beautiful dead woman. They had clothed her too in a fine black robe; she even had a fine scarf of black silk round her, and they told us that when a poor person dies they borrow for her beautiful clothes which she wears to the mouth of the grave.'

With these thoughts of mortal vanity I followed the stream into its valley, and found a place to sleep where a eucalyptus had shed mounds of bark. I heard the double-note of the owl again, and lying beneath the tree I glimpsed the moth-like bird flying between branches. The cold wind scarcely touched this glade and I would have slept well, but I was lying on the home of a family of tree voles, which rustled beneath me in astonishment all night.

CHAPTER FOUR

· · · · · · · · · · ·

The Copper Hills

East of Fontana Amorosa, where the road from Paphos joins the shore, and a few miles beyond the sunken breakwater of Lachi, lies all that is left of ancient Marion. The city–kingdom was said to have been founded by Athenians in the seventh century B.C., but tombs far older are scattered about it and the hills which fringe its bay are rich in copper which was mined long before the rise of Athens.

Marion's prosperity occurred during centuries of unrest between the Greeks and their Persian conquerors, but it survived its unsuccessful wars and was eventually destroyed not by the Persians but by the cruelty of Ptolemy I. Long after the Persian star had fallen, he razed the city and transported its people to Paphos, and now little but its sepulchres – irregular chambers reached by shafts or stairways – tell that it existed at all.

Eighty years ago the copper-workings were visible in the mountains behind. The crater was covered by a great lake which had formed there, and beneath it a labyrinth of tunnels spread for hundreds of yards. For years the vast concentration of water frustrated miners, but early this century it was drained and underneath it the delicate network of ancient shafts was blasted away. The vein of copper runs southward, following the Khrysokou river. The Romans, chasing its richest strata, were deflected only by ore so pure and hard that even modern equipment is scarcely able to excavate it. Among these hill-villages – Pelathousa, Istingio, Melathia – rise tell-tale mounds of slag, and the graves of early miners pock the cliffs.

Early in the third century B.C. Ptolemy Philadelphus rebuilt Marion and named it in honour of his wife and sister, Arsinoe. He even raised a temple to her, but the people associated her cult with that of Aphrodite, and worshipped the goddess instead. A feeling of quiet and independent wealth surrounded the city, and little more is heard of it. In mediaeval times it was nostalgically called Polis-tis-Chrysokou, City of the Golden Land, and a legend persists that from its mines the road was paved with copper to the sea.

Polis, which means 'town', is the oddly minimal name of the successor to all this misery and distinction, and a poor place it is. I strolled among an unsmiling people down streets lined with deserted shops and houses whose roofs hung broken. On the doors a white cross pinned to a black cloth showed where a man had died, and these were everywhere. It was the only town I saw in which the owls dared to come in at evening and cry from the rooftops. In 1964 it was strafed by Turkish jets, and now half its walls were smeared with anti-Turkish slogans: 'Up ENOSIS', 'Bring back Dighenis'. Resentment was in the air. Wreaths were piled high on the grave of an EOKA hero. His glistening white bust was the only well-kept object in the place, which made one feel that people should sometimes forget their pride and think of their children.

Some soldiers loitering in dilapidated barracks followed me at a distance to check what I was doing. But ingrained good manners forbade them to dog me too closely, and I eluded them. So silent and depressed did the town seem to be that I asked a man what had happened.

'Nothing,' he said. 'That's what happens here. Nothing. We have some orange groves and a United Nations post, and that's the sum of us.' He smiled the quick, polished Greek smile. 'Empty? Yes, like a rotten melon. When a man dies his sons go away – to Nicosia, abroad, anywhere. Anywhere's better than here.'

The streets creep down where the river moves among mud flats, without flowers. Animals' feet pattern the silt. I made my way through bamboo thickets, and out where tall reeds waved in emptiness. Nothing recalled Arsinoe, which sent its centuries of copper over the sea and which flourished under Byzantium. But excavators have unearthed countless tombs and filled them in again; in 1885 alone more than four thousand were opened and their contents sold by auction in Paris, without record. But I saw no sign of graves now. Only the acropolis, sloping under abandoned Turkish houses, had shed a few Roman stones, and a single column eased from the mud – more finished and beautiful than anything in the modern town.

The coastal road ran straight and low for thirteen miles before steepening at Pomos point. I set out along it, numbed by seeing so far ahead. The mountain's feet were hemmed in corn, but higher their peaks folded one upon the next in softening tiers, etched with trees like the pines in a Yuan painting. By the shore a few sheep moved, the ewes' udders tied in bags to ensure weaning.

This region has known no peace since the outbreak of the EOKA war when the Cypriots, in their first ambush for a hundred and twenty years, fired on a British jeep in the defile behind Polis. It was a very amateur ambush. The driver was shot, but his officer returned fire with the dead man's sten gun, killed one of the ambushers and captured two others.

The body of the dead Greek was taken in a hearse to Nicosia. The people along the way covered it with flowers. In the capital the two captured men were condemned to death. The telltale signs were everywhere by now, if only they could have been read. To the Cypriots the men were patriots and martyrs; to the British they were terrorists. A few days before the executions EOKA kidnapped an elderly British civilian called Cremer and threatened to kill him if the sentence was carried out. Zakos, one of the condemned, appealed to Grivas over the radio to prevent this death. 'What I did,' he said, 'I did of my own free will, and I am willingly paying the forfeit. Cremer is innocent, and the innocent should not suffer.' Cremer was set free, and Zakos hanged at Nicosia in August 1956.

This long, disenchanted coast, which curls in a bay to Pomos, suffered again during the Greek-Turkish fighting in 1964, when more than three hundred people were killed or wounded. Now the road is blocked by the Turkish enclave of Kokkina, which refuses passage to Greek traffic. The whole shore has fallen silent. The people still live away from the sea in mountain villages, safe from the corsairs who raided them for slaves as late as the nineteenth century. Somewhere here the town of Alexandretta has left nothing but its name on ancient maps, not so much as a shard or stone.

It was late afternoon when the road turned eastward on heightening cliffs. The hills came steep to the sea, sliced by mimosa-filled valleys. A reddish soil appeared. I tramped into a No-Man's-Land where a burnt-out armoured car rusted and a United Nations post flew its flag in the hills. Turkish sentries let me through the barriers into Kokkina, puzzled by my walking, but smiled their slow smiles and eased their rifle-straps on their shoulders as farmers relax their tools, not with the Greek swagger.

Very likely they were mainland Turks and not from Cyprus at all. In 1964, while feeling between the island communities was worsening, the Turks were secretly landing arms and soldiers at Kokkina. In August the Greeks attacked the enclave with three thousand men supported by light artillery and homemade armoured cars. The fighting lasted several days. The Turks only lost their positions after stubborn resistance, and retired on Kokkina itself while the Republic of Turkey supported them with jets using rockets and napalm. President Makarios threatened to attack other Turkish villages if the bombing continued, but he went on pressing his land offensive. Only a mile east of Kokkina the hamlet of Mansoura fell to the Greeks. The situation grew perilous. Greece and Turkey, allies within NATO, came near to war with one another, and even after the crisis cooled, nothing was resolved.

The Greek Cypriots felt that the treaty by which they gained independence from Britain granted the Turkish minority too large a share in the affairs of the island. But the Turks, who lost many villages to the Greeks in the fighting of 1963 and 1964, raised an embittered cry for partition. Their revenge was to come a year later, when all the north-east island – over a third of the country – was seized by their invasion force.

I found Kokkina embattled, but the families which had come here for protection touched it with a nomad look. Small girls sat with goats in the long grass, while their fathers tended the larger flocks or had enlisted as soldiers in the hills. They lived in huts of mud and beaten tin, where the loose-trousered women went about their duties. Even in squalor an air of sufficiency remained. The uprooting of more settled peoples, whose lives are twined in their possessions, can be devastating. But living frugally, and not caring overmuch for business, the Turk, when the time for change arrives, will collect his household on the backs of donkeys and carry it away with as little loss as such a change allows.

I asked the military commandant if I might stay a while in the village, but with the embarrassment of thwarted hospitality he refused me. Might I not stay one night? No, he answered miserably, not even a night. It was against military law. The place was under siege. 'But a mile east of here is Mansoura. You'll find a United Nations post there and . . .' – his mouth twitched – 'units of the Greek army.' He glanced at the darkening sky. 'I'm sorry.'

High on the top of a windy headland I passed a

memorial, a huge wooden bayonet stuck in rocks, where the dead of 1964 lay. The graves of very young men, they were huddled under geraniums in one corner of an enclosure, whose unfilled spaces seemed to be expecting more. The sea, lashing in from the Turkish motherland, cast a grey, hard halo round the promontary, and a notice said that the soldiers buried there had died for freedom and democracy.

It was dark by the time I reached Mansoura, which had been abandoned eight years before. Its houses stood decaying in the moonlight, their doors gone. The grass lapped at their windows. Farther on I found Greek soldiers, as the commandant had said, then the coast was solitary again. The moon shed a cold avenue over the sea. There was no other light. The headlands slipped blackly in and out of its phosphorescence.

These bays were bleak for camping, and I walked on for five miles to Kato Pyrgos, anonymous in the dark. I found a coffee-shop to offer me a room, and ate among its good-humoured customers, answering questions about Kokkina, England and the price of my boots. A robust schoolmaster named Chambi appointed himself my host. This happens in the tiniest hamlet. For no apparent reason some villager – a shepherd or a farmer – makes himself responsible for the stranger.

I warmed to Chambi at once. His laughter detonated in volleys which shook his whole body, and his talking only paused long enough for him to pour jets of wine down his throat. 'You came through Kokkina did you? What a place! May God spit it out – *Pthuh!*' He mimicked the disgusted

Divinity ejecting a gob of Turks. 'You must be feeling awful. Here, have some beer. Beer will cure anything. And have you eaten? You can't drink beer without eating *mezze*. It's unthinkable. Here, Pavlos, bring us everything you have!' His huge arms scooped up an imaginary cargo of food and deposited it on our table. 'Meanwhile, drink this' – thrusting the wine bottle towards me – 'It's revolting stuff – where I come from we wouldn't use it to wash a pig in – but it's better than nothing.'

I guessed that he was from Paphos. That bluntness is special to the south-west.

'Yes, I'm from Dhrousha – two thousand feet up in the Paphos hills.' He leant forward on his elbows and his voice quietened to a confidence. 'We in the Paphos area, you know, are different from the rest. We are a separate race.'

I stared at him. 'You're surely Greek?' The word 'Greek', like 'English', disguises an ethnic chaos, but I had never until now met a Cypriot to whom the term held any complications.

'Of course we are Greeks,' said Chambi, 'but of a separate kind.' The wine trickled at his lips. He said: 'I am an Arcadian.'

For a second I answered nothing, simply relished the cadence in that immemorial word and watched the dark wine dribbling down his chin. He had peopled the air with idling shepherds.

'It came about like this,' he said. His eyes were bulging with intensity. 'The ancient historians tell us that after the fall of Troy the Greek armada was dispersed by a storm. The Arcadian fleet under King Agapenor hopelessly lost its way. Homer himself says that Agapenor was no good at ships; because Arcadia, you see, was an inland kingdom, the centre of the Peloponnese.' He held one hand downward with bunched fingers to indicate a hopeless, land-locked isolation. 'So the Arcadian fleet arrived at Cyprus. Pausanias says they founded Old Paphos here, and built the temple to Aphrodite.'

All this was true. Because of archaeology these Homeric heroes, once considered myths, are beginning to bulk into history. 'The Arcadians were a pastoral people, solitary.' Chambi picked a piece of bone-dry salami from the *mezze*. 'They worshipped the woodland Pan.' Here his fingers curled on his forehead in a rakish pair of horns. 'They left fruit and staves as gifts in his cave sanctuaries. Now when I was a child, my father was a shepherd in the hills around Dhrousha. I remember clearly how he and the others left fruit as offerings in a cave, and stuck sticks in the ground outside it. Once, in a childish fear, I even took one of those sticks away. But who was I afraid of? The people said that the cave was sacred to St Ambaelis. But who is he? Who has ever heard of him?'

I confessed that I had not. I was drowning under the river of his words, as they unfolded a Pan-haunted Arcadia in the hills of Cyprus. Already the massed ranks of *mezze* – cheese, lamb, nuts, olives, were whittled to nothing.

'Who then was St Ambaelis?' Chambi flung a slab of cheese into the back of his mouth. 'Ask a priest and he won't know. Because St Ambaelis never existed!' He clouted the table in triumph. '*Ambaeli* is simply the Greek for a vine. You see? He is the saint of the vine! A simple corruption of Pan! That's typical of this part of the country – dig up a saint and you uncover a god!'

The wine in which Chambi disdained to wash a pig was pouring warmth along our veins. By now I was prepared to accept this rustic, charming man as pure Arcadian. 'According to the Cyprians' own account,' Herodotus had written more than two millennia before, 'some of them came originally from Salamis and Athens, some from Arcadia ...' Arcadia and Cyprus shared a common ancient dialect, a language closer to that of Homer than any other known. From inscriptions in ancient Cypriot have come crowds of words related to those in *The Iliad* and *The Odyssey*.

'And we still use them,' cried Chambi exultantly. He leant forward again in mingled wonder and elation at what he himself was saying. 'In my own village we use words forgotten in the rest of Greece – yet you will find them in Homer. Listen. *Etaraxen o themos tou*. Have you ever heard that? It means "he was moved to anger". It is pure Homer. You will never hear such a phrase outside our own hills.'

It is a strange thought that the shepherds of Dhrousha continue to lose their tempers in the same idiom as Achilles lost his. The Homeric word for 'to blind' was still used by his villagers, he said, for 'to terrify', and the archaic name for a heavy bolt had continued in those backward hills, but had vanished from the rest of the world. 'If Helen had only used that bolt in her bedroom,' Chambi declared, 'there would have been no Trojan war, no *Iliad*, no Arcadian landing at Paphos and no – me!' He banged his chest with delight and speared a cube of lamb as portentously as Hector skewering Patroclus.

'It would be too much to say that Cypriote was the descendant of the language talked by the Achaeans of Homer,' wrote Maurice Bowra, dumping Chambi back on *terra firma*, 'but it was certainly reasonably free of Attic and Ionic.' Another authority has identified a hundred and sixty words common to both Homer and modern Cypriote, and there is a host of words from classical Greek which are peculiar to the island. 'In the Paphos area we still talk about a *pitirion*,' said Chambi. 'It means "a little pine tree". The classical writers tell of crowning heroes with its leaves, but no townsman would have heard of it.' He twisted in his chair and thumped the back of the man behind him. 'I've seen this fellow before,' he said. 'He's from Nicosia. Tell us, Mr Soteriou, what's a *pitirion*?'

The man turned a dark, sophisticated face. His eyes flickered between us suspiciously. 'How should I know?'

'You see!' roared Chambi. 'I told you. And what's a *rimi*?'

The townsman frowned.

'It's a small street,' Chambi answered himself. 'You find the word in the Greek New Testament, and in Paphos. Nowhere else. This poor fellow' – he tapped his finger on the man's astonished nose – 'would only have heard of *strada* which came in with the Venetians, and the demotic *odos*.'

'What are all these words?' asked Soteriou. He spoke with a soft, manicured inflexion, but looked unnerved, as if he was being left behind in a business deal.

'Pericles would have understood,' said Chambi in rebuke. The two stared at one another. For a moment their features were juxtaposed. The townsman showed the hawk-nosed, delicate face of Phoenicia. His fingers were long and faintly effeminate. But Chambi was all shaggy, peasant squatness. His hands looked like blunt weapons. As of the earliest Cypriots, of the Achaeans perhaps, his body was the mountaineer's, built for freedom. Soteriou turned away from him with a shrug: water flowing round stone.

And certainly Chambi's putative ancestry had gone to his head. 'Why should I not be descended from heroes?' he bellowed. And by now, with the dregs gone from the third wine bottle, I too could see no reason why not. I remained in my chair, lolled euphorically against one corner of the walls, and listened to his torrents of words as they poured and splashed into the mist between us. Offspring of Helen and Menelaus perhaps, he boomed in my ears like the sea. Academic truth was shrinking into wine-sodden dreams. Who cared if Arcadia, the mountain heart of the Peloponnese, was not all it should have been? What did it matter if its pastoral inhabitants were lampooned in ancient times for their stupidity, or practised human sacrifice into the fifth century? Arcadia was not fact. Arcadia was the smile of a porcelain shepherdess, the sound of the double flute in watered valleys. Poetry, silence. Idyllic peace.

Where the last ranges of Tillyria steepen to an inaccessible sea, the palace of Vouni rests high up in the sun. Many of the villages in the valleys round about are Turkish, and proclaim themselves by erecting poles fixed with iron flags which stand out stiffly as if the mountains were shaken by continual wind.

But the morning was motionless about me as I climbed

the hill. Along the lower slopes, in and out of wild corn, grew gladioli and bugloss, with mimosa, rose-coloured fedia, and all the desiccated ranks of last year's dead. To the north the sea and sky were hazed together. They shimmered under the sun's furnace and below them the whole bay of Morphou hung in a misty loop, with ships and islands magically suspended.

As I spiralled upward, sweating and elated, anchusa and pink cranesbill appeared, with aromatic rosemary in the higher rocks. It was utterly silent. The air, like a held breath, embalmed the stones in an intense light. Even the anemones, red against crown daisies, shone with a stilled violence; and as if the mountain's pinnacle had burst into some rarified stratum, the very sky had trembled into quiet.

A legend lingers over the ruined palace that a company of nobles dined here and left their silver spoons behind them. It is locally called 'the eating-place of the lords', and the ubiquitous Queen appears to have joined in the feast. 'Queen Philocyprus reigned there years back,' a farmer had told me, muddling the Queen with a king of neighbouring Soli. 'They found her bracelets among the stones. She left them when she ran away from the giants. But where she went to after that, nobody knows.'

In the haunted brilliance, under that colourless infinity of sky, the palace climbed in terraces swept clean by wind and invader. It was almost clinically bereft. The walls were few of them higher than a man's shoulder. They described courts and terraces luxurious for their day, with here and there a graceful ascent of steps or a maze of rooms built in the fair, hewn stones of a more careful age.

Yet it is a palace without history. No ancient writer mentions it, and even its name is lost. 'Vouni' simply means 'a mountain peak'. All that is known of the place has been inferred from itself. Greeks, it seems, built it early in the fifth century B.C., and the king of Marion, a quisling of the Persians, set it as a watchdog over the Hellenic city of Soli farther along the coast.

In these years the palace had a Persian feel. The layout of its state apartments, the frontal entranceway, the elaborate baths whose furnaces and conduits are intact, show an oriental influence. Then in 449 B.C. the dynasty at Marion was overthrown and the palace passed into pro-Greek hands. You may still see where the old entrance was blocked so that chambers could open onto an inner court in the Mycenaean manner. And thereafter the rooms and stores proliferated – until the people of Soli had their revenge and sacked the palace at the start of the fourth century.

Its rubble, I imagine, was carried off to build other homes, until little was left but the hard-wearing plaster floors, which remained like a face whose features had been forgotten. I entered room after room, trying to decipher what each had been, and small things, in those cement foundations, betrayed them: bathroom floors which sloped to drainage conduits, sockets for jars of oil and wine, basements of the arsenal built to bear an upper storey. The great amphora-shaped cisterns – one was more than eighty feet deep – still showed filter rims and pools, and a stele, slotted for a windlass, had been carved with a face of Athene which remained unfinished, her grave features stillborn in the stone. The palace contains no other sculpture.

I sat under a carob tree whose fruit was dropping ungathered. The morning had lapsed into noonday sultriness. Banks of marigolds purred with insects. Beneath the walls stone altars – circular, semicircular, square – showed where sanctuaries had stood, and a road climbed under scrub.

I fell asleep. Nothing disturbed me on that hill. The mountains had kept its beauty secure, and the islanded coast wound beneath it uninhabited in sunlight. When I woke, only the pattern of its shadows had altered. Southward the mountains, bank on bank, rose colourless as glass.

It was growing late, and I wanted to reach Soli before sunset. For days now I had been eager to see this city, which lies under the copper hills by the Kambos river. Its founders, apparently, were Athenians led by Demophon, the son of Theseus and brother to Akamas who in legend had loved Aphrodite. Its name appears on the seals of the kings of Nineveh early in the seventh century, and it was here, about 600 B.C., that the great law-giver Solon came, after leaving Athens for ten years while the people grew used to his statutes. He persuaded Philocyprus, the king, to rebuild his mountain-city in the plain below, which was done so well and swiftly that other rulers followed his example.

The feeling of newness, of a town plucked from its feudal hills and placed confidently in the plain, pervades all the history of Soli. It was a very Greek city. From here came the first known medical treatise on bones (with a scandalous little book on flatterers from the same author), and in the Greek Cypriots' struggle against their Persian rulers during the fifth and fourth centuries B.C., Soli's part was conspicuous.

All this time the inclusion of Cyprus in an oriental empire favoured its Semitic element. Phoenician kinglets replaced the Greek ones in its city-states, and at moments it seemed as if the island would become absorbed into the orient. For to whom, precisely, did the Cypriots belong – to the East or the West?

We have a glimpse of them through the pages of Herodotus, fighting against Athens in the armada of the Great King Xerxes. Their commanders are wearing turbans and their sailors peaked Phoenician caps; but their armour is Greek. No doubt the Phoenician faction amongst them fought with some heart for their puppet kings, but others had been pressed into service unwillingly, and they were the first to break away at the Battle of Salamis. 'And thou who art of all men the best hast bad servants,' wrote the Queen of Caria to Xerxes, 'namely those who are reckoned as allies, Egyptians and Cyprians and Cilicians and Pamphylians, in whom there is no profit.'

In fact the Greek roots of Cyprus had already shown themselves during the Ionian Revolt, in which Soli's king, the son of Philocyprus, was slain. Of all the Cypriot towns, this was the one to hold out longest, and the Persians only took it after a four-month siege, by undermining the wall. Years later the names of its soldiers appear in the campaigns of Alexander, reaching far into Central Asia where Stasanor of Soli was left behind as governor of a wild province, and Nicocles, the king's son, commanded part of the fleet which rowed down the Indus.

But the city's remains are Roman now. A theatre has been reconstructed to a height of seventeen tiers, cradled against the hill, and looks as dull as such reconstructions do. From here, where the Greek looked down upon his city's harbour sending copper to half the world, you now see only a silted depression filled with banana and eucalyptus trees. The temples on the hilltop have yielded statues of their sad, chthonian deities – a cult figure of Canopus, an Eros who turns his torch downward in mourning – and have been earthed in again. They come from a time when the brightness of Soli had faded. Their world is the resurgent orient, Plutonic fatalism. The voice of Solon is lost, who 'grew old, ever learning many things'.

In the gulf below, the freighters idle and hoot. The sea is very close, and the coastal road with all the Morphou plain spread greenly to the east. The copper traffic continues in the wider bay, for an American corporation mines the hills inland; its conveyor-belt loader, projecting into the sea, betrays where the wealth of Soli lay and still lies along after the town is ruined.

'May Aphrodite pour glory and grace on this city,' prayed Solon, and certainly it enjoyed a distinction which its remains lack. Even its sculpture has been crippled by the local limestone, which turns as soft as cheese in the earth and may dissolve at a touch. A yellow or bluish marble was imported – from where, I do not know – but much of it is so coarsegrained that lumps of crystal can be plucked out, and it was worked in an oddly muted way by which the statues' surfaces glide into one another in a narcissistic caress. These pieces are very delicate and Hellenistic. Even their eyes, curiously, are not incised, and the traces of red paint on the hair, quite new to Cyprus, hint an Alexandrian influence.

The second century B.C. 'Aphrodite of Soli', now in the Cyprus Museum, has become a trademark for anything from a table wine to a travel agency and it is sad to discover that she is little more than a conservatory Venus, a product of local Hellenism. Behind her lie all the complications and ambivalent ideals of a civilization grown old, evolved over five millennia from the idols of Khirokitia into something self-conscious and trivial.

This matter of Cypriot sculpture betrays the people. In the sixth century B.C., before Soli moved into the plain, the typical statue was still flat-bodied. The mouth turns up in a sensuous half-smile which belongs more to the Buddha than to Pallas Athene. It is easy to imagine these as stylizations of a heavy-featured people of very irregular looks. Conflicting sculptural traditions – Egyptian grandeur, Syrian force, Greek harmony – melt into a flaccid type with ringleted hair and ponderous chin and nose. And about the faces of the women there is that boneless velour which is still the ideal of beauty in the Levant. Cumbered by ornaments, they look less like human beings than exhibitions of dowry.

As for the Great Goddess, her primitive nudity had long ago been considered a disgrace, and the clothing of statuary – both gods and men – contributes to the dullness of much Cypriot work. The drapery which emphasizes a figure by its tensions is only possible to a sculptor who has already mastered the nude. But the early Aphrodite is simply a cult figurine, conventionally swathed.

Yet it was precisely such a goddess whom the Greeks developed into some of their most celebrated statues. As they undressed her, her body flowered into opulent grace. Praxiteles himself carved her stepping into an imaginary pool – a statue which Pliny called the finest in the world – and even in the copies which remain, her figure is as natural as a fruit. Caught in a moment of poise, her left hand, which in Cypriot terracottas clasped her robe, now suddenly, with a movement of primal innocence, discards it.

But in the masculine climate of Greece, Aphrodite was faintly suspect. Called 'The Cyprian' or 'The Cyprus-born', she never completely lived down her oriental birth. Her rites were tinged with licentiousness, and she was surrounded by an elaborate and slightly disreputable mythology, becoming the mother, by various gods, of some unattractive offspring. In a time of decline she was much worshipped by prostitutes, no longer of the sacred kind, and the word 'Cyprian' in our own language remains a synonym for 'lewd'. Yet even after her deposal by Christianity she continued to haunt the mind of Europe, and for a thousand years survived as a demon and a profligate, before emerging again to balance with a lost, Delphic sweetness on Botticelli's seashell.

After the Ptolemies had extinguished the other island kings, the last prince of Soli was married to a daughter of Ptolemy Soter and the courtesan Thais, and so preserved independence, at least in name, for a few years more. Thereafter the city's fortunes followed those of copper. In Roman times it flourished. Bishops of Soli appeared in the early Christian councils, and a ruined cathedral is under the hill. But by the fifth century A.D. the mines had been abandoned and the harbour silted up, and soon afterwards the first Arab raids began.

Richard Pococke, who travelled through Cyprus in 1745, found traces of a wall and a handsome Corinthian portico; but by the end of the next century even these were gone; shiploads of material had been carried away to build the quays of Port Said, and boats came regularly from Cilicia to take back the hewn stones in exchange for timber.

'For many unworthy men are rich, while good men are poor; but we will not barter with them our worth for their wealth . . .'

So thought Solon, who could not have guessed the destruction of his city, but whose words are remembered after the stones are gone.

The copper mines of Cyprus may be the oldest in the world, and the name of the ore, the Greek *kupros*, derives from that of the island. The Romans, to distinguish it from brass, called it *aes Cyprium*, and as late as the Middle Ages, in the symbolism of the alchemists, copper belongs to the sign of Aphrodite.

It was Cinyras, said the ancients, who discovered the metal, and who was the father of the hammer, the anvil and the lever. But early in the third millennium, long before this half-legendary king, before the first Greeks came or the Phoenician was known, men were digging the mines and leaving in the slag pots and flints which were to betray their age. Smelting works as old as the thirteenth century B.C. have been discovered near Salamis, and Cypriot copper is mentioned in the archives of Mari and the Hittite Empire.

'My brother, behold, I have sent to thee five hundred talents of copper as a present,' wrote one of the island kings to the pharaoh Akhenaton. 'Let not my brother take it to heart that the copper is little.' For the hand of the god Nergal, he said – lord of the underworld and protector of miners – had killed all the copper workers in his land.

It was the Romans who developed the industry. Antony gave it, with all the island, as a gift of love to Cleopatra, and after the Battle of Salamis had decided their end, Augustus nationalized the mines. The Roman slag-heaps, like those of the Mycenaeans and Phoenicians, scatter the foothills of the Troodos. The Mycenaean smelters used manganese as a flux, and it has turned their slag pale brown; the Roman heaps shine black, like coal. Modern miners traced the ore by prospecting near them, and by noticing the red oxidized stains on the hillsides. Wherever they dug they hit ancient shafts and galleries which spun through the mountains to awesome depths.

In Roman times the copper hills of Soli were the richest of all. Augustus offered their management and half their revenue to Herod the Great in return for three hundred talents, and the shrewd king accepted. The Soli mines had already been exploited in the fourteenth century B.C., when the foundries could refine the coarse metal to an astonishing purity, and the Romans themselves were to leave more than a million tons of slag behind them.

This area, called Skouriotissa, is still the most important in the island, although it is becoming exhausted. The American corporation has excavated it underground and opencast, and the hills, already treeless, have taken on a mutilated, synthetic look. From far away I could see the new slag spilling over the hillsides – a green and rose-tinted waste, artificial as a rainbow, where silicate rocks and lava mingle. Beside me, as I climbed to the mining offices, glittered hills of Roman debris; its fragments were sharp and glassy – an imperishable iron residue amongst which lay broken vessels and lamps; and a far older refuse, very red and fine, was drowned beneath it. Nearby, as a charm to tangle evil spirits, the miners had circled in hemp the tiny church of Skouriotissa, 'Our Lady of the Slag', where a bell hung from a wooden frame and touched the wind with a weathered sanctity.

One of the mine supervisors turned out to be a red-haired Cockney. 'The Romans took a mass of the highest grade ore,' he grumbled. 'Their galleries run everywhere, as deep as we go. Four, five, six hundred feet down, and there they are: shafts, ladderways, drainage conduits, everything. And how did they work without ventilation?' The question went unanswered as our Landrover climbed towards the largest of the pits. The first sight to meet us was a hill of glimmering timbers at the side of the track – the props of a gallery.

'Roman?' I asked.

'Yup. They've even found ropes and reed baskets.'

We plunged up an incline, teetered, straightened. I looked back at the strange, frosted pile. How many suffocated slaves haunted it, how many years chipping at the rock's darkness, was futile to guess. The modern excavator had brushed it aside like a heap of fishbones.

'We can't preserve the galleries. They follow the richest

veins. When we strike one, it's bulldozed away.' We swung round the funnel of an underground powder magazine past loitering miners whose aluminium helmets were jerked back from streaming foreheads. And suddenly, where no sound came but the purr of our wheels on the dust, an arena of mountains lifted round us. I looked down and saw with a start that we were circling the rim of an abyss which had once been a peak.

'It's like cutting a cake,' he said 'only we do it in steps.'

Hacked in concentric tiers, it dropped by steps six hundred feet below us to a lake green with copper sulphates. At one side only, like beetles along the cliff's face, an excavator and two dump trucks were scooping up the last pyrites. I asked in astonishment: 'How long did that take?'

'Eight years.' He slapped one hand across his sweating neck. 'We blast with ammonium nitrate, then use excavators to pick up the ore.'

I stared down again where in my mind's eye the maze of Roman galleries, irrecoverable now, went threading through empty space. The mountain-head looked almost organic; its sides were preternaturally greyed, like a skull whose brain had been picked clean.

'We took nearly four million tons of ore from there,' the miner said. 'The Phoenicians and Romans got two and a half million more. So you see what damage they did.'

When work on such a mine is finished, the site takes on a desolate brilliance. The dust clears, and the naked steps become an empty amphitheatre. Yet their look of permanence is an illusion. Within a year or two the cliff face will begin to crack and shudder apart, as a well-excavated mine must, and soon after will crash in on itself and lose its symmetry until it is no more than a bowl of stones washed in liquid sulphates. Already, here and there, the excavation benches were splitting while we circled them. As we descended, hugging the rock, the supervisor pointed. Close to the last excavator, an opening showed. We moved towards it over a thickening lava waste, and he set the Landrover at the disused incline. 'How are your nerves?'

I discovered that they were delicate. We tilted and roared at the disintegrating ramp. 'Bloody machine. We've had too much rain. Ground's like silt.'

I looked down into space. The Landrover slewed. For a moment it seemed to be debating whether to stick fast or to somersault. I saw my own shape spreadeagled in the sulphur four hundred feet below. Then we stuck, reversed and scrambled on foot up the slope. The silence was sudden and unfriendly. A moment later we were at the mouth of a Roman shaft. Down beautifully cut steps it vanished into blackness, a little wider than a man.

'We first struck it eighty feet higher. But where it led I can't say. That part had caved in.' The miner turned his back on it, his hands thrust in the pockets of his overalls. 'It looks like an exploration shaft. But you can see now that the poor devils were tunnelling away from the ore.'

'How would a modern company have done it?'

'In much the same way.' He laughed sourly. 'The Romans were good miners by any standards. There are plenty of people I know who've made a bigger cock of a mining job than the Romans ever did. And the metallurgists in those days knew more than we do now. But their methods are forgotten.'

I crept into the shaft. The miner remained behind, four-square in the dwindling rectangle of light, and shouted: 'Don't stay long down there. The air may be stale.'

My torchlight flickered over a passage, steeply descending. On either side the surface of the walls had been shaken by the blasting nearby; only once or twice did I notice chisel-marks still precise on the stone. The daylight faded. My footsteps reverberated in the vault, echoed ahead of me like the advance of a dinosaur. I shone my torch back up the tunnel. The walls winked and glistened with tiny zeolites. The steps were cluttered by stones. I could still hear the mumble of the excavator three hundred yards away and realized that in a day, or in a week, this passage too would be gone. And I was suddenly struck by my own grotesque-ness here, sightseeing where generations had died. For the first to come had been slaves stabbing at the walls with Roman iron, suffocating from the inhalations of fetid lamps, sulphuric stone-dust, tuberculosis, sickness which no god could heal. The last to come would be myself.

Galen, physician to the emperor Marcus Aurelius and founder of experimental physiology, visited these very mines in A.D. 166 in search of medicinal minerals. He came away with a cure for trachoma which was only superseded by modern antibiotics; and a by-product of smelting, he said, a zinc oxide called *pompholyx*, was a remedy for cancer and ulcers.

Throughout his descent of the mine, he wrote, the temperature equalled that of the first room in a public bath. But 'at the bottom of the mine the smell of the air is suffocating and is tolerated with difficulty, being redolent of chalcitis and the rust of iron. The water has a similar smell. The nude slaves carry the jars with the greatest haste in order not to remain long in the mine. There are lights at moderate intervals, but they become extinguished frequently. The mine was excavated little by little by the slaves during many years. When the dripping water begins to lessen, the slaves dig further into the hill. It sometimes happens that a caving of the ground kills all the men, blocking the passage.'

My torch cast a weak blob. For a few feet the dwindling corridor steered to the left, but straightened again as if its cutters had lost hope of discovering ore in that direction, although there it lay. Beyond, the way was choked by stones.

Later that morning we found the section of another Roman shaft. Its props stood unbroken, their grain patinated with minute lights. Their splicing showed white and new. Even the revetting of the twigs remained, delicate as when first torn from its pines. The supervisor was not surprised. He had once found some grains of ancient wheat and a fossilized egg; and his wife wore a seal, he said, which portrayed the copper god and had been taken perfect from the grave of a Roman miner at Limni.

Underground work at Skouriotissa has stopped. The last project exploited an ore which was sometimes so hard and rich that the Romans ran galleries frustratedly about it at a great depth, but were unable to take it all, and even modern equipment was taxed.

With the rise of heavy earth-moving machines it has become cheaper to excavate from the surface, and I saw only one mine which sent its men underground as the ancients had done. It was run by Greek Cypriots, and for fifty years had been devouring a flock of sallow farmers who worked there part-time to supplement poor incomes. Above it lay heaps of waste left by the Phoenicians.

'So you're prepared to go underground?' The Safety Officer stared at me with pinched lips: a delicate, unhappy-looking man. Mining seems to turn men silent, even Greeks.

'Yes.' It was, in any case, too late to change my mind. I was dressed in overalls lent by the company, and in a helmet whose cat-lamp socket had been knocked off.

'The mine has reached the end of its life.'

'Which means it's not safe?'

'We do the best we can, but . . .' he stared lugubriously at his boots. 'We have almost the worst safety record in the country.' Sighing, he thrust a piece of paper into my hands. It rendered me responsible for any damage I caused, for the death of others, or for my own death. 'You must sign this.'

We went out into the light. The Safety Officer looked more like an academic than a miner, he spoke and moved so fastidiously, and gazed with distaste at the rail cars which squeaked and jangled past us on a medley of tracks. 'We employ thirty professionals,' he said. 'In a force of more than two hundred it is not a happy ratio.'

'And you?' I asked. 'What did you do before this?'

'Oh.' His thin lips seemed to be savouring something ambivalent. 'This and that.'

We passed the ventilation plant and reached the entrance to the mine. A whitened monument stood there, sprinkled with flowers. It was dedicated to the patron saint of miners, St Barbara, heiress to the ancient copper gods, and no more predictable than they.

'Some people believe in her,' said the officer. He pulled down the rim of his helmet as if to close out the sight. 'Some people believe in anything.'

A steering-car arrived at the tunnel entrance, shunting its empty wagons before it. The driver barely stopped for us to squeeze in before he moved it forward, and the flames of our acetylene lamps, so weak in daylight, gave out a mandorla of enshrining gold. Encapsuled in this faint glow, we went jarring and clanging into the hill. The wagons ricocheted together with stage groans and screams, and the sleepers of the track creaked in a near-human anguish. At first the tunnel was lined by iron struts, but these gave way to simple wooden props which glided before us into gloom as the train's weak lights resurrected and forgot them. It seemed impossible that anybody should be living beyond.

I rested on the floor while we travelled more than half a mile into the mountain. We were still a hundred and forty feet above sea level. The driver's small eyes inspected me, his face unsoftened by the light. The mine entrance was now only a white semicircle hung in the blackness. Where the lava above us had contracted and sunk, the props clustered like petrified trees. 'Meteoric clay,' said the officer, glancing at it in a bored yet meticulous way. 'It causes settlements.'

Then the tunnel turned to pure stone about us. We clashed hideously inside it. The cavernous silences seemed to threaten as we took our pitiful light with us, like a centipede pattering into night.

The air was cool when we stopped where the rail divided, and the officer and I got out. We set off alone down the second tunnel. Fresh water and compressed-air pipes ran together beside us. The silicate crystals were so fine that they had become a fur on the ground. They lisped strangely about our feet. We found a leak in the air pipe; when the officer gauged it, it registered a twenty per cent loss. 'Ten per cent is expected,' he said 'not more.'

Had there been any accidents recently, I asked.

The officer's shadow wobbled over the walls in front: such a shadow, perhaps, as was the origin of the Man who terrified lost colliers through the mines of nineteenth-century France.

'Not since Thursday,' it said.

We emerged into a series of lit-up galleries and chambers. Voices sounded. Two men idled by an electric winder, and were unsurprised to see us.

'The air's thin,' they said.

The Safety Officer nodded, pressing his fingertips delicately together, perhaps as a substitute for thinking.

'I'll show you the old works,' he said to me.

As we went, I lost all sense of direction. For three hours we climbed and descended a honeycomb of abandoned ladderways and tunnels, mined decades before. Once only, faint in the silence, we heard the grinding of a laden skip: a pulley still being used. Then came a moan deep in the earth, as if some disconsolate animal were trapped under the hill. Far away it emptied itself.

By now we were both inhaling noisily. 'Nobody's been here for years,' he said. 'But it's all right.' He lit a paper from his lamp and it went out at once. He lit it again, and again it went out. He frowned. He was determined to make it light. After all, he was the Safety Officer. By now something seemed to be pressing at my forehead. And he was breathing in gasps. So we found a shaft, and lit the paper above it in the rush of air.

'You see,' he said. 'These old levels were excavated on a top-slice system. The ore was taken up a central hatchway. But under there—' he jabbed down with his thumb, 'they've undermined the galleries by a railway.'

We descended the ladderways, breathing freer, finding men again, grimy and haggard, moving down to the modern mining. We began to go deep. We were now barely fifty feet above the sea. In the haulage inclines the steps were sunk in oozing clay and the sides of the tunnel bulged against splintered props. It was here, where the walls pressed in on the skip rails, and the timbers were snapped one after another as we descended, that the officer stopped and listened. A haulage wagon was moving down through the darkness towards us. There was no escape in the cramped incline. The officer shouted up shakily: 'Are you coming? Don't come.' The rattle died away. We saw the monstrous truck lingering on the lip of the incline. It seemed, by its own decision, to spare us; but an oil-streaked face was peering down behind it, cursing and turning back a handle.

'These props – you see where they break at the knots in the wood?' The officer continued to step squeamishly down the passage. 'One would like to do a lot of repairs here. But why kick a dying mule? The mine doesn't make a profit, it just keeps people employed. So one had better accept the realities. Less money, less safety.' He kept his sad, liquid gaze on the steps in front of him. 'Of course when I was a young man I wanted to change everything . . .'

We passed a telephone hanging on a wall with a promise of communication. It was the most comforting sight I had seen that day. But the officer said: 'The wires got blown up in blasting . . . What are you laughing about?'

'I don't know.' I was in a Safety Officer's nightmare. 'I've forgotten.'

He shrugged moodily. 'We're coming to the works.'

There was no more light, except our own. Closer and closer, we could feel reverberations and smell the heavy fumes of explosives. Suddenly the passage opened into a maze of galleries, pierced on all sides by the lamps of the miners which glimmered and wandered like fireflies. The whole core of the mountain was a furnace of noise. Pneumatic drills, slusher-hoists, detonators – every sound in the caves was multiplied a hundredfold, shattered and trembled the intestines of the mountain, never seemed to die. These sallow men, stripped to the waist, had not accu-mulated muscle like northern miners. They stood or knelt in isolated pools of light. Their necks and arms, illumined in lonely amputation, showed sickly white.

We followed the rails along the central passage, which disappeared under fallen pyrites. An antique loader stood abandoned on them; its scoop hung toothed and agog like the maw of one of Hieronymus Bosch's half-mechanized fish. And it was Bosch's world which enclosed us – a mediaeval phantasy of Hell where men were announced only by lamp-flames and the whites of their eyes, and where noise and stench were as native and eternal as the rocks; while far above, one after another, the crump and shudder of explosives sounded like the wrath of an unimaginable Heaven.

The Safety Officer received complaints. One man had been laid out by a falling rock. Another grumbled about his eardrums. The officer made dainty notes in a book. As we walked on, a deathly pale youth rose in front of us and said: 'I can't get air. I feel as if I'm dying.' He looked no more than sixteen. His body was slack and narrow. An utter weariness circled his eyes. The next moment we had passed him, like a ghost out of *Germinal*, and the officer was writing 'extend compressed air hose'. Farther on, where the priming cords dribbled in and out of caves, I watched a man boring blast holes in the rock face. He held the drill against his shoulder like an elaborate lance. Behind its juddering his whole body trembled, but the instrument itself, predatory and graceful, sank into the stone with the ease of a giant syringe.

By this system the pyrites are scooped out in a series of caves. Twenty-four blasting holes, drilled one and a half meters deep, bring down a mineral debris which battens against timbers erected in the cave mouth. For three months the mountain subsides and grows firm behind the timbers, before the ore is excavated and carried back to the rail.

Beyond us, at the end of the gallery, a tiny man with a carved face was striking sparks from the rock with a pick. He was, I suppose, some sixty years old, and in his isolation, swinging his iron instrument as Galen's slaves had done, he belonged to any era. Squat and wide-headed as the earliest Cypriots, patient and expendable as they, he, or a man precisely like him, had dug out of Cypriot earth the copper for the sword of Alexander the Great, and from these same mines had smelted the breastplate which a lord of nearby Amathus, said Homer, sent as a gift to Agamemnon, King of Men.

'There's one more level beneath this,' the officer said.

So again we went down. But this time we dropped into silence. The many passages – we never entered them all – were empty. But as we played our lamp-beams on the rock I caught my breath in astonishment. Over every wall and ceiling millions of silver and russet sparks awoke out of the darkness. They shimmered like a night sky of unearthly clarity, covered the caverns with a haze of fire.

'Silicate crystals,' said the officer. 'Almost worthless. The copper pyrite is a grey-green colour, the greener the better.'

I asked why the level was deserted.

'We've finished work here,' he said. 'And there was an accident. Somebody left some old timbers in one of the blocked caves. That one.'

We peered in. Again the stars hung on our light. 'The oxidization of copper makes for a high temperature, and the subsiding waste must have produced a spark. The cave exploded just as two miners were passing it. One of them seems to have grabbed the ventilation pipe to try to hoist himself up. We found the skin of his fingers on the metal. But that was all. They were drowned in molten rock.'

'Just like that?'

'Just like that.'

A silence came creeping over us from the unseen caves. It gathered in the air about. The officer unhitched the lamp from his belt and fingered it meaninglessly. Muffled detonations sounded. Everything faintly vibrated. And as they faded we heard a plopping of rats from walls, and an obscene scuttling along the disused galleries.

'What do they eat?'

'They eat the timbers,' he said 'the props . . . and the remains of the miners.'

I looked at him in alarm. 'The remains . . . ?'

'I mean what they leave over from their meals.'

My laugh was weak in the silence. He began to walk again, slowly. 'The greater part of a mine, you see, is just emptiness.'

True, the miners seem always to be tapping on the fringe of some elusive world. And long after their inferno has been forgotten, it is these emptinesses which obsess the mind: the echoing, long-exploited galleries behind and above, caves and adits sealed up, shafts shut off, the long length of railway lifting back towards the forgotten light. The whole addled mountain, it seems, the mysterious mass itself, contains a heart which is never reached.

CHAPTER FIVE

....

Into the Mountains

Hussein, son of the *muchtar* of Ghaziveran, befriended me the moment the Turkish sentries let me into his village. He had the blunt face and wide-set eyes which are never seen among the Greeks, and although he sported a shirt with a gigantic flowered collar which the whole village thought dashing or indecent, he made an impression of simplicity which did not belong to the Mediterranean but to his native Anatolia.

Settled in the fertile Morphou plain, the people of Ghaziveran are wealthy fruit farmers, but seem content to live in clusters of mud and concrete huts. Hussein's house, the richest in the place, showed nothing on its floors and walls but a coat of tiles already cracking and a few ponderous pieces of furniture. Only in the bathroom, which had no bath, a spin-dryer stood gleaming and alone, like a domesticated god.

By a curious chance the name Ghaziveran, 'The Place of the Veterans', belonged to the hamlet long before its recent battle against the Greeks. But nobody could tell me who these veterans had been, and already in the village imagination the name was related to 1964.

'The Greeks set up floodlights on us in the small hours,'

Hussein said. 'They demanded we remove roadblocks and surrender our arms.' Impassively he told me the story of the battle, while his mother, reared in the self-effacing charity of eastern maternity, served us an improvised supper like a devoted servant.

'My father went out to talk with the Greeks, and the commanders showed a list of the arms they wanted. It was ridiculous. The list read: "So-many sten guns, so-many hand grenades . . ." We didn't have any of these things. We had twelve rifles and a few shotguns.'

'Did you have to surrender?'

His mother let out a barely audible sigh.

'Surrender?' sparked Hussein. 'Certainly not! At four in the morning they attacked us. By that time we had made bombs from lead piping and dynamite and had laid them under the road. The Greeks had no tanks but they'd armoured a bulldozer and tried to force an entry that way. It blew up on the mine.' He went on speaking placidly, almost without emphasis. 'Next they tried to encircle us with infantry. I think they were several hundreds. We were just a few, with only these twelve rifles to go round. So my father drew us into the village centre and we fought from our houses almost until midday. I was only thirteen at the time, but I was waiting to take the place of one of the men with a rifle when he was killed.' He looked up at a silhouette in the doorway. 'But Rashid over there was a fighter – come in, Rashid!'

There was a moment's pause, while Hussein said: 'This is Rashid, my friend and next door neighbour.' Then the huge profile lumbered forward. The first thing I noticed was his absurdly small feet. They seemed to dwindle into the floor. Then my eyes travelled upward to a stomach which burst over a pair of revolting army trousers all of whose buttons were undone. He stood in front of me uncertainly, his hand extended. He was a young man still, but his body sagged with surrendered muscle, and the backs of his hands were scabbed and blistered. He seemed to be self-conscious about them, and held them palm forwards, like a suppliant bear. Yet on top of this wreckage was a velvet face round which the black curls flopped and fondled like those of a debauched Roman emperor.

I shook the hand.

'Certainly I fought,' said Rashid in a gravelly voice. He remained staring down at me as rudely as a child. 'I fired all through the morning.'

'Did you kill?'

'Kill?' His infantile eyes went on staring at me. It crossed my mind that he was unhinged. He said: 'How should I know? I just pulled the trigger.'

I asked if they had been afraid. Rashid's face puckered, as if he did not understand what I meant.

'No,' said Hussein. 'We weren't afraid. If we had died we would have all died together.' He opened his placid hands and laughed. That was the eastern feeling of community: the village ties which are stronger than those of nation or belief. To die alone is terrible. To die with your people is the way of nature.

'At midday Turkey gave an ultimatum to Makarios, and by evening the fighting had stopped. If you like, I will show you the graves of our fighters. They are at Lefka.'

111

'And the cinema's on,' said Rashid. '*Girl from the Swampland*. We'd be fools to miss that.'

Lefka is a Turkish town by the Skouriotissa copper mines. It was ten miles away, and I wondered how we were going to get there. But at one side of this half-empty house Hussein pushed up a corrugated iron door, and a moment later drove out a gleaming white Mercedes.

I blurted: 'Where did you get that?'

'It's my father's.'

There is a legend that every Turkish peasant keeps a hoard of gold buried under his house. He is naturally frugal. His home is undecorated, simple to the point of coldness, as if he cannot shed his nomadic instinct; and his clothes are makeshift — fitted clothes were unknown to the Ottomans, whose love was for something loose and rich. When he acquires money it is spent on things luxurious but utilitarian — an advanced household appliance, a child's higher education or an expensive car.

So we glided up to the little town of Lefka in this glistening tyrant, looking down at dusk on the copper harbour where the boats shone on their lights. At the Turkish enclave soldiers stopped us and squinted in between a cage of bayonets. The police played their torches over our faces. Rashid, sprawled in the back seats, shouted an obscenity at them and they recognized him with jokes and let us through.

We passed the graves of the fighters, lying beneath a stony memorial in the dark, and a moment later were in Lefka. That morning the radio had given out news of two Englishmen kidnapped and killed by Turkish anarchists. Hussein had fallen into a bitter silence after telling me, and he now wanted to make up to me for this. He proposed *Girl from the Swampland*, the only entertainment available, with a meal beforehand and a casino afterwards, and they begged me not to refuse.

'Now the English will think us barbarians,' said Hussein tightly. 'It will take years to forget.'

Rashid grabbed a fold of his own neck and bellowed: 'Anarchists should all be hanged!'

But after three bottles of weak brandy and a dish stacked with kebab, Anglo-Turkish relations looked less hopeless to them. Rashid had dissolved into a beneficent heap, splashing the drink down his throat and rolling his eyes. Hussein's flowered collar was spotted with fat; he grinned idly at the wall behind Rashid, at himself, at me. Would the English forgive them in time? He picked up the last bottle; the dregs gurgled into my glass. What did the English think of Turkey? If you said 'Turk', what did they feel?

I pretended to have my mouth full.

But the English knew, didn't they, that Turkey would never go Communist. Never, never. Communism was of the Evil One. And they understood, didn't they, that Cyprus should be partitioned? And if they didn't, could I say so in whatever-it-was I was writing?

Rashid jerked upright and shouted: 'And can't you put me in? I expect you're writing history, but surely, some-where . . .' The Roman curls danced round his dissolute head. 'I know! Make me a cave-man! That's historical isn't it? After all, I eat with my hands, and I look like . . . well . . . you see me!'

It was true. The degenerate and the primitive coexisted

in him. Neolithic jaw, prehensile stance, overcast eye-sockets.

'Put me in!'

So there he is.

In a basement under the market of Lefka a projector rattled through a hole in the wall, throwing *Girl from the Swampland* over the heads of some hundred men but no women; a Turkish woman, said Hussein (underestimating the species), would die of shame at such a thing. Jungle scenes flickered innocuously back and forth for ten minutes. Then a near-naked girl struggled from the swamp, and in the close, dark room seemed to press herself liquidly against her audience. For long minutes the hundred dark heads ogled. Their cigarettes burnt unsmoked against their fingers. Their lips faintly parted. Then, from somewhere in front, a voice called out: 'Go on Rashid, eat her!'

Laughter hit them from nowhere. Within a second the whole room was an explosion of ridicule. For minutes after, childishly infectious, this laughter detonated groups of spectators. It swirled about us like a lubricant. They hooted at each new absurdity, pulled out bottles of drink, conducted an obscene shadow-play over the screen with their fingers, hurled nuts at it; and as we were returning to Ghaziviran at last, Rashid said: 'That's the first good film I've seen for years!'

The sentries raised their barriers. We glided into the sleeping village and stopped outside a shuttered café. A sliver of light showed under the door. Hussein knocked. In this secret casino – Moslem law forbids gambling – the last flicker of gaiety warmed us into some small hour. The attraction was not of money, but of excitement. Alone in a

114

Greek sea, these Turkish villages suffer claustrophobia. Men with open faces and slight moustaches, their days were consumed by the citrus orchards, guiding water down mud channels. While at evening a tense society developed in the forbidden room. Isolated, they passed the night watching the fall of cards, enveloping in their hands small glasses of brandy – this too is forbidden – playing a game I did not know on a rickety table. When they wanted to replenish their stakes they pulled out wads of money from tattered pockets; the stake on the table rose, as I looked, to fifty-five pounds; but the tension remained solemn and heavy, far from the Greek effervescence. They did not quarrel. Perhaps they felt too threatened from outside. In silences, in the dark at the edge of the village, the sentry coughed and dragged his rifle.

Nobody talked of the future. The Turk, like the Arab, is a natural existentialist. They would go on farming, they said, if God and the Greeks allowed them. 'Who can know the next day?'

At half past five in the morning the *muchtar* shouted for his son to get up. Hussein cursed softly, moaned and dangled his feet blearily over his bed, then came across to mine and nudged me gingerly. 'It's late,' he said. 'You'd better get up if you want to find the tomb-robber.'

I nodded but closed my eyes. The tomb-robber was an old man in the village who dug illicitly for ancient graves, and sold their contents to black-marketeers. Now that most Turkish areas are shut off from Greek ones, the Turks have been pillaging graves of every period down to the Christian era, and near Famagusta an entire Mycenaean city – tombs, walls, houses – has vanished.

I opened my eyes again. The window let in a liverish patch of sun. Hussein was gone. I dressed in a hurry. I could see the old man's house – a mud hut – from the doorway. I had wanted to meet him only out of curiosity, but now I felt heavy and ill-tempered. Remembering those thieves who gutted the sepulchres of pharaohs and ancient kings, thieves who gilded their petty lives by depriving posterity of irrecoverable art and knowledge, my irritation turned to anger.

By the time I had crossed to the old man's home and knocked, I was conscious of my slightly clenched teeth, and of arguments crammed behind them. I felt sickened that even now, when archaeology has become advanced enough to deal tenderly with the past, this treasure-house of Cyprus should lie at the mercy of robbers. The longer he took to answer my knocking, the angrier I grew. How could he dare to burrow among the graves of men more civilized than himself, without reverence or understanding for what he touched? Gold Hellenistic bracelets, Roman ivories, Bronze Age terracottas – to such men they are simply money. Ideas, civilization, beauty – these he would obliterate for ever; because at best the pieces he recovered would turn up in American or European collections with their provenance imprecisely known. At worst they would be destroyed, since such robbers break the fragile ceramics like cobwebs as they go.

'Yes?' The door had half opened. A tiny, wizened face looked out, under a tall woollen cap filled with holes.

'May I see you?' In his room the only furniture was a table and an unmade bed; and half of each wall was plastered over with pictures of fulsome women from Turkish magazines.

'My wives,' he said in English.

I refused to smile. I was deploring obliterated civilization. On the table were fragments of Roman glass, corroded gold, two patterned lamps – perhaps early Christian – and pieces of a dark red polished ware which in Cyprus generally belongs to the early third millennium, but which might have been Roman *terra sigillata*, it was too dirty to tell.

The old man held one up to the light. He was spry and brown as a monkey. 'One pound,' he said. 'Will you buy?'

'No I won't,' I said sharply. 'Do you realize . . .' All the cooped up temper spilled out of me. I spoke about the loss to all futurity through his plundering, the depletion of the world's understanding. He was, in his way, a murderer. Did he know that the importance of the objects on his table depended on their presence in a particular stratum or tomb? Isolated, they were next to useless.

All the time I spoke his pale, bright eyes fixed me from under the woollen cap. And at last, as I finished, he knit his brows and muttered: 'All right, I see.' He dug into his pocket and drew out a Hellenistic coin. 'If you won't buy those, what about this?'

'No!'

'I'm a poor man.'

'Then get a job.'

'I'm too old.' He plucked a wisp of white hair from under the cap. 'Look.'

117

'You must have a family to help. Everybody has a family . . .'

He gazed around his peopled walls. 'This is my family . . .'

I caught myself smiling, and half turned away from him. He crept round to the other side of me, as if I was a building, and fondled the coin under my gaze. His hands were arthritic, like claws. But the coin was beautiful.

'These ancient people . . .' he wheezed 'whoever they were . . . they're dead aren't they?' – from a tomb-robber it seemed a superfluous question – 'They can't feel any more. What's the use of gold if it's kept in the ground? It ought to be used.'

'This gold shouldn't be used. It should be admired and studied.'

His tiny, simian face puckered in perplexity. 'But people will admire anything.' He violently pulled out the table drawer – it was stuffed with figurines – and turned his back on me as if disowning the whole matter. I picked up two of the pieces and spat on them. The smell of terracotta when damp is distinctive. These pieces smelt of nothing.

I asked: 'How did you get them?'

'Well . . . sometimes . . . I don't know.' He wiped his chin with the back of his hand. 'The people at Elea try to sell them to me. They are American antiquities.'

'American?'

'Yes. The Americans buy them in Nicosia. After all, they look the same.'

'But they are fakes.'

He pouted, said softly: 'Reproductions,' and slowly closed the drawer. The hardy brightness had leaked out of him.

For the first time he looked what he was, an old man. 'I don't have the choice.' He crept round to face me again. The tip of the woollen cap reached to my shoulder. 'I don't like the job either . . . dead men's things . . . but I'm poor.'

I sighed, no longer in anger but exasperation, and in spite of myself my gaze travelled round the empty room again, out of the curtainless window, back again into the room and over the mural wives who had brought no dowry.

I said: 'But the dealers pay you a twentieth of what a thing's worth.'

'That's enough.'

'How much can you earn in the orchards?'

'I?' He frowned. 'Perhaps fifty mils a day.' That was fifty pence.

'And as a thief?'

He did not reject the word. 'Last year I could dig only a few times, because our own authorities are getting hard on us.' He put his grizzled head to one side. 'But in five nights I made three hundred pounds.'

I could think of nothing more to say. Scholarship and beauty, in that impoverished room, grew meaningless as dust. The old man simply wanted to eat. He held up the Grecian coin again. The helmeted profile was clear and Attic; from the other side gazed Athene's owl. It was exceptionally lovely.

'Half a pound,' he said.

It was absurdly little to ask. For a moment I could not answer. If I did not buy it – the insidious thought curdled up – somebody else would. I touched its irregular edges. The concubines were giggling from the walls.

'No,' I said, but only from pride. 'Somebody else will buy it.'

When I returned through the market-place Hussein ran out to meet me and we walked together to the edge of the village. I barely mentioned the tomb-robber. It was late, I said. I must be going to Morphou.

'You shouldn't walk there,' he replied. 'Not among the Greeks.' He spoke as if I would be threading through a minefield. 'There are buses on this road. Take one.' He waited with me stubbornly until a bus came. Then we shook hands, he shrugged away my thanks, and with the quaint Turkish farewell 'Smiling-smiling!' he turned his back and was gone.

The bus was a luxury after so many days walking. It trundled the four miles to Morphou with elaborate halts. I sat next to a peasant woman who placed a live chicken between us; after we had disembarked at the same station, I hope the mess which it left behind was not attributed to me.

At Morphou, the centre of this fertile region, I sought out the shade of the monastery of St Mamas, whose walls sported blue and white flags crying ENOSIS, and walked beneath its arcades undisturbed, munching some oranges which Hussein had given me and wondering why I had not bought the Hellenistic coin. Inside, the reconstructed church was dim and cool. The morning came through high windows; chandeliers dripped in the gloom. I sat down, a little numbed. Before me a magnificent iconostasis shimmered in tiers of gold. Fish and griffons fought each other in its carved foliage; dragons dangled lamps; and on the baldachin painted cherubim leant forward with candles, touched by a celestial urgency, to illumine an inscription which asked for reverence before God's altar. I turned from this gilded conflagration to find the grave of St Mamas recessed in a wall under an ornate Gothic niche. The earliest story tells that his body floated in a marble sarcophagus to Cyprus, where a pious Christian led a pair of oxen dry-foot over the sea to drag it ashore. In keeping with many an early icon and saintly corpse, the body signified where it wished to be buried by sticking fast to one spot – the site of the pagan temple at Morphou – and was enshrined here in a church and monastery.

For centuries the saint has exuded a sticky liquid which is sovereign against earache and will calm storms at sea; it is said to dribble into two sockets in the side of the sarcophagus, but I touched them with my unbelieving fingers, and they were dry. The legend, in any case, smacks of Byzantine propaganda, and the Cypriots give the saint a more genial history by which he has become one of the most popular personalities on the island.

St Mamas, they say, was a peace-loving hermit who received no income and so refused to pay the Byzantine income tax. The governor had him arrested, but as the saint was being escorted to the capital, a lion – an animal unheard of in Cyprus – leapt from a thicket onto a lamb which was grazing nearby. St Mamas held up his hand, gathered the lamb in his arms, mounted the astonished lion and rode it to the palace. The governor was so impressed that he exempted the saint from taxes for life, and ever since then St Mamas, as patron saint of tax-evaders, has enjoyed a fervent worship.

Tiny symbols hung in the niche above the grave – mostly silver ears and hands left as offerings by people praying to be healed. Similar ex-votos can be seen all over the Christian Mediterranean, and as I looked I recognized them. For precisely such gifts have been excavated in Cypriot temples where they were left thousands of years ago – clay arms and legs dedicated in pagan ages to other gods.

In the niche an icon shows St Mamas serenely astride his cheated-looking lion. Riding against a champagne-coloured sky, and dressed rather richly for a non-taxpayer, he cradles a crook and a tiny lamb, and looks out at the worshipper with a girlish solemnity.

The citrus orchards of the Morphou plain are fed by underground lakes and thin away in the south-west to a higher cornland and to patches of apricot and almond grove. The red soil turns to grey, and the first foothills of the Troodos reach into valleys, while to the north, above the vivid colours of the plain, the Kyrenia mountains begin.

Hamlets along the way made walking easy. I bought bags of oranges for a few pence, with local bread still warm, and tins of fish – the villagers eat Japanese mackerel and tunny. Along the northern slopes, rambling as yet over near-level ground, I went among an April sheen of flowers through land not beautiful, but faintly eroded and spent. The town of Akaki is here, but has lost the horizontal waterwheels which made it strange; beyond is Astromeritis, said to contain so deep a well that in its bottom the stars showed at midday; and Peristerona, whose five-domed church is one of the most harmonious in the land.

Ten miles beyond, walking over virgin country, I came on the ruins of Tamassos, one of the oldest of the city-kingdoms, which was made rich by its copper mines as early as the third millennium. 'We are bound for the alien-speaking people of Temese,' runs *The Odyssey*, 'with a cargo of gleaming iron to trade for copper', and little more than its copper is known of Tamassos at all. Its name appears fleetingly in the annals of the Assyrian kings, and we read that the revenue of its mines passed from the Phoenicians to the kings of Salamis and to Herod. But soon afterwards it vanishes from record.

Large for its day, the city is buried beneath four modern villages in sight of hills stained russet even now by slag and oxidized copper. But its ruins – stones so friable that they look welded together – have been barely touched by excavation. Nothing could be more dead, more final, than these formless and coagulated heaps. Even a pair of sixth century tombs, probably royal, does nothing to dispel the feeling of strangeness. The stones of their thresholds are scarcely worn. Their friezes are sculpted shallow, repetitive. The doorways stand squat and brutal. They frighten. Nothing foreshadows the dawn of grace. Whoever were the princes laid in this fetid darkness with their sacrifice of horses, they seem unimaginably distant.

I descended the tombs into a stagnant coolness. The sunlight splashed on their steps. Built of sandstone monoliths, their chambers reproduced wooden houses with such fidelity that the roofs were corrugated like logs, and fake stone doors were carved with stone bolts. From wherever they were influenced – Mycenae or Lycia – their barbarism is their own.

A lifesize bronze statue, pulled from a nearby gravel-bed in 1836, has not given to this people a more recognizable face. Some god or votary, stepping naked into another age, all but his head was hacked to bits by the ignorant villagers and sold for a pittance as old copper. That is in keeping with so commercial a city. Tamassos seems to have depended overmuch on business; Phoenicians drifted inland to work here and its miners were often settled from other places. No doubt this interchange and tolerance brought its own weakness, and by the fourth century B.C. the city's king dared to sell it off to another state.

Knowing such things, it is surprising that Tamassos is rich in legend. But to Roman writers, who were distant enough to idealize, the city was pastoral and holy, and Strabo wrote more practically that all this area, now barren, was once so dense with trees that people were allowed to own whatever land they cleared. Thus, long ago, perhaps, the river which sparkles through these fields created a love-liness wider than its own. The poets wrote of its twin fountains, sweet and bitter, in which Eros dipped his arrows; and Ovid placed here the tree of Aphrodite with whose golden apples Hippomenes enchanted the fleet-footed Atalanta. Was this, then, the Garden of Hesperides?

The afternoon was wearing thin. I did not plan to penetrate the mountains for several days, although they were now gathered in the south, but had decided to circle the foothills then to walk their whole length among the great monas-teries to the cedar slopes of the west.

Meanwhile as I went the country grew wilder. The

scrublands lost their level greenness. They cracked and whitened, and dug down like hands into the plain. As the first chill of sunset came creeping over the hills I realized that I was lost. I had been walking carelessly by compass. I did not even know if I was in a Greek or a Turkish area or whether I was not, even now, crossing some military boundary.

The dusk gathered gently, thickening in the valleys. And out of it, as if in answer to my question, yet more beautiful in that quiet than any Caruso, the voice of a muezzin called from an unseen minaret, proclaiming the One God. A moment later I found a track and fell in with a tinkling stream of goats. An old Turk had tethered his cow in a glade and was hobbling after her in circles, seeking her udder with his fingers and smearing the milk over his face. I asked him the name of the village, but he only stared at me in amazement and whispered: 'Unbeliever!'

A sentry stopped me on the outskirts. We stood and talked while the sten gun left his hands and was hitched back on his shoulder. He ended by inviting me to spend the night in his barracks, but his commander arrived and flicked angrily through my passport, seeing that I had been to Greece. 'How can you stay in barracks when you're not a soldier?'

I replied ungraciously that I had recently slept in a clinic when I was not a patient, and in a monastery when I was not a monk. And once I had slept in an ancient tomb, even though not dead.

He looked at me as if he would have liked to rectify this. 'You can't stay.'

125

I should have accepted his excuse as a façade – my presence in the barracks would be a security risk. But for a moment I remained unsure and stood looking foolish in my threadbare sweater and interesting boots, when the village carpenter appeared and invited me to his home. 'That officer,' he said apologetically 'is not from our village.'

Hamid the carpenter, although still young, had a line-scarred face, and shoulders deeply stooped as if they had always been carrying burdens. From under his moustache an unlit cigarette drooped continually – he enjoyed the idea of smoking but could not afford it – and in his poverty an Asiatic fatalism pervaded him. Of all Levantine races only the Turk has not the quicksilver Mediterranean heart. Yet although he could speak little English and I only a courtesy of Turkish, he placed me among his family as if I belonged there.

His home, which he had rebuilt after the Greeks destroyed it, was of scattered huts enclosing a courtyard where fifteen goats and some chickens scrambled. To pass from one room to another was to run a gauntlet of hoofs and horns. The he-goat, whose satanic eyes vetted anyone entering the living-room, had a flattened custard-tin tied on its forehead to give it the advantage in butting; and by the side of the privy a tiny dog called Terrible-Fierce lived in a broken suitcase and would hurl himself, frantic with friendliness, on whoever approached. Not long before, a disease in which worms infested the liver had spread among the island's dogs. Even humans had contracted and died of it. So a law was passed and almost all Cypriot dogs were at once shot. These were not the scrawny half-wolves of the Middle East, but the descendants of hounds brought over by the British; and it is strange still to come upon their survivors in out-of-the-way villages – melancholy and stand-offish, like expatriate country gentlemen making do.

'That's the only thing we ever agreed with the Greeks,' said Hamid. 'To shoot dogs.' But he had taken Terrible-Fierce to Nicosia for an X-ray, and brought him back with a life-warrant.

As soon as I arrived Hamid summoned his nine children, who clustered before me like an embarrassed insect shuffling eighteen tatterdemalion legs. Their black eyes examined me for oddities, and wisps of laughter blew between them. Their shoes were all splitting and their smocks and trousers had the look of clothes frequently out-grown and passed down. Their mother, a quiet woman with a smile full of gold teeth, scowled at their laughter until Hamid pounced on them, cuffing, and exploded a command which caused them to vanish.

'They are only children,' he said. 'They haven't seen a foreigner before.'

Ten minutes later the oldest girl came back with a dried herring in her skirt. Then one of the boys returned clutching eggs. A moment later the others tumbled in with colocassia, fruit and sweets, and I realized that they had been dispersed through the village to assemble my dinner.

'I'm sorry, we were not expecting you,' said Hamid, as if this was his fault, and added without shame: 'We are a poor village. No electricity, no road. We live by goats.'

All through supper the children's eyes absorbed me. To them their father was entertaining the Outer World. They had not seen it before, and they stood in a herd, fascinated and faintly apprehensive. The Outer World, it seemed, was gangling and almost as dirty as them. Inexplicably it was walking, when everybody knew that it had cars. But it seemed harmless and its socks were full of holes which their mother insisted on darning.

They appeared, in this watchful repose, more adult and awakened. The lamplight saddened them. Their foreheads, as a family trait, were oddly tall above sickle-shaped eyebrows, so that they had a look of Renaissance angels – and like these there was something prematurely aged about them. The oldest, who was nine, could already do all her mother's work in the house.

I slept in the stone-flagged living-room on a divan with embroidered cushions. In a nearby room the nine children squeezed into three beds and moaned and giggled all night. I woke several times to find lime cement falling onto my pillow from cracks in the ceiling, and in the small hours Terrible-Fierce started a barking duel with the only other dog left alive in the village. Later I woke in full light to find the children peering at me like puppets through the curtained doorway. I pretended to sleep until the puppet-show had augmented to nine round, grinning faces, then my eyes shot open to screams and scuffling as they escaped into the courtyard.

A minute later an angry Hamid had sent them back. He had told them how to say Good Morning, and this time as each head felt its way between the curtains, it uttered a chastened:

'Gud Murning.'

'Ged Merning.'

After this they were duly respectful. Even when they found me at the courtyard tap brushing my teeth – something they had never seen before (they washed theirs in cold water) – they remained as solemn as if witnessing a rite. And as I thanked their father, and left along the village track, they projected a line of dutiful hands which continued waving from far away.

When I was out of sight I settled under a carob tree to eat. Hamid's breakfast of olives and sweet tea had left me hollow. Pulling bags of home-made food from my rucksack, I realized how often I had been made spontaneous gifts. Even in village shops – dark larders whose stock was predictable – the owner might insist on giving me fruit, or a customer slip away and return from his own home with something which I had failed to buy. Now I had some of the salty white *haloumi* cheese, the remains of lamb rissoles called *koupes*, and an elderly *dolma* whose vine leaves were leaking flavoured rice. All these vanished down my throat in a minute.

Within an hour I reached the Nicosia-Limassol road, and at the hamlet of Perachorio I lingered round the village church, waiting for the caretaker to come and unlock it, and noticing by the gravestones how almost all the villagers died in their seventies or eighties. At last an old man with a huge key flung open the doors. His boots crashed on the paving.

Inside, the twelfth-century frescoes had fragmented, but were an intimation of those to come in the Troodos: not the glories of classical times – the ancients barely penetrated the mountains, their world lies shattered along the coasts – but the splendours of Byzantium.

A sharp wind drove through the doors and into the narrow aisle, lifting the veils from the few icons and blowing back the curtain from the sanctuary. The old man trampled round the apse shouting the names of the muralled saints: 'Vasilios! Nicolaos! Athanasius!'

But the beauty of the church surrounds the dome. Within its bowl the Christ Pantocrator is faded – his eyes are blind as Samson's – but beneath, in a half-decayed circle, the angels pay him homage. They move as in a ghostly pavane, with plaited hair and long, attentive hands. Their wings hover and drip, and their bodies genuflect in courtly reverence. Frescoed late in the twelfth century, they were born of the Comnenian art of Constantinople, which gave a sweet, almond-shaped solemnity to the faces. They do not spring from frescoed space in the Syrian way, but caress and harmonize it. Their rhythm and suppleness are classical.

The old man was still striding about the walls, adjusting his glasses and squinting at the haloed faces. 'Theodorus! Epiphanius!' Then he looked up at the faded Pantocrator in the dome and wrinkled his white moustache. 'Finished!' he threw up his hands. '*Oof!*'

And true, it was as if the eye of the church had been plucked out. Around that indifferent face the angels processed like servants without a master, their hands lifted to nothing.

By now I was turning the easternmost flank of the Troodos, where the foothills scatter into plains at Idalion

– sanctuary of Aphrodite whose wooded heights were sung by Virgil.

Idalion remains, though fearsomely ruined, and the marjoram still blooms here, where Pliny said it grew best. But the woods have gone and the half-submerged walls of the city run over hills covered by a flaking skin of shale. The stones, piled one on another in lopsided tiers, are burnt to dust, and disintegrate piecemeal.

Di Cesnola, the American consul-turned-archaeologist, claimed to have opened more than ten thousand graves in the necropolis, and found forty gold earrings with bull-head pendants, whose eyes had once been inlaid. And while tilling the valleys, wrote a traveller seventy years ago, the peasants 'find in incredible numbers little statuettes of the same stone, from one to two feet high, all female, and holding a flower or other object against the breast, with distinct traces of painting, blue, green and red'.* These were cult-images of Aphrodite and here, as well as in Lebanon, classical writers set the Phoenician myth of the death of her lover Adonis. The pastoral poets wrote that from his blood and her tears grew crimson anemones, symbols of resurrection, and on the eastern acropolis they still bloom in irony among walls slithering to rubble.

What became of Cesnola's graves I do not know. In them he found the dead lying with their heads pointed to the tomb entrances and resting on earthenware plates. But I found none. Graves, walls, temples – all had been rattled empty and the city gone to join a hundred other places

* Ludwig Ross, *A Journey to Cyprus*.

which earthquake and the soft local stone have returned to powder.

That evening I settled on the hillside, unsure if the air might not be too cold to endure. A man collecting snails stumbled on my camping-place and said that the night would be all right 'for Englishmen and flocks'. I curled in my sleeping-bag on a patch of clover, but the ground was too hard for early sleep and for hours I watched the landing lights of airliners winking down to Nicosia.

My sleeping-bag covered in dew, I woke to see dawn clouds over the mountains and the moon still shining in the south. I was too cold to remain. I ate a soggy breakfast, consulted my compass and settled into a striding walk. On these mornings I became prey to a nervous sensitivity. I wanted to see nobody at all. I felt sick with being stared at in the towns – to stare is no offence here – and followed by children through every village. Even the shout of a goatherd to his flock was enough to turn me away from his hillside and from the focus of uncomprehending eyes.

So I waited for the sunshine to ease me back to human charity. Descending to fields where the sugar estates of the Crusader kings had been, I approached the first outpost of the Troodos mountains in the east – a mist-hung pinnacle on which the monastery of Stavrovouni perched remote as a cloud. After two hours I reached the hamlet of Pyrga, where old men sat in the young light, sipping their coffee. One of them came over to me with a glass of lemon juice, as if he knew that the night had sapped me.

'Here,' he said, 'drink this. It nourishes the bones!' His twinkling gaze ran over me. 'Where have you come from?'

'From Idalion.'

'A rotten place,' he said 'a pimple', as if the mere existence of Idalion were enough to explain all bad humour. 'And where are you going?'

'Stavrovouni.'

'Ah, Stavrovouni.' He glanced up to where the great monastery battened against heaven. 'You know what they'll give you up there don't you?' His bloodshot eyes threatened me. 'Beans.'

'Beans?'

'Yes. You go there to worship or to see something wonderful. But it's nothing really. All you'll get' – he puffed out his frosted cheeks – 'is beans. If I were you I'd make do with seeing our church here. It's very old – one, two thousand years or so.' He jabbed his stick towards the dark-stoned chapel, turned to go, then looked back and asked: 'How much did you pay for those boots?'

I invented a sum in Spanish pesetas, but he was not deterred.

'Hah! You were cheated!'

To be cheated is the least laughable thing in Cyprus. I glared at my dust-clogged feet.

'Yes,' he cried. 'You were shaven completely! My cousin in Nicosia could have sold you twice such a pair for . . . But it's too late now, too late.' He took the empty glass from my hand with a look of mournful finality, then added, recanting a little: 'All the same, they will get you to Stavrovouni. Spanish leather you know, comes from bulls . . .'

I turned into Pyrga's little chapel. It rose vaulted and

bare. Its ceilings were blazoned with the arms of Lusignan Cyprus and of the ill-fated Janus, almost the last of the island's Crusader kings, who built it in 1421. In its frescoed Crucifixion he and his queen, Charlotte de Bourbon, knelt very small, their round faces and hands lifted in dedication against the gates of an imaginary Jerusalem. The humility of this perspective – their heads barely reached to the feet of Christ – was oddly touching and sad.

Lord of a kingdom which the Genoese were strangling, threatened by Egyptian invasion and unable to extirpate the piracy among his own people, 'good King Janus' must have built this chapel with foreboding: as vulnerable and puny in a world of greater powers as his frescoed portrait, dwarfed under the Cross. Not far away, in the dried bed of the Maroniou river, he fought the battle which foreshadowed the end of his dynasty. Against a huge force of Mameluke invaders which had already laid waste Limassol, he led the moribund Lusignan chivalry and a rabble of levies.

'The Saracens,' wrote an eyewitness, 'slowly began to come into view on the top of the hill over which the road lies, and our men stood aside and awaited the attack as the king had ordered. The king stood in the midst of his army, and the Prince of Galilee, his brother, on his right, the whole of the troops being in good order.

'Immediately the Saracens perceived our army, they commenced to shout and to beat their drums. Then the king placed his lance in rest, and with his whole army advanced upon the Saracens, and killed so many that they were forced to retreat. Then an old Turk who had been baptized and was in the service of the King, and his friend, shouted "Let us attack them once more and they will be routed, for their trumpets have sounded the retreat". But no one obeyed his counsel and the infantry supporting the knights were inexperienced in warfare, and many of them threw down their arms and ran away, for they were without discipline. All those of the army who were found overcome by fatigue and the heat, were killed by the Saracens . . .

'Thus the King was taken prisoner and carried to Larnaca, and the news was carried to Nicosia; and those who were killed, God will give them Requiem.'*

Later Janus was taken to Cairo, where he was paraded on a lame ass, with his banners reversed before him; but Pope Martin V engineered his release and he was ransomed for 200,000 ducats – a crippling sum to which half Christendom contributed. He was said never to have smiled again. Five years later, after a reign filled with disasters, he died strangely loved and respected at a time when failure in public life was no more forgiven than now.

In the chapel – his only surviving monument – he kneels as a young man, modestly dressed in umber-tinted robes and a houpeland, facing his wimpled queen whose veil falls beneath her crown over fair hair.

After his reign, for more than four hundred years, Cyprus lay in the shadow of Islam.

The Maroniou stream ran several miles to the south, but I emerged through woods of pine and acacia under the peak of Stavrovouni. Erupting two thousand feet, it was

* Strambaldi, *Cronicha del Regno di Cypro*.

ribbed by terraces for the most penitential farming. The track tilted and corkscrewed between them, overhung by Jurassic boulders which had rumbled down the slopes and suddenly frozen, teetering and ominous on the lips of terraces. From above, these vine-scattered shelves, which circled it almost inaccessibly, must have looked like the whorls of a giant fingerprint.

Here and there, along lower slopes, beehives clustered under copses. But as I ascended, the trees began to thin and die. After five miles of toiling up my feet had turned to millstones. I remembered the old man's warning that I would climb up here for nothing. Or for beans. But even beans began to take on a ghostly attraction. They promised rest, and at each successive bend their mirage grew richer and more improbable until at last, so tired did I become that I forgot the proper purpose of my ascent and the whole monastery of Stavrovouni – tradition, sanctity, art – was transmuted into a cool and succouring dish of beans.

As the track levered itself higher the lowlands came billowing into view and the glory of the eastern Troodos rolled towards me in waves, their crests dashed with white-gold, lapping the foot of the peak. I walked through utter stillness, while the afternoon wore old. By the time I had reached the summit these savage ranges had paled and softened on a sallow sky, while to the south I could see Larnaca bay and the crags of Kyrenia marching to their end up the Karpas peninsula.

The ancients imagined this peak to be a meeting-place of the gods. They called it Mount Olympus and crowned it with a temple to Aphrodite. Three centuries after Christ, run the traditions, St Helena the mother of Constantine, returning from Jerusalem with the cross of Dismas the penitent thief, built a church here to enshrine it and set in its heart a fragment of the True Cross of the Saviour.

Beyond this half-legendary foundation the records of 'Stavro Vouni', the Mountain of the Cross, are silent for eight hundred years, until the church becomes a lodestar for pilgrims in the wake of the Crusades. The guardians of the Mountain were Benedictines, but only the shell of one of their black-stoned towers is left. In 1480 a Dominican monk found the monastery by moonlight almost abandoned. St Helena, he said, had left the cross of the penitent thief in a niche beside the altar. 'And there it still remains, untouched, though long since the monastery was utterly destroyed by the Turks and the Saracens, and the monks of St Benedict, who served the church, are scattered.

'Wonderful is the position or location of this cross in its place. It is in a niche dimly lighted, both its arms are sunk in recesses made in the wall, and its foot is sunk in a recess in the floor . . . Yet does not the cross touch the wall, but is absolutely free from any contact with it; and this is the wonderful story about the cross that it hangs in the air without support . . .'[*]

After the Turkish conquest Stavrovouni lay in ruins and was rebuilt only in 1824. How many crosses have succeeded one another here I do not know, but the Mameluke vizier Khalid reported that after the defeat of King Janus troops were sent to destroy Stavrovouni; among the booty captured,

[*] Felix Fabri, *Evagatorium in Terrae Sanctae*. Trs. C. D. Cobham, *Excerpta Cypria*.

137

he added, was a massive golden cross cunningly furnished with springs which set it in motion at the lightest touch.

As I approached I saw that the monastery was not old, but was a patchwork of domes and piers which stared vertically down into space. Nobody answered my knocking. I entered and peered along passages where cats flew in and out of semi-darkness. When I called, my voice died with a stony whisper in locked, Bluebeardish chambers. The cats leered and flitted. In the basements great stones, Benedictine or earlier, showed themselves where stucco had not covered them.

I creaked open a door which gave onto nothing but a mattress laid on flagstones in an abandoned cell. I opened another door and was faced by the skulls of dead monks stacked on shelves, their names inscribed on their foreheads, crosses between their eye-sockets and their bones sorted in boxes behind. I stopped in the passage and listened. A wind touched the roofs, and fell. From somewhere, thin and old, came a sound of chanting. Up some stairs, over an enclosed drawbridge, I found a chapel where two monks were praying. It was early in Holy Week; each icon stood among many candles, and the superior, glistening in silk dalmatics, swung his thurible between them.

I noticed a cross draped in damask and enclosed in beaten silver. Five hundred years old, it has taken on the tradition and magic of the earlier cross. As the last chant ended, one of the monks shuffled over to it.

'Smell there,' he whispered to me. He touched a perforation in the centre of the silver casing. 'That is the True Cross . . .' Through its tiny grille I saw embossed gold. It gave out a heady perfume. The monk's expression had softened to primitive wonder. He breathed: 'Miracle!'

We went out into the courtyard. In its sudden light the two brethren winced like old and withered monkeys. They looked desperately poor.

'Most Reverend,' one said 'we have a guest.'

The superior turned to me. 'Father Athanasius.' His grey beard still held strands of black. His eyes, voice, all his movements partook of an almost female gentleness. 'You must stay as long as you wish.'

He led me to my cell. Beyond its iron-barred windows the mountains were lapsing into twilight. Framed photographs of the Greek royal family, dust-covered and three generations old, hung askew on the walls. The father made my bed and poured out water for my hands, while I tried to anticipate him – shuffling and mumbling with embarrassment as this man who had lately been a god, wreathed in incense, now busied himself with my bedclothes.

'Do not let the cats in,' he said. 'If they get in they will take anything. They have not studied the Eighth Commandment.'

I hung my rucksack out of reach. It occurred to me that for every monk there must be twenty cats.

'We keep them to kill snakes,' said the father. 'They kill them in hundreds – four, five feet long, and some of them poisonous.'

'Are the cats ever killed?'

He looked up in surprise. 'God,' he said with the faintest reproof, 'protects them.'

We ate a frugal supper in the refectory – olives, bread

and the long-promised beans. There was no sign of the sultanas whose vines, it is said, were first cultivated here, nor of Stavrovouni honey, the best in Cyprus. The father cut potato for me as reverently as for an abbot. He had been a monk for thirty-three years, ever since he had joined this most austere of monasteries in defiance of his parents; but the two older men were little more than farmers dressed as priests. Their lives had been spent tilling orchards and they had come here already old, after the death of their wives. Now, the shadows closing in and with a half-savage faith, they waited in this place already lifted halfway to heaven. It was a proper way to end, said one. Up here you felt closer to God than to earth. You looked down and the world was just a map, a faded map . . . Later he took me out onto the parapet and pointed out the stars. He called even tiny ones by name. His aged face, tilted back towards the sky, seemed already to be conversing with eternity. 'Orion . . . Perseus . . . Cassiopeia . . .'

Below us cities and villages, by day invisible for haze, glimmered out of the darkness: Famagusta, Nicosia, Limassol, the bracelet of Larnaca on its bay; while to the west the Troodos mountains were piled with scattered sparks like a fairground canopy.

A cold wind had beaten up from the sea. I groped to my cell down pitch-dark corridors and lit my oil-lamp with numbed fingers. In its glow I saw six or seven cats mounded together on my bed – a pool of fur which gazed at me with variegated eyes. At three o'clock in the morning I was woken by chanting. The rectangle of my window was ablaze with stars. The four-hour liturgy, I knew, would last until day and I closed my eyes again. Praise, glory, penitence: it rose and fell in the syncopated plainsong which existed a thousand years before Bach, almost, it seemed, before creation itself, and pulsed through those corridors with a phantasmal sadness.

After the Crusaders captured Cyprus in 1191 the Catholic church began to displace the Orthodox from its age-old authority. 'The state of our country,' wrote the monk Neophytus 'is now no better than that of a stormy sea lashed by a gale.' The older church lost much of its property, and its bishops, now reduced to four, were exiled to distant parts of the island. Supported by successive popes and by the Crusader occupation of Constantinople, the Latins dominated both politically and economically.

The Orthodox withdrew and bided their time. Their monks took to remote places. While the cities of the plains, under a Western aristocracy, built cathedrals in a hothouse flowering of Gothic, the Orthodox monasteries grew up in the wilds of the Troodos, whose secluded valleys filled with churches. Because they were not envied, they survived, and from this time to that of Archbishop Makarios the Church has stood sentry to the nation's spirit and its leaders have been spokesmen of the people.

Into this defensive world – the Troodos – I was now climbing. The plains, with their flow of merchandise and conquerors, their cities, their vulnerability, lay far below, and the land had risen into hardness and quiet. My map no longer showed a cushioned succession of towns. In eight hours' walking I saw no one. I had the illusion of ascending out of senseless activity into reasoned calm. But in fact the Orthodox quietism has been dead here many centuries. The monasteries themselves are dying. The mountains are not so much a fortress as a reliquary, and the route was steep up stream beds slashed by skeins of water.

On the eve of Good Friday the last sunlight lit me into Pano Lefkara at the easternmost spur of the massif. The white soil of this town was once good for vines, its lace considered unique and its people cunning – 'in the oil-trade they are reckoned very fraudulent, for they mix their produce with mallow-water'.* In summer the women still sit out of doors sewing the elaborate Lefkara lace, the same which Leonardo da Vinci, who visited Cyprus in 1481, bought for the altar of Milan Cathedral; and the menfolk of Lefkara travel for months at a time selling it where they can.

Now the alleys were lined by abandoned Turkish houses whose doors were painted with crescents – nobody had bothered to efface them – and many others had been deserted by emigrating Greeks. But I found the church choked like a market-place; its congregation jostling and chattering. This family atmosphere is natural to a faith in which sacred and secular are one. God and His saints, like senior members of a close-knit clan, are invoked throughout everyday life which in turn is carried into the church.

'Panos was drunk again on Tuesday,' complained the old woman in front of me. 'I said if it happened once more I'd give him lizards for breakfast.'

---

* Ludwig Ross, *A Journey to Cyprus.*

'You give them,' her companion answered. 'Serve them right up.'

Louder than the chanting, this exchange of news and scandal hung beneath the dome in a genial effervescence. The priest stood before the iconostasis and waved his censer cheerfully, fumigating sin. Small boys bounced balls; babies yelled. But through the densely crowded aisles the people faced a single point. Here, on a high catafalque bathed in flowers and under a canopy of trumpet lilies, lay the funeral cloth called *epitaphion*, woven with the figure of the dead Christ. The people queued to kiss its face and naked body. Their joy evaporated. The older women caressed the embroidered feet with a terrible whimpering. Their lips trembled out an 'Oh-oh-oh' or 'Ah Christos!' until the ritual became emotion, and they wept. One woman, whose grief seemed less organized than the rest, would not leave the bier; her red-rimmed eyes filled as she pressed her lips against the hands, the wan feet, the reddened side, and the tears rolled down her cheeks until her friends pulled her away.

Two thousand years ago a pagan would have recognized this festival as the death and resurrection of Adonis, who was mourned by women at the vernal equinox, and his image laid on a bier among flowers. Christianity grew up among such cults, too deeply ingrained to destroy. It absorbed and christened them. In this way the ritual of the Orthodox Church has embalmed Adonis and Christ together, and behind them a whole disguised worship from some dark religious watershed. This earlier god too – a god of many names and countries – died for the

143

regeneration of man, but was a deity of plant and harvest in whose older and more primal cult life was of the body, not of the spirit.

Even Charon, who ferried the dead over Styx, has survived under his own name as the angel of death. The Church has done nothing to soften him. Wingless and old, but liable to sudden metamorphoses, he arrives ferociously armed and sometimes on horseback. Folk poetry perpetuates his terror. In Cypriot song, after wrestling unsuccessfully with Dighenis for three days, he changed himself into an eagle, drove his talons through the hero's skull, and drew out his soul. And if Charon can overcome Dighenis, they say, there is no escape. Some country folk, dying with a priest's absolution and the name of Christ on their lips, are yet buried like their classical ancestors with a bowl of wheat, libations of water, and a coin to pay the ferryman. 'His thread is cut,' say the people. 'Charon has taken him.'

Now, after two and a half hours of requiem, the bier was carried into the night. Ablaze with candles like a vast, tiered cake it lurched and wobbled into the streets above a singing forest of worshippers. The bells clanged in their campanile – the low tolling of one, the silver lament of the other, like man and woman mourning together – while far in front of the catafalque girls sang the funeral dirge.

> *The earth trembled and the sun hid*
> *When Thou O Christ the Saviour*
> *The unwaning light,*
> *Didst in the flesh sink down into the grave.*

The golden fans and lanterns followed them in a river of light, with the priest holding the heavy silver cross, rival to the True Cross of Stavrovouni, under a white veil. One by one the candles were snuffed by the wind, until only the lilies and the white hands of the bearers could be seen in the dark. The *epitaphion* jerked and slithered on its hearse. Flowers fell onto the dead, epicene face.

> *Thou, O Jesus, king of all,*
> *Who didst set the measurements of Earth,*
> *Today dwellest in a narrow grave . . .*

Uphill more slowly, the cortège moved through abandoned lanes, shuffling and swaying. Once, in more peopled streets, men stood at their doorways and sprinkled rose-water onto the bier as it passed, while their women held up little silver incense-burners. But a moment later the procession, circling to the church, was heaving back into the night, its priests and people coalesced into a single blackness, mourning the death of the god who is yet immortal, and will rise again.

From Pano Lefkara to the great monastery of Makheras is no more than fifteen miles through mountain as the crow flies, but by reckoning this a day's walk I had taken no account of the valleys which intervene. Here the watershed of the Pedeios river begins its descent to Nicosia, and the going is very steep. Already some three thousand feet above sea level, the peaks are too cold for night sleeping, and the shoulders of Mount Kionia, lifting far higher, are difficult to traverse and are racked by winds.

But at midday I was still unaware of this. A ridge ran easily from Lefkara, tilting at the massif through acacia and pine, and here and there the slopes ripened into valleys where lupins grew. Below and to the south, but far away, were the villages of Akapnou and Vikla near which the followers of the folkloric Queen fought with an army of negro soldiers; and here at last, where a pile of rocks bears witness, she was cornered by the giant twins and stoned to death.

My walking startled salamanders in the trees. The scuttling of their bodies was the only sound in the stillness apart from the industry of the bees and the scrape of my boots on the water-hardened rock. After ten miles the flowers disappeared – all but asphodel and mats of wild mint. I was feeling pain about my ankles, but the warm light and the mild land reassured me and the tinkle of goats sounded in the woods.

But soon afterwards the track dwindled north-east, and I was left alone. The sun had slipped from its meridian. Ahead the steep ranges flowed one into another with a desolate beauty.

I advanced on them unwillingly. My feet were already cushioned in blisters. I had miscalculated badly. On my map the land between me and Makheras showed a few wrinkled valleys and blue, deceptive streams, but three hours later I was still climbing and descending in vertical zigzags. The mountains heaved in an unbroken swell. The shale poured and crumbled down their flanks, where the roots of pines gripped an impoverished earth or were eased up and slid away. They rarely gave a solid foothold. Above my ankles some muscles which I never knew I possessed had swollen rebelliously. The soles of my feet were so painful that I was setting them down with a halting tenderness where they would least be hurt, trying to avoid stones.

By nightfall I was limping badly. If I had seen shelter, a ledge or a cave, I would have settled there and shivered away the night, for plumes of storm cloud were blowing up behind me. But I found nothing. Ahead of me the trackless hills wore that sameness which is more depressing than the most spectacular obstacle. As dusk obliterated them I could find nothing to curse but my own carelessness.

The sun set, leaving its job to an incompetent moon. No other lights appeared. I crested another ridge and looked over into the same pine-smothered solitude, another range, and another. I thought: I must be lost, nothing could be so far away.

My feet dragged on of their own accord, as if stopping would realize their pain. I kept my gaze averted from the skyline. It was too discouraging. Safer to pick out the knoll, or the step, immediately ahead. That was how I struck the road.

It curved round the mountain shoulder, gently insisting upon itself, while I gaped at it then followed numbly. Under the pines the scree gleamed silver in the moonlight, like a mineral. Half an hour later I was approaching the monastery, watching the headlights of cars gliding up on the metalled road from Nicosia and the northern plains. I was too relieved to feel pity or anger at myself. I was walking on twin flames.

By the time I crept under the walls there were only three hours left before Easter. Some people sat outside at sheltered tables, waiting for the night Liturgy. They murmured and laughed together. A light wind was blowing leaves along the ground. Makheras loomed like a prison from the mountainside. It was built in the accepted Cypriot pattern – a church enclosed in a fortress-like cloister – and its scale was immense; but on Easter eve, I knew, there would be no empty rooms. I lowered myself onto a bench and remained without thought or movement, facing the blackness of the valley. And as I hunched there, sleep came like a thick vapour lapping at me out of the dark.

A small, bright-faced man sat himself beside me, put his mouth to my ear and suddenly shouted 'Grivas!'

I looked up in bovine bewilderment and mumbled: 'What about him?'

'Just a joke,' he said, disappointed. 'You were meant to jump.'

'I can't jump.'

He shuffled uncomfortably along the bench. He looked like a sleek, crestfallen bird. 'I didn't mean any offence. All that's forgotten between the British and us.' He pointed at the valleyside where lights were moving through the trees. 'There's Afxentiou's dugout down there, only half a mile, and the British go as tourists just like everybody else.' He looked at me harder. 'You've heard of Afxentiou?'

I nodded. My tiredness seemed beyond sleep. And my feet had fossilized. They lay stone dead at the end of my legs.

'He was a good man, Afxentiou. A lion of a man.

Everybody that knew him loved him. You know how they killed him don't you?'

I nodded again. Afxentiou, I remembered, was Grivas' second-in-command, a far less austere and inaccessible person. In 1957, out in the darkness of the valley opposite, a shepherd noticed his hideout and betrayed him.

'British soldiers came to the monastery,' the man's voice chirruped through my weariness, 'but the abbot denied any knowledge. "Afxentiou," he said. "Who's he? Afx – who?" And so on. But they found the bunker just the same and shouted into it for his surrender.' The man cupped his hands to his mouth in a soundless order. 'And who came out? All the others, but not him. No. He stayed.'

'That was very un-Cypriot,' I mumbled gracelessly. Previously EOKA men had always surrendered when in hopeless situations. But Afxentiou had decided, as he prophesied in a letter to his wife, to 'fight and fall like a Hellene'.

'Yes,' the man admitted. 'He was something special.'

Wounded by a handgrenade and choked by the smoke of lighted petrol, he had fought for eight hours until explosives demolished the dugout. Soldiers, searching the rubble, found beside his burnt body a copy of Kazantzakis' *Christ Recrucified*, lent him by the abbot of Makheras.

'You'll come with me to the dugout, won't you?' the man said suddenly. 'It is, believe me, an inspiration. After all, you were scarcely born when these things happened. (How young did I look, then?) You were not to blame.'

'It's late,' I said. 'Perhaps in the morning . . .' How was he to know that inside my boots were not feet, but furnaces?

The thought of walking half a mile was a fantasy. I could scarcely walk fifty yards. 'My feet . . .'

He stared at them. 'How much did you pay for those boots?'

'I came over the mountains from Lefkara,' I said, ignoring the question. 'It's fine country but . . . hard.'

'From Lefkara in a day! *Panayia!*' The man frowned and smiled together. 'You English, I don't understand you.'

I didn't either, I said.

'We'll go to the dugout tomorrow then.'

'Yes.' (We would find it like a shrine to a new saint, filled with wreaths and candles.)

'You'll be amazed. No wonder they never discovered him themselves. He could go to earth like a tarantula.' The man sighed. 'But they killed him like a dog.'

The quick, bright eyes flashed over me again as if I might be offended. But I was past offence. I was past anything. 'Mind you,' he went on, 'I'm not one to glorify these people. No, no. Nowadays there's a street named after every pipsqueak who got shot by mistake. Yes, really. Martyrs are a disease here. If your village doesn't have a Victim of Colonial Oppression it's not worth a goat. A second-rate martyr is as good as a miracle-working icon. Why, we had one in our own town. He and I were at school together. And who was he?' He ejected this martyr with a flick of his fingers. '*Po-po-po*. Just a nobody. And now there's a marble bust to him in the village street.' The man gazed up in mock reverence, dilating his eyeballs and lifting his hands like a frescoed saint. 'It makes you sick. Him stuck up there as if he were an archangel. And when I think of him, picking his nose in the back of the class . . .'

My eyelids dropped with the weight of a portcullis. 'Go on,' I mumbled politely. 'I'm just tired.'

'. . . I don't like violence at all,' the voice continued. 'But it's useless to say it doesn't get you anywhere. It does. It has done all through history. A revolutionary is only a terrorist until he's achieved his revolution. After that he's a hero. An outcome makes a morality . . .'

My eyes opened to see if he approved of this, but clanged shut again before they had decided.

'Now if the British had stayed in Cyprus . . .'

I woke an hour later, slouched on the bench. The bells were thundering for the Easter Liturgy. A monk was tapping my shoulder. There were no rooms, he said, but I could sleep in the cloister. Up the valley blew the cutting wind in whose awe the monastery was called Makheras, 'The Sword'. I hobbled to the entrance and along an upper partico. The wind did not penetrate here, but the air was freezing and the cloister looked public. I pushed on a dilapidated door, shining my torch over piles of breeze blocks, cement and rotting furniture, and left my rucksack there, pleased to have a roof at all.

Makheras was founded in the twelfth century with the help of the Emperor Manuel Comnenos, and grew up around a legendary icon of the Virgin; but in 1892 it was burnt to the ground and rebuilt without a trace of its age. That Easter it shielded a varied congregation. Businessmen, travelled up from Nicosia with their fashion-conscious wives, sat dapper and attentive among peasants whose hands spread like crabs over their knees, or were cupped on knotty sticks. But all of them, confronted by the towering icon-ostasis and blinded under the glitter and drip of chandeliers, waited in bowed patience for the pledge of eternal life.

Tired as I was, this immemorial ritual penetrated my memory in confused and dazing images. I remember the abbot bolt upright on his Osirian throne, his black veil on his shoulders and his fingers laced above the pastoral stave, while through the incense-clouds, in gleams of saffron and yellow, his acolytes moved about him with the dreamy flickering of goldfish in a bowl. Pale faces lapped in black hair and beards, they chanted in a lulled abstraction, initi-ates already into the exotic boredom of paradise.

I remember the moment at midnight when the abbot emerged through the Gates of Heaven with the holy fire. The people had surged against the iconostasis, and the chanting had quickened. Then I heard him say 'Christ has risen!' The lights went out. Only the candle in the abbot's hands, held high above his head, glowed with the flame which sparks the eternal wheel of death and resurrection.

As he lowered it a host of tapers jostled forward in trembling hands. They lit from one another. The flames moved and multiplied. An old man with crutches, sitting beside me, tucked a candle between my fingers and lit it from his own. Everyone was smiling and greeting one another with 'Christ has risen!' to which the timeless response went up: 'He is risen indeed!'

All these rites are pagan-haunted. Already by the fourth century A.D. the heathens were accusing the Christians of imitating their resurrection festivals. One remembers the fire of the Eleusinian mysteries; and the myrtle strewn over the tesselated floors, symbol of love and peace in the Church, was once sacred to Aphrodite.

The congregation poured into the biting wind to process around the church. Everybody sang. In the centre of the procession the old man and I hobbled together, like congenital cripples. The doors of the church were burst open in symbol of Christ's breaking the gates of Hell, and the people chanted again, sure in the flush of worship that their lives – rankled and sweated in offices and vineyards – must rise out of their littleness into that radiant and mysterious immortality.

CHAPTER SIX

·········

The High Troodos

The country west of Makheras is cut by valleys where almond and cherry trees blossom in spring. Down their steep glades the streams clatter invisibly and at the head of each, where it flows from the mountain, a red-roofed village stands among hazel or sycamore. Isolating these gulfs of life from one another are uplands where in April the stubble of rock roses is already half burnt away.

The rock rose was once a source of myrrh, and its leaves exude a gum called *ladanum* which early travellers imagined to be dew. 'Sweet-smelling substance though it is,' wrote Herodotus, 'it is found in a most malodorous place: sticking, namely, like glue in the beards of he-goats who have been browsing amongst the bushes. It is used as an ingredient in many kinds of perfume and is what the Arabians chiefly burn as incense.'* Even recently the peasants used to comb it from the beards of their goats and use it as a medicine.

I crossed this country for two days, sometimes dipping into milder valleys where vines grew in a soil yellow with chamomile, and came to the church of Lagoudera beyond Asinou river. These mountain shrines are rudely built and

---

* Herodotus, *The Histories*. Trs. Aubrey de Sélincourt.

are muffled in steep-pitched roofs which ward off the snow and reach so low that a wooden lattice props them from the ground.

The muting of outward grandeur – the growing introversion of religious buildings from early Roman times far into the Byzantine – could scarcely be carried further. Fear may have had something to do with it, for as the security of the great Empire eroded, people learnt that wealth must be concealed. A long decline set in. Pirates infested the shores again, the Arabs reached the sea, Byzantium shrivelled. And Cyprus by the tenth century had suffered four hundred years of invasion from Syria and Egypt.

But between A.D. 965 and the capture of the island by Richard Coeur-de-Lion, a quiet renaissance occurred. The Arab forays vanished like a peal of thunder. Artists, imported from Constantinople and perhaps from Macedonia, built a crowd of churches which were frescoed in the court style of the capital. Curiously transplanted into these secluded hills, whose people were neither rich nor sophisticated, the murals of the Comnenian dynasty set the walls dancing to their elegant vision.

It is a baroque style, which finds its completest beauty in this small Lagoudera church, called Our Lady of the Vetches. From these frescoed vaults the oriental vein in Byzantine art is almost excluded. The prophets do not stare in that familiar, wide-eyed anguish. Instead they are fleshly and susceptible, their foreheads scarcely ruffled, and they move and gesture with a courtly breeding.

The Cypriots, I rather think, were natural members of this dazzling hybrid, Byzantium. They, like it, lay midway between the classical and the oriental. Their softness and conservatism were not Hellenic. To them the character of the Greek mainland was unsympathetically masculine, and all through mediaeval years the Cypriot nobles continued to send their sons for education in Constantinople, which they felt to be their mother-city. They shared the Byzantine's religious intensity, and also his fickleness and suspicion which among the aristocracy could turn to acid wit. The pagan laughter, ribald or gay, was gone forever.

To step into this church is to see the classical world halted in its stride. The figures are still Hellenic in grace, but proportion is distorted, perspective lost and their *raison d'être* is not to express an ideal through beauty, but to act as a channel of numinous power. Man is no longer God's likeness, but his supplicant.

This not only marked the passage from pagan to Christian, but was a return to faith instead of inquiry. By the end of the Roman Empire philosophy had in any case floundered into a syncretic game, in which gods and systems were shuffled like the ingredients of a lost recipe. And the answer to this futile flurry was the surety of Christ. Suddenly wider speculation could cease. All thought, all science, would become a branch of the study of God. Under the centuries-long stasis of Byzantium, belief and art and even the organs of state petrified into an awesome sacrament. There were developments, of course, but they were little more than tidal changes on the deep Christian sea. In the life of mind and spirit people had exchanged freedom for authority and permanence – and for that stagnation which is the price of certainty.

The church itself, even when small like that at Lagoudera, was conceived as a microcosm of the universe. Its cupola, painted with the dread figure of Christ Pantocrator, symbolized heaven. In between heaven and earth, along the upper walls of the transepts, the Gospel narrative and apocryphal scriptures linked man to God; while the lower walls portrayed more worldly business, descending from apostles and prophets to the Church militant parading at eye level.

I found the basilica under restoration, and filled with scaffolding, so I had to ascend these tiers piecemeal. At ground-level the frescoed prelates mingled with anchorites and ascetics whose high-domed faces were strangely tender and humane. Even St Onoufrius, who crawled naked about the desert until his body grew a protective fur, looked faintly academic, his genitals hidden by a fortuitous pine-tree.

I climbed the scaffolding past a beautiful and mannered 'Presentation of Mary' – St Anne leading her tiny daughter by the halo – and lingered before a rendering of the Dormition of the Virgin. In eastern iconography she dies surrounded by the apostles, while Christ rises over her darkened body, cradling her soul. It is a gravely harmonious conception. The apostles lean this way and that in half balletic sorrow. Despite the faith of Gospels and incense they look deeply wounded, oblivious of the ghostly Christ who already clasps his mother's spirit in his arms. This soul, shrunk to a swaddled child, is lifted halfway to his shoulder while an angel flies down from the upper air to receive it.

I mounted to the drum of the dome, where the Evangelists wrote uncomfortably in the pendentives, and the Virgin was seated with spindle and scarlet thread, listening to the Annunciation. Above them a group of prophets stood between windows, and higher still I clambered into the dome itself. I sat down on the topmost scaffolding. From their medallions a circle of angels lifted their hands to the God in shadow above. The fall of their wings did nothing to exorcise their pagan beauty, and the hair fell down their necks in classical coils.

These Comnenian angels were by now familiar to me. In *chitons* and diadems, sometimes elaborately slippered and always expensively coiffured, they approach the status of aristocratic humans. With their wings plucked and their wands confiscated, they could have wandered unremarked about the court of Constantinople in their day – effeminate sons of dukes and polemarchs. The immediacy of the artist's portrayal is extraordinary. It is as if we, in the twentieth century, were to portray angels in suits or dinner jackets. For at any moment, the frescoes seem to imply, one of these creatures may hover into human ken and alight matter-of-factly with a clap of vermilion wings. But we in the West, estranged from the roots of our religion, can clothe the angels only as others saw them, and the longer ago they were conceived the more easily we can accept their likelihood, as if a lapse of time could dissemble truth.

My stare shifted from the drum to the dome itself, whose bowl is filled by one presence. There, above the sweetness of the angels and the brooding of the saints, Christ lifts his hand in a vestigial blessing. His brows gathering faintly as at some distant concern, he gazes in a power-encircled calm, not at the worshipper, but obliquely away. Above the soft twine of beard and bone-like nose, the eyes are merciful. Their gaze cancels sin. His features, in their frame of dark-coiled hair, show a trace almost of tenderness.

To the Byzantines, as to the Greeks, beauty reflected the glory of God, and often dictated the setting of a church or a monastery. Around Lagoudera the way still goes through forests, and the Kyrenia mountains hang over fields which the evening was now beginning to obscure. It was dusk when I reached Spilia.

There is nothing special about the village. From it a track departs for Asinou, loveliest of churches, and a mile to the west runs the main road from Nicosia to Mount Troodos. But I arrived to find the street blocked. The whole populace was standing out of doors, staring up in one direction through the dying light. They had heard crying and shouting on the mountainside. High up, a car had driven off the track and overturned on the edge of the abyss. Saved, it seemed, by a single pine which propped it, at this distance it showed only a precarious point of blue. Around me the people gave out a vague, reverent flutter of sound, a whisper of absent names. Where was Andreas? Was Michaelis coming home tonight? Who else had a blue car? A young woman was weeping.

So the village bus was commandeered and half the male population squeezed into it. Twenty minutes later they were back again, bursting with laughter. They had reached the wreckage to find its four passengers dancing on the chassis, drunk. It was St George's day – their name day – and the car had careered off the road after a celebration. Inside it these four Georges, tipsily chanting, had flopped and

159

somersaulted like dolls and emerged to dance among the debris.

'Glory to God,' murmured a man beside me. 'The saints protect their own.'

'Don't you believe it,' growled a sceptic. 'They were just lucky. They should have been killed, the fools. And the car's done for. No saint protected that.'

'It's covered by insurance,' the other answered stoutly.

'Lot of rot,' grumbled the sceptic, whose name was Loizos: a heavy, middle-aged man. 'Why should the saints trouble if the people don't look after themselves?' He turned to me for support. 'Did you ever hear such stupidity? That road's a torture anyway. You don't have to be drunk to find your death up there.' He went on to tell me of people he knew whose saints had let them down – a caustic impeachment rudened by gestures, which was a relief from the miracles which usually cram the heads of villagers. The saints, he explained, were not powerless, of course, simply overworked and unreliable.

He invited me to this home, which held a little back from the street. Outside, its crumbling walls were chalked with slogans demanding ENOSIS and the return of Grivas. We both ignored them. Even the Cypriots who supported Grivas admitted that they were a minority. For most, ENOSIS was a dream which they cherished; but which remained a dream. They did not want Dighenis and his trouble. They needed to hold the present balance, however delicate, to till their vineyards in peace and to see their children better than themselves. Hadn't the general done his job by throwing out the British? Well then, there was nobody left to hate. Except one another. Yes, it was time for diplomacy – which meant Makarios. Garibaldi must give place to Cavour.

So I was glad when Loizos passed these slogans by and cried out 'This is my home. It is nothing, as you see. But you are welcome.'

His family came and went. I remember a pale, lame boy; the youngest girl, Yanoula, a gypsy elf with golden earrings; and a white cat which lived in the dustbin and was called 'White'. I was used to these houses by now: the few bare rooms, the iron beds, ungainly wardrobes, mantelpieces garnished with cheap china and plastic flowers; the shock of an enormous washing-machine. On the wall Loizos' parents, dressed and waistcoated in the old peasant robes, looked out from the one photograph of their lives, as from a state portrait: he with his gun, his hair parted at the middle in two scrupulously glossy waves. Their faces were faded, as if gazing from some far older time.

But Loizos' wife was decisively alive. Red and robust, she filled the small rooms with a rolling, causeless laughter. She summoned a meal from nowhere, with wine which she had made herself from the vines around the house. Then, her stockings rolled shamelessly below her knees, she sat down splay-legged beside us and bellowed with glee at everything.

'So you've been walking in our country? Hah-hah-hah-hah! I walked to Amiandos once and I nearly died. Hah-hah-hah! That was when I was having Yanoula, and – Holy Virgin! – she kicked me all the way there! Hah-hah . . .' Here her laughter wobbled her violently and she shook for so long that I began to fear for her, but Loizos said there was nothing to be done about it, sometimes she shook all day, and he was lucky to be married to so contented a creature.

He, in the way of sceptics, was a secret sentimentalist, and long before our supper was finished he had opened a biscuit tin stuffed with old letters. A friend of his had emigrated to England years ago. Did I know him? His name was Vassos Phouphoullides, and he was a cook in the Langton Road, Manchester. No? Was Manchester such a big village then? Or what about Sergeant Green? No, again? His face puckered. Why didn't I know him? They had served together in Palestine. Like so many Cypriots, Loizos had left school during the Second War and joined the British Army. ('There was nothing else to do . . .')

By now Yanoula had squeezed beside her father onto a stool so low that nothing was to be seen of her but a plume of hair and two eyes which blinked greedily above the rim of the table. 'She's a terrible flirt,' he said, as she slithered a fork towards his plate and carried away cucumber. 'Even a Turk would love her!'

The eldest son brought in the main dish with self-conscious pride and poured out half its contents for me. Everyone beamed with pleasure. I stared down at my plate. On it were five or six tiny birds. Their legs and wings showed no more than pointed stubs, but their necks were long, and from their skulls the blackened eye-pits looked out resentfully. I tried to smile back at the circle of faces.

'What are they?' I asked.

'*Strouthos.*'

I lowered my smile – by now frozen – to the birds. I did not know what *strouthos* were. Could they be robins? Or the yellow-breasted swallows which fly about these hills? Their grey death's heads reproached me. I poked one with my fork. The skull fell off the neck with a tiny clatter. I scraped away a little of the chest and ate its dark, high meat.

'Eat it all!' Loizos shouted, picking up one of his birds by the head and dancing it in front of my eyes. 'Look!' He threw it into his mouth and crunched up the bones like a mastiff. I nodded in a sickly way. It was ridiculous; I would happily eat chicken but not *strouthos*. And even if *strouthos* was a robin, chickens have a more likeable character. All the same, when I crunched one of the tiny skulls, and felt the brains spilling in my mouth, I thought I might be sick.

'Good! Good!' the woman burst into her monstrous laughter. 'Scrunch it!' Her red knees shook. 'Swallow it!'

Almost every small bird in the countryside is shot – more for sport than for food. The price of a cartridge would buy twice as much meat as a *strouthos* provides. I decided not to inquire any more about the bird (was it a bee-eater?) but managed to slide three of the skulls into my pocket when nobody was watching.

Then Loizos asked: 'Do you have *strouthos* in England?'

'Yes,' I said, not knowing.

'But you don't know how to eat them.' He paused cannily. 'You don't kill them, do you?'

'No.'

'Why not?'

'They're small . . .'

163

'But so are crabs. You eat crabs in England. I've heard it. So why not *strouthos*?'

'I don't know.'

He was looking at me slyly. 'I know,' he said. He leant towards me and lowered his head and his voice together in conspiracy. 'In England,' he murmured 'you believe that birds have human souls in them. Isn't that right? It's a superstition.'

'No . . .'

'But I've heard it.' He scaled his voice to a gossamer thread. 'No need to be loyal. Every nation has its superstitions.' And from time to time, for the rest of the meal, he would squint at me confidentially as if to say: 'You're just being patriotic. I know. And you know I know. But we'll keep it a secret.'

To sleep, there were half as many mattresses as people, and everybody was redistributed so that I could occupy one alone. The villagers do not wash at night. They go straight to bed. Yanoula cuddled beside her father, stared secretly across at me from between the threadbare blankets, and whispered in admiration: 'He's got pyjamas.' Loizos, like all the village poor, slept in his vest and underpants. He had worn two pullovers under his shirt, I noticed, which may account for the cold-impervious appearance of many of the mountain people – they are padded underneath.

For half an hour the other children moaned and bumped in the darkness of the next room, reminding each other to keep their arms still or to wash their feet in the morning. Outside, the village fell silent, for there were no dogs left to bark. Only a low wind blew up from the north and rattled the door.

As soon as the room was quiet I reached for my pocket dictionary and torch and looked up *strouthos* under the bedclothes. It merely said 'Sparrow'.

Next morning, in an old car crammed with labourers, we arrived at the asbestos mines of Amiandos where Loizos worked, and here I thanked him and said good-bye. The quarries are sliced in dazzling fields, where the whole Troodos massif gathers to a head six and a half thousand feet high. The rock is so soft that the miners rarely blast, but bulldoze it loose and smooth it out, so that the landscape is turned to a tundra where the whining of the machines is muffled in a snow-like earth. Conveyor-belts criss-cross the desolation, and above the crushing plant and the screening mill dust and fumes blot out the sky.

I found myself covered in tiny threads of asbestos, like worms, which worked their way into my pullover and dusted my hands. In its natural state the mineral mingles here with a lustrous, serpentine rock, but when the stone is broken these tiny fibres appear. Asbestos was mined in early times, and the ancients knew the secrets of spinning and weaving it. The Greeks spoke of a magic stone, *amianthus*, 'the undefiled', which could be set alight but never quenched. Its fibre formed the fireproof 'Carpasian linen' of Cyprus, as well as the napkins of Persian kings and the lampwicks of the Vestal Virgins in Rome which were said to be everlasting. The longer-fibred mineral was woven into cremation sheets. The funeral pyre would clean the sheet white while the body inside burnt to ash and was thus preserved and folded into an urn. So Pliny called asbestos 'the funeral dress of kings', and centuries later Marco Polo described with astonishment how the Chinese, wishing to clean their table cloths, hung them in flames. The stone from which this cloth was woven, he said, had produced the legend of the salamander which dwelt in fire; and the Great Khan sent him back to the Pope with one of these cloths, in which to wrap the shroud of Christ.

I was now close to the summit, the island's highest point, which is called – like many others through the Greek world – Olympus. I followed a winter stream, a scar of flinty stones. Under the pine forests, whose trunks were silvered by wind and branches glossed with lichen, last year's needles covered a ground which was poisoned and flowerless – although Aristotle wrote that the mountain in his day was rich in healing plants.

After an hour's gentle climbing the land levelled and the great heave of mountains – which began thirty miles to the east under Stavrovouni and dipped twenty miles north-west into Tillyria – lifted at last to the rounded glory of Olympus. All about hung that fading and overlapping of mountainous profiles, like successive stains upon the sky, which gives the Troodos its dense, static beauty. The sun seems not quite to reach them. They roll in a raw silence: waves which never break.

Like Ararat in Turkey, this peak was said to have been the resting-place of Noah's ark, and was a haunt of dragons. The Venetians built a fort here, which was surrendered without battle to the Turks who awarded its commanders by dressing them from head to toe in silk. But I could find no trace of early building. Instead the mountain summit held a Royal Air Force radar unit, whose satellites and antennae were covered by a white glass-fibre dome like a giant golf-ball.

During the British occupation Troodos became the summer resort for military and government. A woman visitor in the 1920s described days spent loitering in the club house, which was filled 'with select parties of gossiping ladies who forget that the windows of the turrets are wide open and that their conversation can be plainly heard below.'* Others passed the time driving round the hills, playing tennis, getting bored or organizing motor picnics, which were generally an excuse for young couples to escape chaperonage during games of 'sardines'.

A few miles south of Troodos the valleys brighten into streams, where the pines and glens reminded British servicemen of Scotland. The country falls steeply. Pink cranesbill gathers out of the fern, and the rivers lurch through gorges to flash down fifty feet into green pools.

Here a summer residence for the British governor was built in 1880, reserved now for the country's president. I found the sentry-boxes empty at its gateway, and stepped unchallenged over a barbed wire barrier and into the drive. I tried to walk quietly, but my feet clashed outrageously on fallen leaves. The house looked like a Scottish shooting-lodge, perfectly undistinguished. At the front a few apple trees blossomed, and a plaque on one side of the door read in French: 'Arthur Rimbaud, French poet and genius,

* Gladys Peto, *Malta and Cyprus*, (1928).

despite his fame contributed with his own hands to the construction of this house, 1881.'

I listened for a sound, but even the birds seemed tongue-tied, and the building was shuttered. I felt intrigued by anything to do with Rimbaud. He came to Cyprus in 1879, after deserting from the Dutch army and escaping through the rain forests of Java. Already at the age of eighteen he had given up poetry for ever. He worked as a foreman in a stone quarry near Larnaca, earning thirty shillings a week, but caught typhoid and returned to France sick and almost unrecognizable except for his peculiarly beautiful eyes.

> *'Mais, vrai, j'ai trop pleuré! Les Aubes sont*
> *navrantes.*
> *Toute lune est atroce et tout soleil amer . . .'*

This was his last year as a total wanderer. Afterwards the endless flight from himself, the burning out of pain and genius together in penitential escapades, grew less explicit. He seems to have become bent on a career. He returned to Cyprus the next year and supervised the building of the residence, commanding fifty men, but quarrelled with his employer. Examining the plaque, I saw that like so much written on Rimbaud it made nothing clear. He was not famous at this time and he built nothing with his own hands, and by 1881 he had already left the island for the Red Sea and Ethiopia. In fact it is odd that he should have supervised the building at all. He hated the so-called progress which an empire like the British valued, and nothing seems further from the inspired drunkenness, the 'flowering blue abyss', than this sensible residence in its suffocated glen. It is teasing to think that on the slopes nearby a young lieutenant of Engineers, later Lord Kitchener of Khartoum, was at the same time carrying out a land survey of the island, and must often have passed Rimbaud with his train of tents and men. But what they could have said to one another is unimaginable.

Towards twilight, making for Trooditissa Monastery, I found a path which circled the shoulders of Olympus. I had not gone a hundred yards when I came face to face with a beautiful buff fox. We stood stockstill and stared at one another in astonishment. Then it loped fifty yards, stopped and turned on the steep mountainside to check on me, and vanished.

It was growing late. Below me dusk merged the valleys, and the sky had melted to mauve-grey, quieting the sea. Here and there the path choked with rocks where the mountain had slid over it. They looked newly fallen. In other places the crags had almost broken away. Once a few lights appeared in the hills a thousand feet below, as a village warmed itself against the dark. I considered trying to reach them, but the mountainside was too steep and the view, drowned in that liquid sky, became ever more strange. So I wandered on.

The path ascended in semi-darkness now, and the moon shed serrated shadows through the pines. It seemed as if I was walking along the edge of the tangible world. On one side, above me, the mountain rose exact and heavy, but my path was the limit of its reality, and on the other spread a mirage filled with swimming lights and vague, moon-crossed hills. From here I heard foxes barking. The sea itself was invisible, traced by the winding of Lilliputian inlets and all the country in between had darkened to chaos.

I knew that I had lost the monastery, but I no longer cared. I would sleep wherever I reached, and the night was warm. My mooncast shadow strode strangely in front of me, and the owls called from every valley, echoing one another or relaying my progress by their sudden silences.

I arrived above a village where a greenish light showed the wall of some enormous building. I believed that I had, after all, reached Trooditissa Monastery, so I sat on the slope and ate a frugal supper. But my stillness provoked rustlings and slitherings in the surrounding maquis. I did not trust the slitherings, and after warming myself on a half bottle of wine given me by one of the Amiandos miners, I prepared to go down. By now the stars were sharp and abstract above the village lights, and I descended slowly, flashing my torch in front of me down five hundred feet of wasteland, until I smelt blossom and saw apple branches pushed out along a road.

I approached the entranceway under the green lamp, but the place turned out to be a mammoth hotel, abandoned. Two men, standing in its shadows, ran away. So I went into the village where I found a barber sitting alone in his shop, and asked where I was.

'Prodhromos,' he said. 'We're the highest village in the country. Where were you going to?'

I said sheepishly: 'Trooditissa.' (How was he to understand that I had walked along the perimeter of the world?)

'And where have you come from?'

I did not dare say Olympus. I was almost back there. I had gone in a tortuous arc. 'Somewhere,' I mumbled irrelevantly 'somewhere . . . up there.'

He found me a bed in an empty shoe shop. I tumbled into it without a thought, and knew nothing until I woke up in the morning to find myself lying at the back of the window, with several curious shoppers staring in.

The older monasteries of the Orthodox world lay claim to supernatural beginnings, and generally an icon is responsible. Makheras was built around a holy painting preserved in a cave, with a sword buried in front of it. The monastery of Chryssoroyiatissa enshrined an icon which had floated over the sea from Asia Minor. And the Virgin of Trooditissa was found bathed in an eerie glow on the mountainside, awaiting a fraternity to care for her.

'Shepherds discovered her a thousand years ago,' said a monk, shadowing me through the monastic church. 'Here at Trooditissa she is older than anything else. She was painted, you see, by St Luke.' He spoke in a shy, wheedling way, as if expecting contradiction – perhaps some rational-minded tourist had once refuted him. 'While he was not doctoring, Ayios Loukos was painting.' Encouraged by my silence he added: 'Our Virgin may even have been done from life.'

We stepped along the iconostasis, he in an eddy of robes and holding up a taper, I as discreetly as I could in my heavy boots, with my rucksack attached to my back like a hereditary hump. The saints gazed down on me with brackish disapproval, but the monk looked familiarly back at them, and his face, with its dark brows and wincing innocence, seemed a troubled reflection of theirs.

'Here,' he murmured. 'The Panayia. Our Lady of Troodos.'

The light of his candle fell on the icon. Like all the most sacred and venerable of its kind, it was encased in a panoply of repoussé silver, beaten out in the image of the painting beneath, and pierced by an aperture which showed a square inch of blackened and indecipherable wood whose pigment had long ago been worn away by kisses.

The monk gazed at it with love, then at me with hesitation. 'Our foundress,' he said. He kissed the tiny, vacant square. 'When they built the monastery farther along the mountain, she pulled it down during the night. She wanted it here, where there was a spring of water.'

In early Christian times many churches were built on the sites of temples, either to exorcise them or to harness the sanctity of the place. Trooditissa Monastery may be one of these, its Virgin replacing that older goddess whose features are embarrassingly discernible, for it is still sometimes called the Aphroditessa Monastery, and its Virgin is well known as a bringer of fertility to women. 'Even the name of the old goddess,' wrote Frazer in *The Golden Bough* 'is retained in some parts of the island; for in more than one chapel the Cypriote peasants adore the mother of Christ under the title of Panayia Aphroditessa.'

'No one has looked on her real face for two hundred years,' the monk said, smoothing the veil against the silver. 'It is better like that. Sometimes the blaze from heaven is too bright.'

For an icon is no mere portrait. It is a shadow of its archetype in heaven, a window through which the divine is looking out and by which the worshipper can gaze into paradise. To some, the very wood and oil and egg white are a living incarnation of the saint portrayed. Several portraits of the Virgin are believed to have miraculously painted themselves, and others, it is said, she left behind her after visitations. Occasionally saints too have appeared before their artists and stepped into the waiting tablet, limning themselves onto its wood.

Such icons, and hundreds of others, become legendary for their miracles. They burn with celestial light. They weep, they fly, they spurt blood, they are washed up on the tide, dug out of the earth, handed down from heaven. And with a little coaxing and adoration they induce rain.

But above all they effect cures. Conceived in a time when medicine could do little, they once had to cope single-handed with the fears and sickness of half the Christian world. Cyprus alone is filled with these immemorial doctors whose bedside manner is one of numinous and infallible strength. They nestle propitiously behind spinneys of candles and drip with ex-votos: silver arms, legs, ears, eyes, hordes of coins and necklaces, wax statuettes. They cater for even trivial ailments. St Yennadios of Moronero, who was frozen to death by the Cypriot winter, can cure the common cold; St Antipas soothes toothache; St Procopius will banish boils; and the lion-riding St Mamas at Troulli, as well as dealing with tax matters, will relieve sore throats.

A host of other icons – some obscure, others known all over the island and beyond – are sovereign against more severe afflictions: for epilepsy you must make a pilgrimage to St George of Gypsos, for dumbness to the Virgin of Glossa, for leprosy to the Christ of Chrysorroyiatissa, for insanity to the Archangel Michael of Lemona. The Virgin of Makheras heals wounds, while St Andreas ministers to blindness, indeed to almost anything, and guards those at sea (his shrine in the Karpas used to be cluttered with wax votive boats). The Virgin of the White Hill at Pyla cures ophthalmia by loaning a silver eye to her petitioners. The Panayia Zalagiotissa subdues varicose veins. St John the Baptist, in his ruined chapel at Silikou, will heal malaria in children if they are rolled up and down the aisle. The lamp-oil burning beside the bones and icon of St Eliophotes eases rheumatism, and the Panayia Aphendrika dispels the disease of any youth uninhibited enough to undress outside the west door of her chapel and smear his whole body with candle grease. Once, in the middle of the Holy Liturgy, St Heracleides of Tamassos (who never existed) even cast out a demon; his petitioner, a small child, fell to the ground and vomited out the ghoul in the shape of two crabs and a snake, which were hung up in the church for the edification of the faithful.

'The Virgin of Trooditissa? She cures teeth-grinding,' answered the monk, who still wore a wounded expression.

'Teeth-grinding?'

'Yes.' He ground his teeth in the dark. 'And aches in the bones, and rotten kidneys. And she brings fertility.' Again his gaze drifted over me for signs of apostasy. Then he unhooked a bronze-studded belt which hung beside the icon. 'If a barren woman wears this,' he said 'she cannot fail to have children.' His hands described a pregnant stomach in the air. 'It has happened time and again. I have myself known two women made fertile by their faith since I was here. In the old days, if the baby was a boy, the mother had to dedicate him as a monk in the service of Our Lady.'

The whole island is scattered with these procreative Virgins, heirs to the nubile Aphrodite, who not only ensure fertility but ease childbirth and increase milk at the breast. The Panayia Galatoussa will even renew the milk of goats and cows. In fact the Virgin and saints are co-opted into a variety of activities which might be thought beneath their attention. St Marina of Mesa Khorio, for instance, is sovereign against nagging wives, and St George of the Black Hill reactivates broody hens.

There is no cranny of domestic and emotional life into which a saint may not helpfully pry. Many are the St Georges who will return lost children and animals, and the Virgin of the Phaneromeni near Temblos points out suitable sons-in-law to anxious mothers, both Moslem and Christian. Strangest of all, the Panayia Chrysorroyiatissa, like an echo of the sanctuary granted by some pagan gods, has compassion on criminals, who pray to escape arrest, or send their families to plead for a light sentence.

The eccentricity of the icon of Trooditissa lies in the large stone wedged in the back of its wood, and in the story which explains it.

'It was the father's fault,' the monk insisted, stroking it with his fingers. 'He tried to take away his child, who had been dedicated as a monk here. He came from Beirut, you see, not from our people at all. No sense of duty.' His beard quivered angrily. 'Arabs, you know . . .'

'He threw a stone at the icon?'

'God protect us! Even a demon wouldn't do such a thing! No, no. The parents were arguing with the abbot, trying to get the child away. You know how some people go on – they'd wear the horns off a goat. Then suddenly a stone detached itself from the church wall and fell on the boy!' Once again I felt his eyes on me, probing for disbelief. 'It wasn't in my time or even in my grandfather's, but it happened all the same. Just because we haven't seen these things . . .'

I looked away, but I could feel his hurt gaze trailing round my features. So I shook my head sorrowfully. 'The poor child . . .'

'But that is where the miracle comes in.' He revolved his amber beadstring in a turmoil of nerves. 'The boy was not killed, he was not even hurt. No. The icon leapt forward and took the blow upon itself! The stone is there to prove it, stuck fast. And the boy's father accepted it as a sign, and let him stay. May God so protect us all!'

Many are the icons which, when pressed too hard, have taken a violent and sudden revenge. Like the statues of ancient gods which they replaced, they are only slighted at peril. They wither arms, and strike men dumb or blind, lopping off the hands or noses of interfering Saracens. They can become immovably heavy, and stick fast to walls – the icon of the Virgin of Yiolou has repeatedly refused to be taken into the fields to bring rain. Some, armoured in silver or veiled, assail those who attempt to gaze on them, and broken vows bring a terrible nemesis. St Andreas of the Karpas has been known to reimpose the blindness he cures, and if there are thieves in his church he can cause the doors to disappear, enclosing them in blank walls.

But most of these touchy, even vindictive icons belong to the Holy Mother. The Virgin of Lagoudera killed a Turk with hailstones the size of cricket balls (hail is only averted by the Virgin of Troodos) and the Panayia Valheriotissa frightened away intruders by boiling a whole river. The Eleousa of Salamiou has roused snakes to avenge her, while the Virgin of Kliron punishes ingratitude by striking down cattle, crops and even children. Our Lady of Makheras struck dumb the Lusignan queen Alix d'Ibelin; and when a painter persisted in retouching her icon, the Virgin of Lophos killed him stone dead – a healthy warning to restorers.

'You see, God is justice as well as love,' said the monk. By now we had emerged into the courtyard, where a tabby cat sat insolently watching us. 'You will not find everybody in heaven. Not the Jews, no, nor the Arabs nor the Russians who believe in nothing, nor . . . but the Americans are Christian aren't they?' The cat squinted up. '. . . nor the Egyptians . . .'

We stopped near one of those prints of the Last Judgement which clothe the walls of Orthodox monasteries as a *memento mori*.

'The future,' he said 'is all there.'

I looked politely, and saw the righteous spiralling upwards in a column of lymphatic faces, while cupids puffed and angels blew and the apostles sat on little curled wigs of cloud. For them St Peter unlocked the doors of a castled Eden leading to pleasures which could not be depicted, since nobody can imagine a pleasure compatible with Byzantine ideas of holiness. As for the rest, soundlessly screaming, they were somersaulted down to Hell. Their faces poked in amazement from the maws of scaly or leonine monsters endlessly masticating them – hypocrital emperors, pretty women, Arius and Judas (still clutching his bag of talents) chewed and regurgitated forever.

'This life,' said the monk in the same strained, fragile voice, 'is only for a day, but afterwards is for ever.' He placed one hand vertically on the edge of the other and slid it down. 'You see how easy it is to fall off . . . we walk always on this edge – paradise or damnation.'

But the monastic life, as far as I could see, left little time for interesting sins. The monks rose at three in the morning and prayed between four and seven. Through the heat of the day they farmed the terraces or worked in the kitchens. For an hour in the late afternoon they prayed; then came Vespers, and bed at eight o'clock. This life is very different from that of the Western orders with their pragmatism and scholarship. It is closer to the ascetic and contemplative rule of the earliest fathers, with no learning except for a little mystical theology: a life of praising God, not of bettering man.

'Of course it is hard,' he said. 'People who say that monks are lazy should come here and see. The first few months as a novice you think you're going to die. But we cannot grumble. A man chooses his own path.' He smiled his diffident smile. 'And we will have eternal light.'

The explorer Samuel Baker, who came in 1879, called this monastery 'the first step to Heaven', for it is the highest in the land, more than four and a half thousand feet above the sea. Like all the older monasteries, it has been ravaged by fire, and although founded a millennium ago, its buildings are young. The clink and scrape of hoes sounds along terraces under the hill, where the veteran monks work their orchards, standing up now and again to hold their backs or to lean on their implements and stare at what has yet to be done. They look weathered and old as trees. Their robes hang torn on them, and their hair is a jungle around faces wrinkled to dignity by years of quiet. Water slops and gurgles along the slopes, and in spring the apple blossom appears, with the softer cherry and the tinted pear whose waxy flowers have barely opened while the rest are blowing over the valley. An elysian restfulness pervades the place, as if all that existed was its own trudge of days and the procession of the sun and stars around its mountain.

That evening the monk brought me half a loaf of bread in my cell, a dish of beans and an onion. In the morning he came again with a plate of olives.

'You in England,' he said. 'Do you grow olives?'

'No. It's too cold. We import them.'

'Where from?'

'Some from Cyprus,' I guessed.

He lingered in the doorway, his eyebrows locked in thought. At last he ventured: 'You mean to say that if I bottle an olive here, it may reach you in England – I mean *you*?'

'Yes, it could.'

The vision of this much-travelled olive absorbed his thoughts for a full minute, conjuring lunatic coincidences of space and time. Then he whispered: 'We must try it.'

We both suddenly laughed, and he produced a piece of bread from his pocket and tucked it into my rucksack. On the way his fingers collided with my battery-operated razor which he picked up and scrutinized. 'Can you get the BBC on that?'

'It's not a wireless. It's a razor.'

But he did not understand. He frowned at its teeth. He had never shaved. 'What about Voice of America?'

'It shaves,' I said. I held it against the side of my cheek.

But the man's dark, injured expression did not change. 'You are listening to it.'

'No, there's nothing to listen to.' I switched it on so that it buzzed. 'You see?'

He clucked worriedly. 'Something strange is happening at the BBC.'

'Yes,' I said.

It was a little after dawn when I prepared to leave. The place asked nothing for its hospitality – monasteries never do – but an offertory stood in the church under the veiled and censorious eye of Our Lady of Troodos. As I placed my money, I saw that the monk was praying there. He did not turn round, but seemed to be addressing the Virgin in front of him as he said: 'I hope you fixed the BBC.'

I set out for my long traverse of the southern mountains. Already, touched by the early light and a mandorla of blossom, the monks were trooping to work, following one another along the terraces with the faces of saints at peace.

Lazily I took the road down through the summer resorts of Platres, lapsing into a long, slow stride which after three days would carry me, I hoped, into the western hills. I went through villages of whitewashed alleys, two donkeys wide, where old men slumbered on chairs, their heads buried in their elbows or tipped back to show yellowing teeth, and I tramped out again into a vine-speckled country which produces some of the best wine in the island. By now I was going parallel to the heart of the Troodos and was being rocked up and down on the valleys and foothills which bleed away from it. To the south-west was the village of Arsos, where the loveliest of ancient Cypriot sculptures was found – a female head with veiled hair and faintly parted lips.

I left the road and struck out across fields. There were no farmers among the vines, only orange-rumped grass-hoppers which gnashed their wings in a hot and endless din. High above me, on the summit of Mount Olympus, the golf ball of the radar station looked as if it must roll down at any puff of wind. One by one, during my descent, these mountains had dropped behind me, and now their billows haunted the sky again so that I felt as if I had never truly penetrated them.

I entered more barren country, making for Kykko, the island's sovereign monastery, two days' march away. Dogs bawled at me from the rooftops of Ayios Nicolaos – a Turkish village despite its name – and from the last house a pretty, grey-eyed girl came out and gave me water. Dusk showed a planetary landscape. The sun, misted in cloud, was pale as chalk, and ahead of me the terraces were white with stones. A blind woman, led by her son, came round a slope driving goats tied together in pairs, whose bells jangled tiredly.

'Englishman,' the boy said.

The woman turned her eyelids to the sound of my feet, and smiled. The next moment they were gone into the dusk.

I came down by moonlight to the river Dhiarizos, which flows out many miles southward below the ancient temple of Paphos, and bathed my feet in its waters. These feet had forgiven me for the trek to Makheras, and had paled to a watchful shrimp colour. The river was piercingly cold. I crossed it on stones which split the waters in a moon-golden stubble, and lay down under a plane tree among whose branches a family of owls fluted and whistled feebly to itself. Hours later I awoke to the tattoo of rain on the leaves, but the storm passed within minutes, flashing over the mountains and leaving a river whose rocks glistened under the moon like the casques of drowned soldiers.

A family of tree rats, breeding irresponsibly in a hole lower down than the owls, scuttled among the branches at dawn. They were the first wild animals which I had seen since the fox of Trooditissa. Grey hares, tortoises and the elusive mountain sheep all live in these forests, but I did not find them. Nor did I glimpse that chameleon mentioned by the eighteenth-century Doctor Hasselquist, which is 'very subject to the Jaundice, especially if it is made angry,' and which starts to change colour on the soles of its feet. But his dog-eared monkey of Ethiopia which 'makes an horrid appearance, and is very ugly towards the back parts' is recognizable in Limassol Zoo.

Along the forest track, salamanders lived in the trees. As I passed they would inflate their jaws and let out a soundless caution. Lizards appeared too, with delicate feet which they sometimes trailed indecisively behind them. But the days are gone when Rider Haggard, on a Cypriot hunting expedition, fired wildly into the sky in the dark and heard the thump of falling birds. 'On they came in thousands and tens of thousands, the air was full of the rush of their wings, and the earth echoed with their different cries – the deep note of the geese, the unearthly call of the curlew, and the whistling pipe of the teal. Sometimes they seemed to pass so close to me that they nearly struck my head . . .' Today I saw only the Cyprus warbler, with partridge, a pair of francolin, and swallows.

I passed a single man all morning, a woodgatherer asleep on his donkey. The track I followed, which used to link a Greek and Turkish village, was abandoned. Its bridges lay broken in the pine forests. No footmarks showed in its dust. At Vrecha, Turkish and poor, I encountered only dogs and a sentry, and was seen by nobody except a small boy squatting in the track and screaming with the pain of constipation. Two hours later I was walking over Mount Panayia, four thousand feet high, and down again through fields of corn. The daylight had suddenly gone.

I arrived tired at Chrysorroyiatissa Monastery for the night. During the refectory supper, under the eyes of several savage-looking monks and while a novice recited the scriptures, I almost fell asleep. Like all the large monasteries its position was beautiful and its buildings rambling, half empty and younger than they seemed. Its heart was the miraculous icon, beloved of criminals. She is the Panayia Chrysorroyiatissa, a name – said to derive from the pomegranate or from the 'golden breasts' of the Virgin – which speaks of Aphrodite; and her icon, like the elder goddess, floated over the sea and alighted on the shores of Paphos.

North of the monastery was Pano Panayia, the home town of Archbishop Makarios, and beyond, a forest track climbed into the peaks of the western Troodos. More than twenty miles intervened between myself and Kykko, but the softness of the track invited me up next morning. After days of struggling over scrub and rocks, nursing an angrily swivelling compass, searching for points of reference already lost, streams long desiccated, it was pleasantly idle to take this woodland path which would lead me along unthinking.

But ahead the ranges were formidable, and I had not gone five miles before a storm threatened. It unfurled itself in crackling scrolls of thunder which lashed the eastern peaks and chilled the sun. Every tree on the farther heights was picked out against it. The heights themselves sharpened. Gloomy plinths of mountain, the colour of verdigris, they lifted a seemingly impassable palisade. Their shaley flanks, pitched this way and that, were forever overlooked by higher crags, as by the towers of a concentric fortress. Their spurs interlocked like wrestlers in the valleys, limb to limb. And all around the other crags rose heavy with storm: Tripylos, Kaloyiros, Aphoriti, black fists shaken at the sky.

I looked for shelter. But pine and arbutus are the everyday

clothes of the mountains – little else will stand their erosion – and these are meagre. Even the Maritime Pine thins away above four thousand feet leaving the Karamanian alone, with an underbrush of golden oak peculiar to the island. But the rain did not come. The track nosed its way upward and finally tossed me onto a plateau from which I saw the storm hanging still over Olympus.

Around me the slopes were spread with little more than slag. Erosion had splintered their very tegument of stone, pulling up the trees and sliding them away into gullies. It sometimes seemed as if whole mountainsides were on the move. Helpless in shifting scree, the pines could not bind the soil and were themselves too frail to decompose to anything more than sapless slivers which the rain washed away – its course obvious wherever the shale tumbled in rotted arteries to a valley. This is an ancient cycle. Before Roman times, wrote Strabo, the land was 'covered with forests run riot, choked in undergrowth, which prevented cultivation'. But every conqueror since has cut down without replanting. Goats have perpetuated the wilderness by gobbling the green shoots, and the mountains, scraped to the bone, are left to glitter and die.

But now that reafforestation was beginning, wide areas had been forbidden to goatherds, and in the valley which was opening beneath me I saw the shelf-like branches of *cedar brevifolia*. Leaner than cedars of Lebanon, their foliage and trunks were white-green, almost mildewed, and in this gully alone thirty thousand of them grew, as if underwater, their branches floating on some melancholy and invisible current.

185

All day, a Landrover of the forestry service was the only vehicle which passed me. The driver, who had a monkey orchid stuck behind his ear, called out when I refused a lift: 'It's too cold to camp out here!' But Kykko was less than ten miles away, and I did not want to drive. On foot, the slow emergence of the mountains imparts character to each. It is the difference between a glimpse and a stare. This interest makes light of miles, and today I saw anchusa among the stubble, with sea lavender and a rare purple honeywort. I glimpsed rock doves, a hawk, and once – in and out of trees – the flash of a blue-tinted bee-eater. By the time evening and storm had darkened the track I was at the gates of the monastery where the strangely bent pines, according to local peasants, are bowing to Our Lady of Kykko.

'Lucky you came now,' said the monk at the gate. 'In another minute the clouds will descend on us, and when that happens everybody up here falls down cliffs.' I tried to imagine a hecatomb of monks tumbling over a precipice. 'Sometimes,' he went on, 'it comes down thicker than a sheet and you can hardly see a pace in front of you. For days on end you might as well be blind up here . . .'

This man was plump as a partridge – the prototype, I thought, of Chaucer's Canterbury monk, 'ful fat and in good point'. He led me through a confusion of rooms and cloisters. Only a few passageways sliced through it to arrive at irregular courtyards flanked by cells for pilgrims.

'Sometimes the people come in thousands,' the monk said, 'literally thousands. On the night of the September *panegyris*, when Our Lady is carried out to make the rain, it seems almost like the old days . . .' In the twilight of the corridors his spectacles gleamed like the blank discs of an owl. 'Oh yes, there were better days . . . I'm not an old man, but even I can remember.'

Kykko was built for its icon, growing round this core of miracle and sanctity for nearly nine hundred years. Of the seventy paintings attributed to St Luke this one, with the *Panayia Soumela* near Trebizond and the *Hodegetria* of Mega Spelaion in the Peloponnese, is especially venerated, for it is believed that the Evangelist received its panel from the Archangel Gabriel. The Emperor Alexius Comnenus, it is said, gave the icon to a Cypriot monk who healed his dying daughter; but as for the monastery, four fires have cleaned away successive buildings on the site, and almost nothing older than the nineteenth century is left.

Yet the feeling is one of immense and inscrutable age, of an enigma heaped upon itself. Kykko's lands in Czarist Russia are lost, but it owns chunks of commercial Nicosia, and its monks are touched by a worldly finesse and circumspection. Their beards no longer gush and tumble, but are neatly barbered; nor do they wear their hair twined in a ball behind, like English nannies, but keep it short and fussily curled. The refectory table stretches for forty feet in jointed marble, and a feeling of plenty surrounds the monks who assemble there. Even the beans are washed down with olive oil and lemon juice, and bolstered by onion-flavoured croquettes.

'Money,' said the Canterbury monk later, sitting in his cell, 'is not the trouble. After all, life is comfortable now. We have electricity and drainage and so on, things which would have shamed us a century ago. Yes, shamed us! We live in luxury.' He gestured round the room as if it were paradise: a chair, a bed, a table with a book and two medlars lying on it. 'Before this we had nothing. The monks could travel nowhere. They worked to the bone. Yet then there were many and now we are few.'

'Very few?' I asked. A traveller in 1683 reported a community of four hundred, but by 1891 it had dwindled to ninety.

'There are rarely more than eight of us up here now,' said the monk. 'We could house all the brethren of Cyprus in our empty cells!' Under shiny brows his face, with its circular cheeks and old-fashioned spectacles, was all polished curves and orbs. He shook his head. 'Where have the faithful gone? What is happening to us?'

The questions dragged out their silence, heavy with a whole decaying world. I thought of the dying monasteries of Meteora and the Peloponnese, the emptied sketes of Athos, the dispersed Russian fraternities, cloisters falling quiet in the Balkans, Syria, Egypt.

'Even I,' said the monk, 'can remember that in 1963 we had twenty-two novices.' He passed a hand across his brow as if the memory might be an illusion. 'Yet now there are only three. It is a disastrous decline . . . disastrous.' Again he rubbed his forehead, violently. 'Is the world forgetting God?'

In the silence we heard the wind round the monastery walls. He went to the barred window and peered through. 'The cloud's coming down,' he said. 'As I told you.'

'But if the community dies out, what will happen to this place?'

'I don't know.' He turned his back on the window. 'But I believe it may become a nunnery one day. Or perhaps a school.' He looked a little surprised at what he had said, but repeated, as if to himself: 'Yes, I dare say a school.'

'Who would come to school up here?'

'I don't know, my child. I will not be here to see. It's useless to torment oneself with these questions. God will find a way. Leave it to God.'

Perhaps the monasteries in the strained and metaphysical West will outlive those in the Levant, where monasticism was born. The urban Cypriot can reject religion in the same simplicity with which he held it. To a practical people God, within a generation, may seem meaningless and unnecessary.

'But it won't happen,' said the Canterbury monk. 'Decline yes, demise no. Our people still believe. They have never doubted.'

Perhaps that was the trouble, I thought. Nobody doubts. Faith is either accepted or forgotten, and the distinction can be slender. Whereas a living belief must survive questions.

'But there'll be a revival,' said the monk. 'Eternity is a long time. People will tire of the material world. Those things will pall, and then the monasteries will return into their own. That will be a time, *paidi mou!* They'll fill up again like wine in bottles, in barrels . . . they'll overflow.' Yet his eyes, plunged in their lairs of flesh, remained deeply unhappy. He spoke as of a time which he would never know, as if it scarcely needed his belief at all. It was merely a talisman.

When I returned to my cell the cloud already hung thick and the rain splintered through the cloisters. Later that night a terrible storm burst. The monastery was trapped in the heart of the cloud, which poured out sheet lightning like a huge flash-camera. The wind cut along the corridors and blasted through broken windows. Under its lash the vast building went cold, but all its trappings, from corrugated iron to old pots, were shaken and rolled about, and the mist was filled with the clang of ghostly semantra. Peering from my cell I saw the usual huddle of cats under the blob of my torchlight, their bodies pressed together and their eyes gleaming like a multi-headed demon, which exploded into the dark.

At dawn the bell-tower was still wreathed in cloud, but the courtyards were dripping and clear. Forgetting breakfast, I wandered into the church to see the famous icon, the Eleousa, and found the Canterbury monk and several others chanting the Liturgy. The Eleousa, 'the Compassionate', enjoys all the powers of her kind. Encased in silver for two hundred years and oozing black wax through a tiny hole, she punishes horribly anybody attempting to gaze on her, and her Child is not the coddled *bambino* of the Renaissance, but the premature adult of Orthodox tradition.

The elevation of the Virgin Mary from her muted role in the Gospels to the status of a near-divinity confirmed the position which she already held in popular worship. For she had inherited the groundswell of devotion to a primaeval goddess: the many-faced Aphrodite. With the coming of Christianity the metamorphosis of Aphrodite Urania, the pure and celestial Mother, into the All-Holy

Mother of God, was often less a conquest than a painless welding, while Aphrodite Pandemos, her sexual aspect, vanished with little recorded fuss. On the sites of her temples were built churches to Mary. From the torchlight processions of the goddess' mysteries grew the Virgin's Feast of Lights. In some regions she even assumed Aphrodite's duties as a patroness of sailors. To complete her Pyrrhic victory she regaled herself with much of the insignia of the elder goddess – the dove, the anemone, the pomegranate, the crown of stars – and in at least one Cypriot village, where the peasants unearthed a statue of Aphrodite, they cried out that she was the Virgin and set her with prayers in the apse of their church.

None of this, of course, was troubling the brethren of Kykko. The Canterbury monk leant back in his stall, smiling at nothing. Clocks chimed and tinkled in the aisles, and an almost picnic air of worship was about; apostles and saints filled the iconostasis with their adoration, culminating in a Crucifixion like a shout of victory. For the death of Christ means only triumph to the Orthodox. Not for them the grief and the passion beloved of the Roman church, nailed hands and broken heart. These, instead, are turned into an intellectual and mystical vision, whose protagonists are portrayed as figments of heaven, floating in an abstract calm.

Softly, like drowsing bees, the voices asked forgiveness – the same cry as has punctuated the Liturgy for thirteen hundred years. 'Peace unto all; love we one anothe' One by one the drama unfurled its ageless be Litany of Peace, the Cherubikon, the Triple Gre the Hymn of Heavenly Victory, reaching at last to consecration and the awed hush of the Metousis.

The brethren looked comfortably settled into their chanting, as if it would last all day, or all eternity. The Canterbury monk stifled a yawn. Along the iconostasis, I noticed, the saints were not all impeccable Christians. Here and there a pretence had worn thin or a mask had slipped. St Demetrios on his red charger is understudy for Demeter the corn-goddess; St Dionysios stands in for his heathen namesake; and the white-horsed St George may have ousted Adonis. Reconsecrated pagans, they have put on the dress of Christian sobriety.

Beside the Virgin's icon, like tribute to her older self, a wax baby lay on its back: a votive offering either in thanks, or in hope, of childbirth. But she herself, flanked by her ambiguous saints, was half veiled in a cloth of seed pearls. Only her lap and hand were visible, enclosing, in glimmering repoussé, the disturbingly mature Child.

CHAPTER SEVEN
• • • • • • • • • • • •
The Glory of Byzantium

An enclosed and verdant mildness covers the northern valleys into which my path had now tipped. In April the rivers feed apple and peach blossom, and are muddy with rain. The cherry blossom of Pedoulas even draws a few visitors from Nicosia, who enjoy it with a sensuous delight rather than with the critical delicacy of the Japanese. But now, in early May, the petals had gone and the rivers tumbled through a dense greenery of orchards.

'The hail did for the fruit only yesterday,' a farmer said, 'knocked off the raw cherries and almonds in a morning. You can see them rotting under the trees.' He glanced at the window. The hail was rattling again on the roofs. 'And this will be the end of what's left.'

'Are your own orchards ruined then?'

'Yes.' He looked entirely resigned. 'For this year.'

'What will you do?'

'I have other jobs. I make bread-ovens – the old domed kind – and I work bottling the Moutoullas table water. You haven't heard of it? But it's better than Evian! It comes from a mineral spring a few miles down the river. They're healthy as rams down there.' He thrust out a chest whose grey hair lapped at his neck. 'A man has to have several jobs up here if he wants to get by.'

How the Cypriots were accused of laziness I do not know, but travellers in the last century often decried them. Perhaps this was due to the islanders' excessive sociability – their leisure was always public and spent in cafés – or perhaps to the country's legendary fruitfulness (once called Macaria, the Blessed Isle) which prompted thoughts of Polynesian indolence. But other travellers, usually those who stayed longer, noted that the peasants lived sober and frugal lives, as they still do, and that this apathy, at least in the countryside, was a myth.

'We can't afford to be idle,' the farmer said. 'If we're idle we rot.'

But conservative they are. In this their character has not changed since classical times. Serious civil crime is still as unusual as it was in the day of the British Vice-Consul who reported more than a century ago that theft, murder and political agitation were alike almost unknown. The pitilessness of EOKA, both against others and within itself, was extraordinary for Cypriots, whose peaceableness has made them the natural subjects of empire. They have always been mellow, masters of flexibility – 'the most subtle and artful people in all the Levant, nor have they more veracity than their neighbours'.* Their intelligence is quick and practical. The eyes see sharply, but not far; even today, unlike dozens of Greeks and Lebanese, no Cypriot businessman is a force in Mediterranean commerce.

---

* Dr Richard Pococke, *A Description of the East.*

'But things are changing so we don't know ourselves,' said the farmer. 'Some of us old ones can hardly believe what our children have become. You'd think we'd spawned centaurs!' He jabbed a finger across the room. 'Look at that for instance—'

Among the farmers a young man flaunted himself in black corduroy, with a lilac shirt and cravat, and hair crinkling elegantly at the neck. A cigarette holder balanced between soft-looking fingers.

'Now who is he?' demanded the farmer embarrassingly loud – several faces turned to us. 'Is he the mayor of Pedoulas? *Po-po-po!* Nothing of the kind! No, he's the son of a butcher. You see, everybody goes to secondary school now. A bit of education and that's what you get.' He made as if to spit, but did not. 'They all work in Nicosia. And the younger women won't even help in the fields.'

'Why not?'

'I don't know. They just sit at home and look after the house.' He seemed genuinely puzzled. 'But it's not like that with the older ones. My wife goes out with me every morning at dawn with a hoe – and she's had eleven children.'

He was pretending sourness, but when he stared at the young man again he could barely suppress his laughter. All the wrinkles poured into the corners of his mouth, as if he was trying to suck in his face. 'May God forgive me, how beautiful . . . the shirt . . . the shoes . . .'

This time the man turned, faintly flushed. 'Are you talking about me?'

The farmer asked blandly: 'How much did you pay for that suit?'

'Twelve pounds.'

'Holy Virgin!'

'You think it a good suit?' (The Greeks are hypersensitive about their appearance.)

'I don't know. I've never bought a suit. It seems much to pay for anything.'

'It is not much to pay.'

'Then it is a cheap suit.'

A rattle of good-humoured laughter went up from the semicircle of weathered faces. The youth turned his back on us.

But I realized that the old man was secretly envious. Later he asked me quietly: 'Can he have paid twelve pounds for a suit? God protect us! What was it made of then? Gold thread?' He himself had a son who was an electrical engineer in London, and who 'dressed like an emperor'.

Education is the new-fangled god of all these villages, the door to a bourgeois paradise which is welcomed by men whose fathers have broken their lives harrowing rock-filled orchards. The Cypriots take easily to the towns. As soon as they have shed their mountain robustness, they soften to a Mediterranean suavity, almost a voluptuousness. Doubtless they have been accused of this ever since the first Athenian tourist returned home from the temple harlotry of Paphos. Without the Arab's harsh intensity, nor that spine of Greek pride, their hallmark is this nascent sensuality and gentleness (shade of Aphrodite) which has not altered since recorded time – 'voluptuaries of the sun and sea,' wrote a critic 'holding on by simple animal tenacity through tempests which have wrecked the nobler races of mankind'.*

The influence of the West is deep and perpetual, deeper than it has ever been. Materialism comes quickly to the Cypriot, and as quickly destroys his qualities. He is entering in thousands that trough – of how many generations? – between peasant honesty and urban refinement. 'To be civilized,' a Nicosia friend told me, 'our people must first be vulgar. It is the bridge between simplicity and culture.'

This leap to modernity out of an Ottoman feudalism is unique in the island's history. The last Western influence, that of the Lusignans and Venice, had barely gone skin-deep and only touched on local culture in eclectic leftovers, like the decaying monastery of St John Lampadistis whose pitch-roofed chapels are crammed side by side in the valley at Kalopanayiotis.

They were built during several centuries, and to walk through them is to move out of Byzantium and into the Renaissance. A rood-screen carries faded coats-of-arms, the lions and dragons of the Crusader kingdom, and beyond is a complete Latin chapel, now disused, where the murals glide into naturalism and an almost Florentine love of colour. Wedged among scenes of Greek abstraction, these explosions occur all over the walls in a beautiful and patternless schizophrenia. Sometimes the two styles – Byzantine and Renaissance – are mixed in a single panel. An apostle of *quincento* fleshliness may pose against a geometric landscape, a formalized angel alight on a Tuscan courtyard.

* W. Hepworth Dixon, *British Cyprus*.

Flamboyant figures in a dark corner, the Magi straddle horses which are supple and eager, and break purposefully into three dimensions. They are not hieratic symbols but worldly statesmen – turbaned Sforzas and Gonzagas – and as they trot back to Babylon they journey through a new perspective. The countryside, to be sure, is desert, but Babylon has become an Umbrian hill town, crenellated and high. The horses gaze back frontally at the viewer as a concession to the older aesthetic, but the riders' faces are turned homewards and their robes flutter behind them with their going.

After the heady world of Orthodoxy this is rather a relief. The human opulence is reassuring. But the whole experiment, like the Crusades which were distantly responsible for it, at last defeats itself. The two traditions are juxtaposed rather than harmonized. In the severe and linear Byzantine style, colours are only blended when portraying flesh. But the Italian art is rich in blending. Its naturalism can make clumsy the floating, rarified world of Constantinople, or else may come to look decadent beside it.

There are other churches here, but none more remarkable than this, and by noon I was climbing among almond groves towards the Solea valley, most prolific of Orthodox strongholds. The spent hail lay about my feet like decaying blossom, and the sky was still densely overcast, its clouds warm now, and dark with rain. But I had always avoided storms before, and when the first drop splashed on my hand I felt astonished and resentful.

The next moment the cloud, like a black-petalled flower, opened and burst.

I spent an hour under a dripping dwarf oak tree in the hope that the rain would exhaust itself. Instead it settled into a cataclysm, falling out of a platinum sky unbroken from end to end. There was no sign of fuller shelter, not the gentlest overhang of rock or denser tree. I slowly became soaked; and it was growing cold. The rain squelched in my hair, trickled off my eyebrows, oozed in my boots. I searched in my rucksack for anything waterproof, but there was nothing; I had been careful to carry a light pack. So I put on my two pullovers, buttoned another shirt over them, and waited. But soon the water was seeping inward towards my vest, and in the end I unzipped my sleeping-bag, slid it over my head, and walked on. Marching through the downpour under this blue canopy, with its cowl and flapping wings, I must have looked like a fanatic from some obsolete order of friars. But two miles later it was already heavy with water. Even my trousers stuck to me. And two miles beyond that the rain seemed to be falling unprevented on my very skin.

At twilight I came to a church sitting tight in a valley. The tiles were sliding from its eaves like scales off a rotting fish, and it was surrounded by a deserted military school. I recognized it as the Church of St Nicholas of the Roof and realized that the nearest village, Kakopetria, was still more than three miles on, and the storm deepening. The church was locked and without a porch, and there was not a soul anywhere. The sky had darkened with more than rain. Dusk was becoming night. I squeezed through the padlocked turnstile of the barracks, rattled the bolted doors and peered through the windows. Then I ran to the verandah of a cottage, which must once have belonged to the commandant, and knocked futilely on the door before settling in its shelter to watch the rain thicken and the daylight leak away. I had no idea what to do. I was too cold and wet to sleep, and began to argue my chances of pneumonia.

This threat made me pull tentatively at one of the shutters of the house. To my surprise it opened. When I pushed at the window inside, that opened too. And there, as if I was dreaming it, stood a bed with two soft-looking blankets folded on a pillow. For a second I gazed as if into a mirage, then almost incredulously started to scramble through the window. The next moment I had dropped into the house on all fours and was pulling my sleeping-bag after me. The room did not look military, but seemed to belong to somebody's weekend home. Did today fall on a weekend? I did not know. But when I eased open the door, half-expecting to encounter a furious or terrified family, I found the place empty. In any case *philoxenia*, the law of hospitality to strangers, might even have extended to a housebreaker; they would very likely have welcomed and fed me. I shuttered the window and peeled off my clothes. When I took off my trousers – Cypriot corduroys of an odd, purple-grey colour – I saw that the dye had leaked down my legs in superb varicose veins. But my pyjamas were dry, so I curled up thankfully and respectfully in the blankets, and fell asleep. While all night the rain poured down.

The church of St Nicholas of the Roof belonged to a monastery which vanished a century ago, but its history, like that of most of the mountain basilicas, is all but lost. While the cathedrals of the plains were built or sacked in tragic uproar, these pastoral chapels stood in their valleys unnoticed. Over a century or two perhaps, a narthex was added or a wall newly frescoed, but the changes were friendly and organic, and went unrecorded but for a few inscriptions.

Feeling delicate from the previous night, I was in the mood to savour its stillness, but a grunting young caretaker from Kakopetria threw open the doors as if exposing a cowshed, and followed me about with a transistor radio attached to his breast-pocket, turned full on. No, he said, jerking a dismissive head at the vaults, the church was not usually open; people didn't need such places any more.

The shrine is too isolated to serve any village. It has to content itself with the visits of stray tourists. But it contains a museum of fresco conceived over six centuries. The intensity of the Macedonian renaissance, the pagan quirks of the Comnenians (including a nereid perched side-saddle on her sea-monster), the naïvety of the fourteenth century – all lavish their mystic propaganda on the walls. Some of these scenes loom with a sudden emphasis which catches the heart. I shall not forget the sweet and archaic Transfiguration, nor the shepherds playing their weird bagpipes in the angel-haunted mountains round the Nativity. But the feeling which surrounds them is one of eerie obsolescence. The worshipper is awestruck, but lost. Godhead, redemption, eternal life – the whole hierarchy of paradise is spread above him like an opaque and glimmering womb. Innumerable hands point to heaven. God is born and dies in the dark.

But the end of it all is the guide with his transistor radio, lumbering back and forth after a foreigner who is more impressed by belief when it becomes art. All this certainty, this world-eclipsing charge of faith, has somewhere trickled away, and the frescoed people look indescribably old and different, like a race which has passed from the earth.

I walked to Kakopetria in the sun. The poplar-filled valley, old houses along the river – how mellow they seemed! A cluster of village patriarchs was sipping *ouzo* under the plane trees, and the girls smiled at me, walking in safety together, arm in arm. I rambled to Galata, whose churches lay in the fields looking like country barns, with their roofs pitched steep against snow and reaching almost to the ground. Beneath them the churches were built of a grey local stone – the kind of haphazard masonry which gathers charm with age.

Somewhere in the hamlet I ate my first cooked meal for days – a piece of charcoal-roasted lamb and a carafe of dry Othello wine. An inspector of schools sat himself beside me, and the afternoon wore itself away indolently in talk about the failure of the humanities in education. The prestige of classical studies, he said, had strangled breadth of knowledge. No Cypriot student, apparently, had heard of a philosopher more recent than Aristotle.

It was almost evening when I abandoned the road and struck out for the village of Nikitari. I planned to walk the few miles to Asinou next day – to the most beautiful of the churches of the Troodos, and the last which I would see. By now I was no longer in the mountains, and the valley where I went showed an early summer land, filled with corn. Jumping over a rock I almost landed on five feet of coiled black snake, which thrashed in terror about my boots and vanished into scrub. For the next mile I went more slowly, occasionally tapping a stick in front of me, until I came to Pano Koutraphas where I had hoped to spend the night. But as I approached I did not see so much as a homing shepherd or hear a dog bark. A few minutes later I was walking in a ghost village. The mud walls were decaying and scarcely a roof hung intact. Not a person was left. I realized that it must have been deserted during the Greek–Turkish battles. And I walked on towards Nikitari.

But now, as if in compensation, the evening was dropping golden out of the sky, anointing the whole valley. These moments, if a man is walking, can touch him profoundly. No machine or person intervenes, and he moved inside their radiance. So now, surprised by this bathing of light over the cornfields, I felt as if I had intruded on a moment of primal solitude, forbidden to men. Beyond the hills shone a sky like the backdrop to Florentine Madonnas – a campanula blue blazoned with clouds. Far away the mountains lifted and poured. While behind me the village lay tawny and calm in its ruin like an innocent Gomorrah, the pointer to some unjust moral.

It was night when I reached Nikitari. In the coffee-shop the card-players were already slapping down their trumps with histrionic fierceness, or had settled on the rush-covered chairs with their coffee-cups set on other chairs in front of them. A woman is never seen in such a place. The men wrangle politics or local gossip, play backgammon, cover the floor with cigarette stubs, press pale brandy on one another with insane generosity, and finally heave themselves away to their families leaving a sediment of veterans lolled asleep.

'You will spend the night in my house,' said a farmer dictatorially. 'We have a television.'

This gloomy prospect was countered at his doorstep by a beaming wife, who offered me traditional *gliko*, fruit embalmed in syrup which must always be accepted – for to reject *gliko* is to reject the family. The house was built of mud, but a facing of red brick had been added neatly to the front, disguising it, and inside were all the signs of emergent status: tiled floors, cheap furniture, kitchen apparatus. The television stood like a pampered baby in the centre of the sitting-room, regaled with plastic flowers. And flowers were everywhere – all plastic – tulips and chrysanthemums, and tropical blooms which dropped their waxen foliage out of plastic boxes or sprouted from synthetic earth. On the walls hung the usual photographs of self-conscious-looking relatives, and a cabinet was stacked with decorated plates, never used.

But in the back yard the façade of gentility crumbled. Pigeons gathered and relieved themselves on a safe fetid with cheeses, and a dead crow was hung up by its claws. The clay oven, proudly disused, had cracked into pieces. The only sanitation, as usual, was a privy, a hole in the earth; but its door was the one craftsman's work I saw, plucked from the house for being out-of-date, and carved with geometric designs.

The farmer had three daughters – the eldest fifteen years

old and pretty. He commanded them to speak English, but they stood in front of me in a bleak, embarrassed line and made no sound.

'I pay eight pounds a week to send them to a special school in Nicosia!' he exploded. 'And this is what I get! Speak!'

Not a sound.

'Haven't you learnt *anything*? What's the English for *odos*?'

Silence.

'*Panayia!*' he fumed. 'I ask you, once and for good, have you learnt a single English word?'

They shuffled their feet in a miserable dance.

'What's the use of education if . . .'

'They're nervous,' I said. 'Perhaps later . . . when we're more relaxed. English is difficult.'

A voice from the wavering line whispered: 'English easy.'

'Ha!' cried the farmer, as if he had been hit. 'Who said that?' He darted glances from one to the next. 'Who's going to speak to our guest?' The eldest daughter flirted a little with her eyes. The youngest giggled and picked her teeth. But the one between them, with near-perfect pronunciation, suddenly said: 'Good morning, sir. I hope that you are in the love with our Cyprus country where the sea is hot and the nature is beautiful . . .' and so on.

At the speech's end the farmer burst into a delighted 'There!' and kissed her resoundingly. 'See what education can do for a girl! She goes on like the Queen!'

'She *works*,' said his wife, glaring at the other two. She herself, although feeling ill – her donkey had fallen under her that afternoon – had prepared a supper of every food in the house: eggs, artichokes and cucumbers, lamb and fried *haloumi* and 'bullybeef' – the word has passed into Greek – with mounds of peas and fruit. I had not faced such a meal in weeks, but when I told them so the farmer said: 'You are very kind. Of course we do our best. But we know it is nothing much. A meal for cats.' His hands fluttered in disparagement. 'You are used to hotels and such places . . . service . . .'

'But I've been walking,' I protested. 'I have no car.' This had usually been enough to convince people of my poverty. Few Cypriots could imagine walking for enjoyment (and in chastened moments I had agreed with them).

'But tourists are rich,' the farmer said simply.

I remembered slabs of bread and fish munched on hillsides, tinned luncheon meats, penitential monastic suppers. 'I haven't eaten an egg for a month.'

'Ho-ho.' He patted my shoulder, then mounded the bullybeef onto my plate, casting a hunk of cheese on top with a deprecatory twirl of his fork.

I felt a sudden nausea – it was due, I think, to the cooking-oil – and for a long time I was able only to stare at the heap and mash it into more digestible-looking shapes. But the man's scrutinous gaze forced me to eat, while his wife and daughters served us and surreptitiously finished what we had left, in the kitchen. In the villages this patriarchy scarcely ever varies; males, even tiny boys, are the first to eat and are served by the women, who finish the scraps in another room. Tonight the mother and younger daughters went quietly to bed, while the eldest washed her long hair under the kitchen tap, combing out the ringlets with a secret smile.

'And where would you have slept tonight if not here?' the farmer asked. 'This part is not good for strangers. A man must know his way about.'

'I'd planned to stay at Pano Koutraphas.'

He stared at me. 'There is no more Pano Koutraphas. Our people came from there, many of them. But when the trouble started they ran away. And the Turks too – fled.' He began to scowl at the floor. 'They're ready to kill one another now. Yet they'd lived together for centuries in one place. You would see them sitting – Greek and Turk together, Turk and Greek.' He aligned his forefingers in a gesture of concord. 'It's very strange.'

I said bleakly: 'I've liked the Turks.'

Always before, in other families, this opinion had been greeted with silence, the nearest to a rebuke which a Greek will show a guest, or else had been swept away in a gale of political recrimination. But now I heard the farmer say: 'Yes. The Turks are all right. They are a decent people.' I smiled back at him in amazement, a great warmth spreading through me. His remark was like one of those comets which burst in a summer sky – lonely among thousands who allowed the Turks no human quality, but a promise that other worlds and other possibilities existed, however remote.

'This trouble . . .' he began, shifting uncomfortably in his chair. 'This trouble . . .' He held out his hands, clenching and unclenching them, until they drifted back onto his knees. 'I don't know.' He bowed his head. 'I simply don't know.'

* * *

Asinou – the word has an ancient music. Only this name betrays the site of a city founded, apparently, in the eleventh century B.C. by emigrants from the Argolis, the Asine of Homer and Seferis. Loveliest of Cypriot churches, Our Lady of the Pastures is all of Asinou now. Not an earlier stone survives, and no sign of modern habitation except for the two-mile track which climbs through cuckoo-haunted woods from Nikitari.

Crowning a hillock and shaded by eucalyptus trees, the little church stands in the pastoral simplicity of its name, of russet stone against the pine-dark hills. In the way of Greek buildings, it seems to be coeval with its landscape, as if each was created for the other. The woods die away at its knoll. A river falls through a glade below. For nearly nine hundred years the church has gone unscathed, protected by its modesty and the quiet valley. Nothing has changed since Byzantium fell.

'Having been blessed in life with many things,' runs an inscription of the church's founder in 1105, 'of which thou, oh Virgin, wast seen to be the provider, I, Nicephorus Magistros, a pitiful supplicant, erected this church with longing, in return for which I pray that I may find thee my patron in the terrible day of Judgement.' Kneeling in fresco over the south door, he presents his basilica in miniature to Christ, like a child handing over a favourite toy, but gives it in memory of an unknown woman who kneels behind him in a diadem with jewelled pendants.

Spanning a period from the early Comnenian to the late fifteenth century, the frescoes end in a powerful rustic and popular style, the work of refugees from Syria and Asia

Minor whose bent, in life and in art, was for forceful expression rather than refined balance. Half early Christian belief spreads in brilliant colours here, as if folding the worshipper in the leaves of an illuminated bible.

For Byzantium enshrines a mysticism. Although the empire has gone which was once the image of Celestial Jerusalem, and the emperors are dead who reigned as regents of God, the Church which has been left behind is a symbol of heaven and its bishops rule in Christ's place. Here the faithful are gathered to immortality while still in the flesh, born by a Liturgy whose glory battens of paradise, and at every service the Universal Church – apostles, the All-Holy Mother, Christ Himself – are witnesses, shining through their icons or their frescoes. 'Eyes stir up the depths of the spirit. Art conveys through colours the soul's prayer.'* This is why the Byzantine portrait is always frontal; both eyes must be seen to ensure the mystical presence of the saint. Only Judas and pagans are portrayed in profile, shutting out their souls.

So, where the vaults of Asinou press close, the worshipper stands under the severe and dazzling witness of all heaven. A thousand saints swarm up the walls and throng the lunettes. There is no arch or lintel or pendentive which does not throw up a cross-fire of inquisition. What a scowl of archetypes is here, what furrowings of brows and liftings of declamatory fingers! Enough to bring the hardest unbeliever to his knees.

Above the sanctuary the stern and ageless Christ floats

---

* Agathias, *Palatine Anthology*.

in a star-filled mandorla, his right arm raised in a vanished blessing, his eyes staring away. Here, in Ascension, he is majestic and awful: the God of Israel. But from the dome of the fourteenth century narthex he looks down as the mild and beneficent Christ of a later tradition. His thumb and third finger are touched together in the eastern benediction, while beneath him, ringing the cupola, a troop of angels flies with ringleted hair and eagles' wings.

In the half-dome of the apse Our Lady of the Pastures stands between archangels, and the tiers of heaven meet the upper slopes of earth on pendentives where the apostles and evangelists sit in an agitated splendour.

Meanwhile, all through the church, the rank and file of the holy surge in their hundreds – teachers and hermits, warriors and prophets, vicars of the Church terrestrial – an army of God, strictly disciplined. From an early time the delineation of the saints was all but regulated by dogma. Their beards, their hairstyles, their books or swords became an unvarying equipment which serves to identify them. Everything has been formalized, like the Liturgy itself, into the hierarchy of a faith which would last forever. 'We do not change the everlasting boundaries which our fathers have set,' wrote St John Damascene, 'but we keep the Tradition, just as we received it.' And so they did. There is no comparable record of religious conservatism since the time of ancient Egypt.

Yet what dissensions lurk behind the façade of this painted eternity! What doubts once racked its authority! Its peace was bought by centuries of subtle and tempestuous dialectic in which the nature of the young religion had to be established. Ritual and dogma only emerged piecemeal from the ponderings of bishops and theologians in debates which crushed heresies and split councils. Half the civilized world was thrown into an academic turmoil in which the price of defeat was anathema or death. The Two Natures and the *filioque*, the dissecting of the *hypostaseis* and the Definition of Chalcedon – these arcane battlefields occupied the empire for five hundred years, from the Council of Nicaea in 325 to the last flicker of the Iconoclasts in 843. 'If you ask someone to give you change,' wrote Gregory of Nyssa, 'he philosophises about the Begotten and the Unbegotten; if you inquire about the price of a loaf, you are told by way of reply that the Father is greater and the Son inferior; if you ask "Is my bath ready?" the attendant answers that the Son was made out of nothing.'* The Greek love of philosophy was airing itself for the last time – no longer beaten out of gold, but filigreed in silver. And after the dissension was all over, and the mammoth theology complete, succeeding generations worshipped in a petrified forest of dogma and symbol. The Church had become eternal.

The saints reflect this triumph. Saints militant and ascetic, gorgeously apparelled or clothed only by their own hair, they fill the sanctuary with their initiate gaze. The cunning theologians and inspired composers of the Liturgy are here, the dark-robed founders of monasticism, anchorites with withered breasts and corpse's ribs, god-crazed stylites balancing on their columns, bishops, beggars, virgins, sages.

* *On the Deity of God.*

211

St George straddles his white horse with the little coffee-boy perched behind him still pouring (Cypriots claim that the saint was enjoying coffee when summoned to fight the dragon) and here is the furtive-eyed Baptist with his flimsy shepherd's cross. Here too are the saints whom Orthodoxy honours and the West scarcely knows: the hoary Cappadocian fathers – expounders of the Trinity, the Cypriot saints Barnabas and Epiphanius, St John the Almoner, St Mamas the tax-evader, Dionysios the Areopagite, St John Chrysostom and Ignatios the Bearer of God, St Anastasia the Poison-Curer, St George the Knifed; while the forty martyrs of Sebastae shine in their frozen pond (except for one, shorn of his halo, who makes a discreet getaway).

But even with these, and legions of others, the microcosmic world is not complete. In the narthex, above a paradise where saints cradle in their laps the souls of the blessed, the personified Earth and Sea sit dimpled and crowned like playing-card kings. Only a single note is struck which is not an echo or a preordainment of centuries before. On the arch of the east door, very small, a pair of hounds and two wild sheep have nuzzled their way onto a frescoed hill. Their freedom brings a sudden smile. If the muralled saints speak of an imagined heaven, these humble creatures are ambassadors of the natural earth. In all this painted glory, only their chance landscape reflects a bearable joy.

CHAPTER EIGHT

· · · · · · · · · · · ·

Poseidon's City

Lolled on a chair by the sea-front of Limassol, sipping a glass of wine, I felt the rain-scarred valleys of the Troodos ebb away. All that lost and heady world was suddenly strange enough for me to have dreamt it, while dozing on the promenade.

Limassol is to Cyprus what Osaka is to Japan – cheerful and rather vulgar. It has a useful port and some light industry – fruit canning, wine distilling – and in late summer the air is filled with the smell of carobs. The town still accommodates the families of two thousand British servicemen from the bases of Akrotiri and Episkopi, half of whom seemed to be strolling up and down the seafront that day or sitting in the open cafés drinking and turning pink in the sun. Some Cypriot youths lounged along the wharf, watching the cargo ships anchored half a mile offshore; a Limassol businessman was arguing a deal with an Englishman, who refused to be cheated, and some United Nations soldiers, buttocks swelling out of their shorts, lumbered among the sun-softened populace.

The city's shabbiness is not that of decay, but of a too-quick growth. By Cypriot standards it is young. When an English vessel of the Third Crusade was almost wrecked

213

on its shores in 1191 this was only a small town, overawed for centuries by ancient Amathus a few miles to the west. On board the ship were Berengaria of Navarre, the fiancée of Richard Coeur-de-Lion, and Richard's sister Joanna, Queen Dowager of Sicily. The self-appointed emperor Isaac Comnenus, who had ruled Cyprus harshly and independently of Constantinople for seven years, came to meet the royal women, and attempted to coax them ashore. But when they demurred, he refused them fresh water, and a week later the bulk of the English fleet appeared on the horizon 'and found the ladies outside the port of Limezun, exposed to the winds and the sea'.* Richard, seasick and fuming at the insult to his betrothed, landed his men and prepared for a full-scale invasion. Hastily he married Berengaria in the Chapel of St George at Limassol, and the same day had her crowned Queen of England, and himself King of Cyprus. She, it is said, was dark-eyed and delicate, and her cenotaph in Le Mans Cathedral shows her beautiful, dressed as a bride, with her hair parted down the middle in the way of mediaeval virgins.

By now Richard must have realized the strategic and commercial value of Cyprus, and he subjugated the whole island. Isaac surrendered, it is said, on condition that he would not be put in irons, so the king threw him into silver chains and had him taken to Palestine, where he died in the dungeons of Margat.

This was how Cyprus fell to the Crusaders. Soon afterwards Richard, ever short of money, offered it to the

---

* *Chronicle of Benedict of Peterborough*, Trs. H. T. F. Duckworth.

Templars for a hundred thousand besants, but the knights could not control the populace and a year later he gave the island to Guy de Lusignan, who had been king of Jerusalem before Saladin's reconquest, and who founded here a long and eccentric dynasty.

Limassol enjoyed two centuries of prosperity. Both the great knightly orders held property there. Its castle became the Templars' headquarters after the Holy Land was lost, and from it their leaders sailed away to France to die at the stake as heretics. But by the end of the fourteenth century the town was in decline, shaken by earthquake. In 1373 the Genoese half destroyed it, and soon afterwards it was twice sacked and plundered by the Egyptian Mamelukes. 'Only one wretched church remains standing, without bells,' wrote a traveller in 1480. 'Its ornaments are of the poorest kind, and they call to prayer with bits of wood. A few Latin clergy still live there but their habits are not edifying. Ruin in many forms has stricken the city.'* The Turks levelled it in 1539 – a portent of full-scale invasion – and twenty thousand citizens were slain. Only under the British, late in the nineteenth century, did Limassol start its unattractive recovery.

The sea is the sum beauty of the town now. Inland it fattens into the bungaloid wasteland which disfigures all the cities of the island. Vernacular building – sandstone mansions, the long fishermen's cottages – is being replaced by villas which might be fragments of Beirut or Malaga. All is pastel-painted concrete, windows fussy with cheap

* Felix Fabri, *Evagatorium in Terrae Sanctae*. Trs. C. D. Cobham, *Excerpta Cypria*.

wrought iron, spindly columned verandahs. And because of tourism the price of land has leapt up, land which a few years ago was worth almost nothing. I met a shepherd who owned twenty-six sheep; his family had been grazing flocks for centuries on the narrow strip of shore which belonged to them. Now, he said, he had been offered guess-how-much for the land?

I proposed a ludicrously high figure.

'No! Higher still!' The ebony eyes glittered beneath his battered cap. 'Two hundred thousand pounds!'

My gaze roamed in disbelief over his threadbare jacket, his boots, his grinning, unshaven jowls. What had he done with the money?

'Done?' he echoed. 'You don't think I sold, do you?' His face was swallowed by a timeless Cypriot cunning. 'The price'll go up!'

I strolled in the lazy morning from one end of the seafront to the other. A castle squatted among warehouses and ironmongeries, but a very rusted and permanent-looking notice said that it was temporarily closed to civilians, and above its ramparts the bored faces of soldiers looked over longingly into the streets below. On the promenade when I returned the same people were dozing or drinking, but the Greek and the Englishman had reached an agreement, and were walking silkily together along the quay.

I came to a notice which said 'Zoo-garden', and wandered in. I wanted to see a moufflon, the wild sheep which has become a national symbol and is portrayed on state coinage and even on Cyprus Airways jets; there are moufflon chocolates, moufflon cafés, moufflon launderettes. I ran a gauntlet of other cages from which stooped heads and dejected eyes accused me. Only the Imperial Eagle squinted down his beak like exiled royalty. I passed them, as through all zoos, in a state of regret – apology to the racoon which used its feeding-bowl as a lavatory, to the dromedary which walked on concrete, to the scowl on the face of the Patas monkey, to every stinking den and lax muscle. The specimens of Cypriot animals looked pitifully small. Even the head of the griffon vulture, which used to rip out the intestines of dead donkeys, was tucked miserably into his ruff: and the wild and furtive Cypriot foxes, newly caged, were no longer beautiful.

I found the moufflon and his wives at the back of an enclosure, sitting with his horns swept grandly over his head. A German pilgrim who came to Cyprus in 1333 wrote that 'There are in the mountains of Cyprus wild sheep with hair like that of goats and dogs, which are said to be found nowhere else. It is a very swift animal and its flesh is good and sweet. When I was out hunting I saw several caught by dogs, and especially by the tame leopards of Cyprus.'* Yet what is distinctive about the Cypriot breed I could not discover – a similar sheep exists, ignored, in Iran.

'But the moufflon,' its keeper tried to explain, 'is peculiar to Cyprus.'

'But you find them in east Turkey and Afghanistan and . . .'

'But this is the Cyprus moufflon.'

'What is different about it? It looks the same to me.'

* Wilhelm von Bodensele, *Hydoeporicon ad Terram Sanctam*. Trs. C. D. Cobham, *Excerpta Cypria*.

'The difference is that it lives in Cyprus. That distinguishes it.'

The moufflon, watching us, shook its crown of horns. It had a dark brown, deer-like skin, and its self-conscious wives resembled mouse-deer. The main distinction, I was later told, lies in the elegance of the horns; but the reason for the fuss is the scarcity of animals indigenous to the island. Cyprus has been overlaid so much by other cultures that anything native is eagerly grasped. The endemic warblers and jackdaws are rather dull, so it is the moufflon, for lack of more spectacular game, which has been frog-marched into patriotism.

The ruins of Amathus, oldest of the city-kingdoms, lie on a hill five miles east of Limassol. A submerged tilt of walls, some tombs to the west, a few shards tinkling underfoot – over this poor but universal pastureland a goatherd was driving his flock, singing one of the sad *manes* which were borrowed long ago from Syria.

Amathus, it is said, was founded by a son of Hercules, or by Amathusa, the mother of Cinyras. The city was known for human sacrifice and temple harlotry, and its lascivious women so disgusted King Pygmalion that he was perverted into wedding a statue of Aphrodite. But these legends spell Phoenicia. Even Hercules developed from a local god of Tyre, and a huge statue unearthed on the site betrays his disreputable origins, for it shows him half monster, massive and bulging-eyed, tearing an animal and already knotted with his lionskin.

Another such legend is that of Ariadne, the Cretan

heroine whom Theseus abandoned on an island – whether Naxos or Cyprus is unsure. Returning to find her dead, he in his grief endowed her cult in the grove of Amathus where she was buried – a grove called Aridela, which has passed out of the memory of the islanders. Yet the name Ariadne, 'very holy one', betrays a goddess, not a human, and the Cypriots melted her cult into that of the Great Mother.

Amathus was haunted by these primal deities as late as Roman times. Its temple of Hercules flourished, with a famous shrine to Aphrodite and Adonis where the legendary necklace of Eriphyle hung. Its people were never deeply Hellenised. They spoke a barbaric language into the fourth century B.C. and they were, wrote Scylax, 'auctothones', 'sons of the soil' – the descendants of the original Cypriots. This allusion, tantalizingly brief, is the last we hear of the men of Khirokitia, of the clay graves and smudged idols where my journey began. Doubtless they lost their identity among the Phoenicians, but the antiquity of Amathus was remembered, which Tacitus called 'most ancient'.

A single sarcophagus discovered here shows how lightly the Hellenic spirit had eaten into the East. Its longer sides are carved with processions, and even here the conical caps of the horsemen, the fan-shaped plumes and the parasol above the head of a king, are Asiatic; while on the other side gambol four defaced creatures which seem, across the centuries, to hold up their short petticoats in derision. These turn out to be Bes, the dwarf-god of Egypt, who once played consort to Aphrodite. A symbol of laughter among the Egyptians, whose humour must have been coarse to indulge him, only a still barbaric goddess would have submitted to his embrace. And so she is – portrayed here as a jewelled and pot-bellied girl, fingering her breasts in licentious self-applause.

The city's people were natural allies of the orient against Greece. Of all the island kingdoms, only Amathus refused to join Onesilus of Salamis against Persia in 499 B.C., and after the defeat of the Greek confederacy, wrote Herodotus, 'the people of Amathus, in revenge for his having laid siege to their town, severed the head from the dead body of Onesilus and hung it up above their gates. In time it became hollow, and was occupied by a swarm of bees, who filled it with honeycomb. In consequence of this the townspeople consulted the oracle, and were advised to take the head down and bury it, and, if they wished to prosper, to regard Onesilus thenceforth as half divine, and their country's protector, and to honour him with annual sacrifice. This was done, and the ceremony was still observed in my own day.'*

Again in 391 B.C. the city sided with Persia against Salamis, and won. But soon afterwards it took up arms for Alexander, and in Byzantine years we hear of it as the seat of a bishopric. St John the Almoner, founder saint of the Knights Hospitallers, was born here in 609 and here returned to die; pious history records that he was buried between two bishops whose corpses, at the funeral, involuntarily rolled aside to accommodate him.

The tombs of Amathus lie to the west, reached by deep

---

* Herodotus, *The Histories*, Trs. Aubrey de Sélincourt.

stairways; but they have mostly been filled in again and were rifled as recently as the last century, when the skulls fetched a shilling apiece in Limassol. The city has never been excavated. Its walls run and dip on rock-hewn bases, criss-crossing a hill where some later age, Byzantine I think, circled the crest with a chaplet of towers. Even the land has changed. The valleys are stripped of all but carob and a few olive trees, clustered like apostles along the shore. Earthquakes have wrenched the littoral out of true. The ancients probably never knew the double curve of the eastern headland, like a taut bow.

Over the acropolis the ground is covered by a sombre haze of shards. A faded inscription can be seen in the cliff-side, recording the erection of some vanished building by Lucius Vitellius – that sycophant of emperors. Everything else has been returned to thistles.

But on the shore the walls erupt startlingly in a sea-tower forty foot tall. I clambered round it, astonished at its size, momentarily seeing the whole city in the scale of its ruin. Yet the grandeur vanishes into nothing. The waves have sliced it clean from top to bottom. It remains a stub, pointing at the deep, and the huge rectangle of defence, starting far inland, is aborted. I sat under it and stared in disquiet at the water. How much of the city lay under the sea? It was impossible to know. When the earth covers a ruin it shows tumours and veins – the grass will still grow thicker over graves four thousand years old – but the sea folds over everything with an impartial brightness.

I walked frustratedly up and down the shore. Beyond the breaking waves, under a green stillness, some columns glistened like whitened fingers, where earthquake and tidal wave had toppled them sixteen centuries before. Somewhere far out, I thought, many such pillars must lie; yet nobody had ever seen this sunken Amathus.

The chance was too tempting to relinquish. I had never tried to skin-dive, but I spent the afternoon searching for someone to teach me. I found a Greek diver, an amateur, who promised to bring a second diver next morning: I think he had ideas of sunken treasure. So, after a single intimidating lesson, I found myself becalmed in a boat half a mile offshore, staring into the depths. One of the two men said that he had once noticed signs of buildings far out. 'There were black rocks near them which you could see from the surface.' So we gazed over the edge of the boat with our eyes close against the waves.

It was very still. The sun threw golden lances into the water, which met and separated far down. After a long time the diver shouted 'There they are! Black rocks!' and threw in the anchor. I glanced back at the shore where the walls showed on the acropolis: ruin of a ruin. We were almost half a mile out.

We somersaulted into the water. The spongy divers' suits let in no shock of cold. Our oxygen cylinders and leaded belts were suddenly weightless on us in the sea.

'All right,' said the older diver. 'We'll try it.' He looked uncertainly at me. 'You stay between us.'

We descended into the blue, following the anchor rope down through the bottom of the hard-cut world into one embalmed for sixteen centuries. I dropped cautiously, adjusting the pressure in my ears. Above me a shaft of sunlight exploded strangely on the water, like an impotent star. Far below, the light reached the ocean bottom, straying in dappled patterns over a plain of sand, filtered and dimmed. Down twenty, thirty, forty feet, I was preoccupied with my ears; a careless descent can burst an eardrum. At fifty feet I alighted on the seabed, and began to swim. I could hear only the nervous rasp of my own breathing, unnaturally loud inside my head.

We were flying low over the sand. The wrinkled expanse showed no sign that anything existed but itself. Our odd, wavering glide left it untouched. We must be too far out, I thought: almost half a mile. Surely nothing of the city, not even a harbour wall, could have been engulfed so deep?

Then, some forty-five feet down, the sand came rippling against a barnacled structure which stretched far away. Its stones were invisible under grasses and flowers which stood up more delicate than could any flower in the air, and it was crusted with a shell-like growth which came away soft in my fingers. I did not know what I was seeing; I imagined it to be a rough breakwater of the ancient harbour. The thickness of weed concealed precise shapes. All russet foliage, it flamed beneath us like an autumn wood, but moved with a telltale straightness over the sand.

Then, without warning, it broadened and grew high. It swayed above us in the owl-light, a true rampart, and as if in a dream its towers appeared – square chambers blurred with plants. We swam down into them, as into small craters. Great clam shells littered their bottom like silver ears. And I realized with awe that we had struck a wall of the ancient city.

I forgot even my fear of drowning. Ruined rooms spread round us, where the damsel fish lay in rainbow splinters, suspended oblivious to us in a sleepy light. I drifted between them almost in disbelief, brushing against ramparts unseen since Rome fell, which the last hands had touched at a time when the Parthenon glittered complete and Constantinople was scarcely yet a city. Somewhere under my hands, perhaps, was the gate where the skull of Onesilus filled with bees on a summer day.

The walls began to turn towards the shore, marking the western limit of the battlements which had kept the little kingdom safe. Whether they were the sea walls, sunk so far out, I could not tell – or perhaps a towered arm of the harbour, built in the years when the Roman grip was slackening at last, which had held half known civilization in its peace.

Then the vision in front of me turned brown. I thought my hair had floated into my eyes. I put up my hands to my forehead. There was no hair there. The brown had darkened to red. I realized with bewilderment that my mask was filling with blood. I tried to release it into the sea the way divers expel water, by tilting back their heads and exhaling hard, but it began to splash in my eyes. I lost sight of the walls. The diver below me was oblivious of my trouble. As I began to surface he was the last thing I saw, dwindled to a starfish on the sea bottom. I pushed the air from my lungs as I had been told, ascending behind the bubbles of my own frightened breath – too quick an ascent can even mean death. And after eternity the daylight burst about me, I ripped off my mask to discover the humiliation of nothing more than a bad nosebleed, and there was

Amathus, desolate on its hill with the noon sun storming against it.

That evening I found a goatherd wandering the ruins. He was collecting the snails which emerge from rocks after rain. Tired from the sea, I sat and watched him, planning to sleep by the walls as soon as night came.

'Here,' he cried. 'Are you English?'

'Yes.'

'A pity.'

'Why?'

'If you were French I'd have given you some snails.'

'The English eat snails too.'

'So! Is that right?' His wizened face peered at me from the halo of a straw hat. 'Nothing stays the same. Please take some then.' His eyes were like hazel buttons. He held out a cellophane bag and when I said that I had no way of cooking snails he demanded that I come to his home. 'The Government will cook them for you.'

'Who?'

'The Government.' He thought this was explanation enough, and I was left with a vision of the Chamber of Deputies preparing me supper. So I helped him gather the last snails, and we drove the herd back towards his village, whose few lights brightened before us in the dusk. The goats scampered in anarchic gangs, their tails curled at us, gnawing the ripe wheat to either side while he pitched rocks at them with savage cries. He could not count this herd; when I asked him how many he had, he did not know. But he realized instantly if one was missing, because he knew each animal individually. Small though he was, he threw stones at them with such force that I asked in alarm what would happen if he hit one.

'Watch,' he said.

He picked up a jagged rock and threw it, ululating. It bounced off the haunch of a harvest-chewing goat with a wooden thud. The creature took no notice at all.

'There,' he answered. 'That's what happens. A goat is immortal. You can't kill Satan.' He added pensively: 'All the same, their milk fetches a pound a kilo in Limassol.'

They flowed up the street and into a yard whose walls, like half this village, were built from the ruins of Amathus. In one corner stood the pedestal of a vanished statue, inscribed, which was propping up boxes of vegetables.

The goatherd opened a door of the two-roomed house. 'This room is yours.' Its floor was covered with drying beans and was furnished only by a carved peasant wardrobe, which looked as if it had never been opened. I saw a ceiling of fire-blackened beams. Yet in the walls shone the flotsam of ancient Amathus, immense and beautifully cut stones which might once have held the roof over a Phoenician god or merchant. And as if in confirmation a female voice boomed beyond them: 'Heracles! Heracles!'

The goatherd jumped. 'That's my wife,' he said. 'She wants me.' I could hear the oncoming tread of heavy, authoritarian shoes.

'Heracles!'

I glanced at his shrivelled frame, the scrawny arms and brown head. So that was his name: Hercules.

'There you are!' She loomed in the doorway – a crimson-faced giantess who appeared not to see me but hustled her husband away. Poor Hercules! Her face had not the quixotic brightness of his. No feature upset its bland monotony, and it was impossible to tell whether or not she was annoyed at my presence, or whether she felt anything at all.

She stood in front of the sink, her working hands tiny against her huge body. 'Get the cucumber, Heracles,' she said. 'No, not there. The shelf above. There are only two shelves and you choose the wrong one.'

'All right . . . yes . . . all right.'

'Pull the table out.'

He flitted round her like a fly around an ox. 'The Government's in a bad mood,' he whispered. 'I'm sorry, but what can I do?'

I laughed in realization. The Chamber of Deputies dissolved itself instantly.

'It's not really funny,' he said. 'She might go on like this for days. She's always worse when it rains.' He gestured helplessly. 'And to think we considered emigrating to England . . .'

She sat with us for supper. There was no escaping her. I had secretly hoped for the snails, but instead we ate goat's meat, which she apportioned frugally. I managed to slip some under the table, where a cat bolted it in tactful silence leaving me with a litter of chips. How Cypriots preferred to cook potatoes before chips appeared I do not know, and Hercules could not remember.

At first, except to demand whisky, the Government scarcely spoke. Hercules poured the drink neat, and they drank from the same glass, she more than he. But soon I noticed something happening to the huge, eternal face of the woman. It was splitting across. It was smiling. It was creased, yes, with a ponderous, friendly smile, and once this smile had arrived it remained as a permanent emotion, like the peace on the face of the Buddha.

The eyes of Hercules, too, grew gay and swimming. He talked of how his six children were all well married and gone. Sometimes when the goats did not pay enough he took a job whitewashing walls in Limassol, while his wife tended the herd. Yes, it was a good life. And he had plenty to remember. He had fought with the Cyprus Regiment in the war, had been captured in Crete and spent four years in prison in Bodenbach.

'We were set to work mending the roads with pneumatic drills. God help me, I'd never seen such things before.' He swallowed a jet of whisky to exorcise the memory. 'Then American bombers strafed the road, diving on us like tomcats. The first time I just stood staring. But I swear I was more scared of those drills than of the bombers!'

I spent the night on a bed which he wheeled in from the other room. I think it was his own. But something in my eardrums opened and closed, unsettled by the pressure of diving, and for a long time prevented my sleep. I lay staring at the blackened ceiling. In their cellophane bags, now sealed, the snails were beginning to die. Through the silence I could hear them crinkling and wheezing, and I regretted having gathered them.

Next morning Hercules could not eat dry toast for breakfast because he had no teeth. But the Government did not produce anything else. At dawn he went away to wash the walls of Limassol, while I walked westward through the town and along the shore towards the peninsula of Akrotiri.

By afternoon a blustering wind was pouring off the hills. It cut uninterrupted over the flat headland. I passed the works for the new harbour and crossed a littoral sordid with miles of rubbish which was being blown piecemeal towards the sea. This was the same tainted coast on which the soldiers of St Louis had died of malaria by thousands at the start of the Fourth Crusade. Somewhere I crossed into a British Sovereign Base area. The knowledge that I was amongst my own countrymen was not a happy one. They broke the Mediterranean ease with the cold of officialdom. Notices warned of low-flying jets, and barbed wire steered me away. The military radio antennae already showed lights in the sunless evening.

I found an abandoned hut where I slept, with the wind screaming through its fissures. But in a dawn which came mauve and tranquil over the dunes, I woke to walk along the shores of a salt lake, where flamingoes fly in winter from the Caspian Sea. This new stillness set me at ease. My rucksack was full of fruit from Limassol; I was making for Curium, loveliest of ancient sites; and beyond the rich plantations near the lake I could sense the headland's tip very near: the Cape of Cats.

'I heard a marvellous thing,' wrote a Venetian monk who came in 1484. 'From the said city of Lymisso up to this Cape the soil produces so many snakes that men cannot till it, or walk without hurt thereon . . . At this place there is a Greek monastery which rears an infinite number of cats, which wage unceasing war with these snakes. It is wonderful to see them, for nearly all are maimed by the snakes: one has lost a nose, another an ear; the skin of one is torn, another is lame; one is blind of one eye, another of both.'* The monks, he said, would summon them to eat by tolling a bell, and afterwards the cats would troop out again to attack the snakes, as those still do at Stavrovouni.

But I found the Monastery of St Nicholas of the Cats in ruins. It was abandoned after the Turkish conquest, and the cats died of starvation. Now only its church was standing, with scarcely a trace of ornament but the Lusignan lion on its lintel. Inside even the altar was bare except for some candles stuck in rusted tins of 'Babies Modified Milk'. I wandered outside again. In the debris of the cloister, under banks of convolvulus, columns filched from some pagan shrine lay in a self-contained perfection. The beauty of their workmanship put the mediaeval stones to shame.

Many are the fables of the cats of St Nicholas. It was said that St Helena herself had imported them and that they numbered a thousand. But the snakes retaliated with lusher fantasy. The poisonous kinds are in fact only two: the short *kuffi* and the long, dirt-coloured *saittaros*. But Cypriot lore has elongated them to terrible lengths and thickened them to the circumference of a man's leg. They were rumoured to be blind and deaf alternate months and to crush the bones of lambs and kids against trees before swallowing them. Alternatively they have been reduced to six inches, like the fearful *Galera*, 'furnished with a quantity of legs

* Fra Francesco Suriano, *Trattato di Terra Santa*. Trs. C. D. Cobham, *Excerpta Cypria*.

which it moves all together like the oars of a galley, whence it takes its name'.* According to one especially enterprising chronicler there were man-devouring, quadruped snakes, as long as horses and with almost bullet-proof skins; but even these the cats hunted, leaping on their backs and tearing out their eyes.

As long ago as classical times the island was famous for its serpents, and in the sixteenth century a family immune from snakebite claimed descent from the Cypriot Ophiogenes who would suck the wounds of bitten victims and heal them. 'One of the race,' wrote Pliny, 'Exegon by name, was sent to Rome and by order of the consuls, to try his power, thrown into a casketful of snakes, which, to the wonder of all, fondled about him.'

Serpent-worship may have something to do with this reputation, for by Roman times Cyprus was the purest repository of the snake-loving Mycenaean culture. But some have conjectured that the monastery replaced a shrine to the Egyptian cat-god Bubastis, and that its tabbies and tortoiseshells were descendants of some remote deified tom a thousand years before Christ. More certain is it that after the Knights Hospitaller left Cyprus for Rhodes, they carried away cats to fight the snakes there, and these squalling shiploads must have come from the Cape of Cats, where the knights had set up headquarters.

Their castle of Kolossi is not far away. Momentarily shuffled between the two great orders, it passed to the Hospitallers after the Templars were indicted for heresy.

* Giovanni Mariti, *Travels in the Island of Cyprus*.

Here, swamped by refugee knights after the loss of the Holy Land, they dallied in bewilderment, split by dissension and deeply criticized in Europe. But they escaped the Templars' end. Shored up for years in their Syrian castles, the knights suddenly adapted to sea-warfare and transferred to Rhodes in 1310; but they kept their rich Commandery at Kolossi with a fief of sixty villages, and as late as the fifteenth century rebuilt its castle in flaxen stone.

Their sugar refinery remains, although empty, with an aqueduct and a mill-race where the water still runs. The keep rises seventy-seven feet high to its crenellations, whose machicoulis looks too delicate for war, and is blazoned by the coats-of-arms of two Grand Masters, with the shield of the Grand Commander Louis de Magnac who built it. Its chambers keep a massive symmetry, and are set with gravely elegant fireplaces like those of Renaissance châteaux.

Here, on the red-soiled foothills, the knights cultivated vines of the Commanderia, oldest of all named wines, which is still drunk. Thick and sweet, almost a liqueur, it was famous throughout European Christendom, and fuddled successive Plantagenet kings. It was said that the Ottoman sultan 'Selim the Sot' was so intoxicated by it that desire for these vineyards caused his barbaric invasion of Cyprus. But the grape had its revenge. Three years later, drunk on Commanderia, he slipped on the floor of his bath and smashed his skull.

In Roman times Cypriot wines were highly esteemed. Pliny called the island's vine the oldest of trees, although why he thought so he does not say. In the fifteenth century

Portuguese traders transplanted shoots of the Commanderia to their homeland, where it became the ancestor of Madeira. And even the origins of champagne, in French romance, are ascribed to Cyprus; the vines, it is said, were taken from the island by Thibaud IV – 'La Chansonnier' – king of Navarre and Count of Champagne, on his way back from Crusade. The flavour of goat and tar which used to permeate the wines – they were transported in goatskins and stored in pitch-lined casks – has gone from the factory products, and the dry Othello, the sweet Aphrodite and the red St Hilarion are pleasant, if not distinguished wines, grown from the chalk soil of Troodos.

As I went westward young vines spotted half the hills, where the Kouris river lingered to the sea. Below me the cliffs repeated themselves in white bays, until beyond Episkopi the promontory of Curium rose. I saw that in the north and east, where the rock lifted sheer for three hundred feet, the marks of chisels showed all over its face – a whole cliff which had been scarped by hand. How much love or pride had inspired this labour, or how much fear, was impossible to tell; but the acropolis was beautiful as well as safe, for it lay above the sea with corn on the alluvial plain, where the people buried their dead.

Herodotus says that Curium was founded by Argives, which is probably true. But during the first revolts of the city-states against Persia, in which Soli distinguished itself and Amathus refused to join, it was the treachery of Curium at the height of battle which ruined the Hellenic cause; for 'Stesenor the ruler of Curium, with a considerable body of troops under his command, played traitor;

and his lead was immediately followed by the war-chariots from Salamis'.*

Many ages scatter their ruins over the bluff. I walked through a Roman palace levelled to nothing higher than my shoulders, and in its garden pavements saw an inscription to Eustolios, builder of 'this cool refuge sheltered from the winds'. An air of ease and affection pervaded it. The mosaics spread into baths where the water channels and air flues were still in place, and portrayed fish and birds in pastel pinks and blues. Their motifs were all of peace; their inscriptions invoked temperance, modesty. An aqueduct ran to a fountain house. A theatre looked out to sea.

Yet the wealth of Curium in its heyday was startling. The American consul Di Cesnola, who was not so much an archaeologist as a systematic plunderer, discovered a series of underground chambers sealed with dust which had perfectly preserved a priceless treasure. As in a fairy tale he found one room to contain objects of bronze, another of silver, another of gold. So extraordinary was his story that many doubt if he discovered such a treasure in one place, but believe that it came from thousands of pilfered graves.

The pieces were not only Greek, but Phoenician, Egyptian, Assyrian and Chaldean. There were bracelets and amulets, jewellery in electrum and agate, jasper, sard, chalcedony; beads of rock crystal still strung on golden wire; silver bowls and ewers stacked one inside the next; a gold-leafed diadem. Many were exquisite. The intaglios of the

---

* Herodotus, *The Histories.* Trs. Aubrey de Sélincourt.

archaic Greek ring-stones are among the loveliest known. Animal-headed pendants came to light, with arm-bands inscribed from a king of Paphos; ruby and amethyst earrings, necklaces formed of gold acorns or carnelian and onyx bugles. Here too was found the sceptre-head of the Curium kings, crowned by two eagles whose filigreed wings and gouged eyes, once inlaid, had whittled to golden bones.

But the great age had passed even before the rise of Rome, and Christianity established an early hold in the city. By the third century it could boast a martyred bishop. 'This house now rests on the support of Christ', runs an inscription in the villa of Eustolios. 'A new protector has arisen for Curium in place of Phoebus Apollo.'

The foundations of a cathedral near the western gate betray a new magnificence and care. The capitals show already the fastidious touch of Byzantium; and a hexagonal fountain, a form strange to early Rome, has left its broken star among the thistles.

Westward along the cliffs I passed a stadium with seats for six thousand, all turned to rubble; and beyond, a track led through woodland, the preserve of deer in ancient times, to a temple of Apollo Hylates. Precisely who this Apollo was, I do not know. His worship centred on Curium, and he seems to have shadowed Aphrodite as a servant-lover – but never as more than a shadow. Called 'Apollo of the Woods' his shrine resembles that in Greece, whose devotees would tear up giant trees and leap from precipices without hurt.

It was a rustic sanctuary, complex and mysterious, whose stones marked out arcades and many rooms. Old as the eighth century B.C., but rebuilt in Roman years, its porticoes showed Doric columns, primitive and surprising in an island so devoted to the Ionic.

As I walked on, the precinct narrowed. A street wavered to the long-profaned altar, and I mounted its steps to where a chamber crowned the podium. It was like a shrine for shepherds, open and very small. Yet whoever so much as touched its altar, wrote Strabo, was hurled from the nearby headland – a place dark in myth – to propitiate the god. Aphrodite herself, despairing for the slain Adonis, is said to have leapt from this awesome precipice, and to have perished in the waves from which she was born.

CHAPTER NINE

Nicosia

I approached Nicosia with dread. Sudden wealth – and the prosperity of this whole island was sudden before 1974 – destroys the most solid character, and Nicosia is the lodestar of thousands who have abandoned the rough graces of the countryside and acquired a higher income in exchange. Through its concrete labyrinth, a wilderness more profound than any tract of the Troodos, I found myself a stranger, trudging in boots so worn that nobody any longer enquired after them. The fever of building and demolition, the sprouting of hotels and offices, the straggle of Cubist suburbs, looked at once new and shoddy.

I found myself a room in a run-down hotel of the kind which is disappearing. It stood on the edge of the inner city, and from my balcony I looked over the walls into the fortress-town of the Lusignan kings, and thought: surely this, at least, has been saved?

Closed in Venetian ramparts which were built unavailing against the Turk, it looks from the air like a many-pointed star, intricate and hopeless. Fifty years ago it enclosed a sandstone city of Ottoman grace, its rooftops mingled with domes and palms. But now the walls have been breached by viaducts, a British innovation, and this priceless town too has been shredded almost to nothing, barely distinguishable from a thousand others.

I walked until I reached the barriers which isolate the Turkish sector. Beyond the United Nations cordon the streets were flanked by houses whose roofs and doors had disintegrated. Within ten years whole gardens had erupted through their floors. I squeezed past a barricade of overturned cars and sandbags. Beyond the ruins a Turkish soldier cradled a sten gun.

But where Greek enterprise has destroyed, Turkish sluggishness has preserved. The quarter was quicker to patch a building than to replace it. Yet its streets had a loosened, unstable look. Shutters and balconies were weathered to a sapless pallor, ironwork rusted in the windows; where the plaster fell, mud bricks showed behind.

Now, through the debris and easily to be seen, the ribs of an older skeleton were pressing, left from a time when Nicosia was the Lusignan capital and Cyprus the last Christian kingdom close to the Holy Land, the haven of Crusaders awaiting a reconquest. I passed the moulded windows of a chapter-house, saw the lift of Gothic arches, a rose window shining in decay. A line of escutcheons marked the last fragments of the Latin Archbishopric which had so persecuted the Orthodox, and the vaults of the Church of St Catherine still rose from their wall-columns like a dream of the Île de France.

These Gothic visions, the fruit of a Northern imagination and unrest, arrived by a freak of history – the Crusades – but their pitted stone looks almost decadently sumptuous: a softening which echoes that of their builders. By the time they were raised the Holy Land was already lost, and the life of the Lusignans had grown mellow with time and the sun. All the female trades of the East – spices, perfumes, silks – flowed through their kingdom. The French nobles intermarried with the Greek and Armenian aristocracy, while Byzantine and Italian, as well as French influence permeated the court. The style of living grew closer to that of a Syrian emir than a Norman baron. 'They were brought up in luxury,' wrote James of Vitry, 'soft and effeminate, more used to baths than battles, addicted to unclean and riotous living, clad like women in soft robes . . . They have so learned to disguise their meaning in cunning speeches, covered and bedecked with leaves, but no fruit, like barren willow trees, that those who do not know them thoroughly by experience can scarcely understand their reservations and tricks of speech or avoid being deceived by them.'

The city, seven miles in circuit, was walled into sections and the alleys barred by gates at night. Its houses were turned inwards upon courtyards set with fountains and trees, and their furniture, inlaid in mother-of-pearl, was the most luxurious of its day. The aristocracy was rumoured to be the richest in the world, a heady compound of the arrogance of France, the effeminacy of Syria and the cunning of Greece. 'An annual income of three thousand florins,' wrote an astonished German priest, 'is of no more account than an income of three marks to us.'[*]

For weeks at a time their hunting expeditions would vanish into the mountains with a train of falconers, laden

---

* L. von Sudheim, 1350, *Excerpta Cypria*.

camels and packs of perfumed and anointed hounds, a servant for every two. The king himself rode in pursuit of moufflon, balancing on the croup of his saddle a spoilt leopard which would turn on its own keeper if it did not instantly catch its prey.

Under their black capes, worn in sign of mourning for the lost Jerusalem, the dress of the court ladies was richer than any in Europe, and scandalously *décolleté*. The fashion, of course, was French, but the native silks – damask, samite, golden *marmeto* – were elaborately beautiful, and both in clothes and in their jewellery the refined patterns of Constantinople were still copied.

All this brilliance, of course, lay sugar-like on the rotting cake of Greek peasantry. Wealth depended upon trade, upon the energy of Italian merchants and the docility of a half-enslaved populace. For 'the poor Cypriots are much-enduring people, and God in his Mercy avenges them; they are no more rulers than the poor serfs and hostages are; they make no sign at all'.*

But the dazzle of the Lusignans was not only of sensual splendour. The kingdom enjoyed a model constitution and a legal code which subtly balanced the power of king and state. For long periods the island was at peace. Alone in a Moslem sea, an aura of romance encircled it. It inspired the poets Philippe de Novare, who fought in its civil wars, Chaucer, Petrarch and Guillaume de Machaut. Thomas Aquinas dedicated his treatise on kingship, never finished, to the young Hugh II, and Boccacio his *Genealogy of the*

---

* Leontios Makhairas, *Recital concerning Cyprus*. Trs. R. M. Dawkins.

Gods to Hugh IV. The island royalty held a half mystical appeal. In the cathedral of Famagusta, nearest of their cities to the Holy Land, the sovereigns on their accession were still crowned kings of Jerusalem. They were heirs to the dashed hopes of the waning mediaeval age, the lost conscience of Christendom. And despite the littleness of their realm they married into the royal houses of Europe.

The palace in Nicosia, of which only a window remains, was set in a citadel whose ditch was flooded by the Pedeios river in spring. Beside it, in the Abbey of St Dominic – the Saint-Denis of Cyprus – most of the Lusignan kings were buried. Together with them, their names reading like a last roll-call of Crusader chivalry, lay the seneschals and constables of the kingdom, princes of Galilee and Caesarea, Antioch and Tripoli, all the ambitions and darkened ideals of two centuries.

When the Venetians tightened the city walls, this abbey was demolished to allow an open field of fire against the Turks; but Nicosia cathedral, St Sophia, whose parvis had once been the centre of the city, was turned into a mosque by the victorious Ottomans, and saved.

As with people, so with buildings, the forced conversion went only skin-deep. The Turks crowned the cathedral with twin minarets and cluttered it in Moslem paraphernalia. But over the parvis the glory of mediaeval France breaks in shadowed throngs of pillars, where the central archway lifts. Among the richness of its moulded orders fly bishops and kings, mitred and crowned, their hands grasping sword hilts or folded round staves, and above other niches, whose saints and apostles have gone, the fingers of

God still descend out of carved clouds and poise their crowns over empty space.

Carved with biblical narrative and allegory, such feats of the High Gothic are themselves like mammoth works of theology. In pinnacles and arches, buttresses and tympana, they rise in a fastidious intellectual balance – the counterpart, it has been said, of those works of thirteenth century scholasticism, the *Summa* and the *Specula*, which were compendia of all existence.

The Gothic cathedral, like the Byzantine, was built with symbols. It was itself designed in the shape of the Cross. But where the mysticism of Byzantium seems passive, almost domestic, that of Catholicism yearns and cries. Over the carpets of St Sophia, through a whitewashed light, the aisles march with restless solemnity. Nothing sounds but the faint dinging of a grandfather clock. But peace, the Islamic and Byzantine completeness, is absent. The linear tension of the building urges the worshipper forward. He is caught up in its awesome longing, for the apse hangs inviolate beyond him, and the whole cathedral seems to mount towards it, making for some unimaginable point of light.

St Sophia recalls the churches of the Île de France. It was raised in the fine early pointed style, and the arrival of St Louis in 1248 quickened its building. Here and there the Islamic whitewash has peeled from its walls like a false expression, and above the ladies' gallery has revealed a carving of the Lamb of God. A few tombstones stand in a chapel, the remnant of hundreds which the Turks plucked from the floor before scattering the bones beneath. Their slabs show little but fragments: the fall of a lady's sleeve, armoured hands touched in prayer. Only the stone of Arnati Visconti, who died in 1347, is magnificently complete. Laid in his barbed plate armour, the ringlets of mail cascading over his shoulders, his moustache tickles a military mouth, while two dragons vomit smoke at his feet.

The gravestone of the Lusignan princess Eschive, heiress to the dukedom of Athens, is a reminder that even in this feudal time, female influences obtrude in the island's affairs, and that several of the country's queens eclipsed their husbands. Catherine Cornaro ruled in her own right. Helen Palaeologina dominated John II to the point of ignominy, and when he dared to take a mistress she bit off the woman's nose. Her daughter Charlotte held out for four years in Kyrenia castle against her own brother; and the wife and mistress of the celebrated Peter I were responsible for his end.

The reign of this extraordinary monarch, Peter, marks the zenith of Lusignan Cyprus. Cultured, handsome, idealistic, he was the paragon of his age. As a young man he had fought successfully in Anatolian Turkey and had founded a new clan of chivalry, the Order of the Sword. Dedicated to the reconquest of the Holy Land, he travelled the courts of Europe to gain support for his Crusade, and in the summer of 1365 a formidable but cosmopolitan fleet assembled under his banner at Rhodes. Its destination remained unannounced until it had set sail not for the Holy Land, but for Alexandria; for Mameluke Egypt was the body of Moslem power, and Alexandria the mouth by which it was fed. So well was the secret kept that when the armada appeared off-shore the Alexandrians thought it a huge merchant fleet and came out to bargain. The city was cruelly sacked, the king unable to control his knights. After three days, glutted with plunder and faced by an army marching north from Cairo, the nobles demanded to return to Cyprus and Peter had bitterly to consent.

He did not give up hope of permanent conquest, but travelled to Italy to renew his plea. There he learnt that his wife, Eleanor of Aragon, who had once loved him with a violent and demanding passion, had been unfaithful to him in Cyprus, and that his favourite mistress, Jeanne l'Aleman, a woman loved for her goodness, had been tortured on the queen's orders for carrying the king's child. 'She ordered her to be brought before her,' wrote the historian Makhairas, 'and they brought a handmill and stretched her out on the ground and put it on her womb, and they held her firmly and ground two measures of flour upon her womb; and still she did not miscarry.'

When Peter returned he brought the queen to trial for adultery, but his nobles refused to condemn her. They were starting to fear his despotism. And Peter did not forgive them. Instead he turned savage. Soon after, while he lay in bed with his other mistress, Eschive de Scandelion, a party of nobles inveigled themselves into the chamber and hacked him to death. 'And for no thing but for thy chivalrye,' wrote Chaucer generously, 'They on thy bedde han slayn thee by the morwe.'

His murder sent a chill through Europe. The hope of another Crusade was gone, and the Lusignan power already corroding. During the next hundred years Nicosia was sacked both by the Genoese and the Mamelukes, and was convulsed by earthquakes; and eventually its rulers grew so weak that Venice was able to seize the island by a dynastic *coup*.

The years of Venetian supremacy added little but their walls, built in a snowflake pattern round the city. Their bastions still lurch out in wind-darkened shoulders, and straighten again to ramps which are pitted as if some rock-eating bird had plucked out the most savoury stones. The deep Venetian entrances remain; the woodwork of the Famagusta Gate swings dreamily on its hinges. And crowning the Constanza bastion a ruined mosque-tomb marks where the Turkish standard-bearer fell in the siege of 1570. Close by, after seven weeks, the Ottomans finally took the Podocataro redoubt, where the exhausted defenders were asleep, and poured into the city. Some twenty thousand Christians were killed in the street fighting.

'And now indeed that terrible roar of artillery and musketry ceased to thunder in our ears,' wrote Angelo Calepio, superior of the Dominican convent, 'but the change was a sad and mournful one, for on every side we heard nothing but the ceaseless wailing of poor women parted from their husbands, the shrieks of children torn from their mothers' arms . . . The victors kept cutting off the heads of old women; many of them as they marched along to prove their swords split open the heads of men who had already surrendered. Did a prisoner try to escape, he was caught up and his legs cut off, and as long as any life was left in him every Janissary who passed had a cut at him.

'Among the slain were Lodovico Podocatoro, and

Lucretia Calepia, my mother, whose head they cut off on her serving maid's lap. They tore infants in swaddling clothes from their mothers' breasts, dashed some down on the ground, others by the feet against a wall: of whom I could baptize only one. To be brief, this sack lasted three days.'*

Now in Nicosia the Turkish sector is besieged by the resurgent Greeks. It is insulated and old-fashioned. A few caravanserais keep a dilapidated charm – the Khan of the Gamblers and the falling Büyük Khan with its multitude of gnome-like chimneys. A library of Ottoman manuscripts stands near the cathedral, and in a mosque garden, tender with oleander and jasmine, a caretaker points out the graves of important men.

As for the great house of Lusignan, heirs to the crowns of Cyprus, Jerusalem and Armenia, it ended in obscurity. The last known descendant, a tiny spinster called Eliza de Lusignan, passed away her life as a governess and died in a London suburb at the end of the Victorian age.

* Fra. Angelo Calepio, *Chorograffia*. Trs. C. D. Cobham, *Excerpta Cypria*.

CHAPTER TEN

·········

The Orchard Coast

The villagers of Kormakiti were starting to feel responsible for me. I was sitting in one of those coffee houses which seem in no way to differ from one another, and it was growing late. Discussion had faded. The village elders had relapsed into stillness, seated like icons of themselves, on rush-bottomed chairs. They considered my plan to camp as a slight on their village. 'You can't camp among bears,' they said, although there were no bears, and murmured amongst themselves, lapsing into a strange Arabic for the purpose, to decide whose house was most respectable for me. This Arabic was filled with words from Aramaic, the language of Christ, which is almost extinct, and it was soft and slurred. Kormakiti is the last Cypriot village to speak it, for its people are descended from the Maronites of the Lebanon, a sect of Christian mountaineers, and they probably came here in the ninth century.

Eventually it was a young man's voice behind me which said: 'Come to my house. My parents will be sleeping but my sister will cook.' I turned to thank him. The Maronites are stocky and round-headed, but they have mixed with the true Arab and it was one of these faces which looked at me now – the eagle nose and slightly withdrawn forehead and chin of Syrian tribesmen. But his limping gait – he was almost a cripple – was his own. 'I'm Spyros,' he said simply.

We walked out into the dark street past the twin turrets of the village church. Spyros said he had never been to his native Lebanon. It was his ambition to go.

'Greece is not our homeland.' He seemed to hobble with pain over the rutted track. 'In all these political troubles we stay silent. We just hope to be left alone. In the old days, I've heard, our colony was strong here. But now we may number three thousand . . . not more.'

I mentioned that from the eastern tip of Cyprus, on a clear day, you can see the Lebanese mountains white with snow above the sea. His lips parted in astonishment. 'So near?'

'Ninety miles perhaps.'

He lapsed into silence, dragging his foot. In mediaeval times the Maronites had furnished the Crusaders with archers and guides, and after the Arab resurgence many more had fled to Cyprus. They lived in the Karpas peninsula, nearest to their homeland, and around Kormakiti. But their Church, although it acknowledges the Pope, is at heart closer to the Orthodox, and through conversion and inter-marriage the community dwindled. The liturgy at Kormakiti, said Spyros, was still held in Syriac, the church Aramaic, and when he greeted his sister at the door of their darkened house he spoke again in that strange language which is a last relic of Lebanese dialect at the time of the Crusades. She looked at me in alarm, and touched her hands to her shoulders as if to draw a coat round herself;

but she only wore a nightdress, so smiled faintly and slipped away.

'That's Despina,' Spyros said. 'She helps in the house.'

The house was so small that I could only say: 'Is there enough to do?'

He gestured round the room with the faintly sad Arab flamboyance. The walls were blackened with smoke from the open fireplace; lizards lived in the cracks of the stones. 'These old rooms need more work than ten modern ones, but . . . yes, it's true, there's not much to do. She's already seventeen and we can't afford secondary school.' He trod on a passing lizard. 'But a pure girl must work in the house. That is how it is. And there's weaving to do. She weaves like a spider: beautiful things.'

'And you?'

'I'm a joiner. That's poor work, but it's God's will. My leg, you see . . .'

Despina returned, wearing a dressing-gown which did no more than the nightdress to conceal her willowy legs and white slope of neck; but she looked oddly old-fashioned in her prettiness, more like a picture than a person, and she blushed when I looked at her. Spyros opened the food cupboard to make sure that she ransacked everything that was best, while I asked myself in embarrassment: Why should they? Among Cypriots the only duty of a guest seems to be grateful acceptance.

Despina said: 'I'm sorry the tomatoes are small.'

'They're not small . . .'

'And we have no cucumbers,' she went on.

'I don't like cucumbers (a lie), tomatoes are better.'

'I thought you didn't have tomatoes in England.' She smiled her judged, tentative smile. 'What don't you have?'

'Good cooking.'

She received this as a compliment to her own, which it might have been, and laced her hands nervously together. 'My mother taught me.'

But Despina would not stay with us, and I ate with Spyros, whose speech had slumped into a goulash of Arabic, Greek, English and Syriac, so that I was glad when he yawned and pulled out two steel-framed beds which had stood against the walls. He shook the blankets.

'No lizards.'

Greeks and Arabs can both be very delicate about physical things. He looked away while I undressed, and waited until I was in my bed before saying: 'You know what is good before sleep?'

I said doubtfully: 'No.'

He crawled from his bed in his underpants and gambolled lamely out under the stars to the next room. 'Music!' he shouted. My heart sank. He would return, I was sure, with a transistor radio, which all the villagers use to fill out the awfulness of solitude. In a moment I heard his hardened feet thumping on the cobblestones, and he ran grinning back into the room. To my surprise he was clutching a flute which he had made from arbutus wood, as the ancients did.

'At country festivals,' he said immodestly, 'I win half the prizes with this!'

Then he propped himself in the bed, smiling whimsically, and began to play. He played the songs whose origins go back to Syria – primitive sounds like the ghost of some other, fuller music, songs which are sung by goatherds on the lonely mountains – and all the time he was laughing over the instrument, his chest lapped by a curly flotsam of hair, like a satyr enchanting himself.

Cypriot families feel dreadful in the early morning. The hospitality and enthusiasm of the previous evening are only blearily mimicked. They grope and blink, cradling their fragility, and sip sweet tea, dipping in hard bread – a Lebanese custom. Spyros' father was a big man whose boots were laced with thongs below his knees. He saluted me heavily, and burped, while his wife flew about him on tiny, noiseless feet and shooed away the lizards. Despina had changed into a blue dress and fashionable white stockings. She had bought a cold sausage from somewhere, which she put beside me, and smiled her Victorian smile.

'Where was your sister going?' I asked Spyros, when we left the house.

'Despina? She doesn't go anywhere.'

'She was dressed up.'

He smiled. 'That was for you.'

We parted on the edge of his village without pretence that we would meet again – he waved away my thanks with a simple farewell – and I set out through the pine forests. This north-western shore has been forgotten, isolated beyond the orchards and the copper hills to the south. Between the darkness of glades the sea showed green. The mist was lifting from Morphou Bay, and all the mountains behind, with the remembered beauty of Vouni, were rising in softened tips. After an hour I emerged from the woodland. The air was very clear. At my feet the coast wound in horseshoe bays. There was nobody in sight.

Now, while I wandered eastward in the direction I would follow for many days, the glory of the Kyrenia mountains filled the horizon. By afternoon I was walking where the nearer slopes burst from their foothills three thousand feet above me and showered the sky with igneous crags: Mount Kornos with Kyparissovouno, its echo, behind; the profiles of St Hilarion and Trypa Vouno; the battlements of Buffavento; Pentadactylos like a mailed fist, and many more, on and on for a hundred miles, castled by the Lusignans with a fairy-tale madness on their razor peaks. At a distance their beauty looked intended, almost sculptural. From softer uplands and bays edged with sunlight they circled one beyond another as if each was the shadow of the last, falling to waves, to mist, at last to nothing.

There could be no greater contrast to the Troodos, which seem physically to sympathize with the Byzantine culture which they preserved and whose peaks, endlessly absorbent and enduring, roll in a rounded calm, like the domes of churches. For the Kyrenia ridge, which the Lusignans loved, is Gothic, pinnacled, an armoured and inflexible order. The villages are withdrawn from the coast a little way up the slopes. Lapithos – redolent name – is sprinkled through lemon and medlar groves where the fruit was still hanging in May. Tombs nearby are more than five thousand years old, but the classical city was founded by the Spartans of Praxander and was famous, apparently, for its amphorae and homosexuals. With a population of ten thousand it remained wealthy in Lusignan times and had left mediaeval churches and a monastery on the shore.

Army notices, which warned me away from the littoral, looked so old that I ignored them, but where the track met the coast I saw that the monastery had been turned into a military school, grotesquely painted and neat. A sentry stopped me; but I produced a letter given me by the Ministry of Tourism, which entitled me to nothing in particular, and walked on with a show of importance. Around the cloister, fragments salvaged from the ancient city lay meaninglessly about. A corporal was cleaning his gun on a stone inscribed to Tiberius Caesar. All along the shore the centuries had elided and eclipsed one another. The port was quieter than it had ever been. A few fishing boats dawdled under a derelict wall. On the twilit headland chambers and doors had survived where cut in solid rock – dead and eternal, with the spring flowers wilting in their rooms. Whether they were tombs or houses I did not know – they had probably been both – and at night I settled in their shelter. A Scops owl haunted the ruins, as owls should; it whistled sadly, alighted on the rubble and stared at me with an ancient, furrowed face whose eyes were invisible for feathers, but which hypnotized me at last into sleep.

The darkness was warm now. All this littoral holds a caressing softness. The northern winds bring rain from Asia and a summer mildness of nights, and have turned the foothills green.

I woke to find a cluster of woolly faces ogling me through the long grass, and a shepherd leaning on his staff and looking down in wonder. With my hands clasped over my chest, and my head covered against dew, I must have looked like an immense chrysalis and he gave a start when I moved, and called away his sheep with a high 'Cuyp-cuyp-cuyp'.

The light was thin, and far away the Lycian Taurus had woken out of the sea. The days were now so hot that dawn gave the easiest walking, and I wandered towards Kyrenia through a corridor of lemon groves, to doze under the orchards of Ayios Georgios at noon. Early in the century this village was peculiar for the fossils of pygmy hippopotami, but I could find none left because the villagers, thinking them to be the bones of their patron saint, and sovereign against disease, had powdered them down and drunk them.

Alone, because of its castle's strength, Kyrenia survived centuries of mediaeval piracy, hugging its harbour and towered wall while other communities were cringing into the hills. This charm of history on the water's edge is unique in the island. Along its wharf the Venetian mansions have been turned into restaurants, or replaced by buildings in the local stone. Boats laze at anchor: coloured toys on glass. The castle, softened by time and the wind, throws out a huge, cylindrical bastion across the harbour, and a Lusignan lighthouse bathes its crumpled feet in the sea. Nothing real, one feels, could ever have happened here. The scene might have been conjured as a backdrop for the English community which occupies villas all about, escaping income tax and cold: a Sunday painter's harbour. Yet within a year, under Turkish bombardment, it was to become a desert.

Kyrenia had been the favourite of retired civil servants since early in the century, but their leisured existence was less noticeable now. To the disgust of the English colony and the delight of the Cypriots a land boom and a tourist influx had begun. The town was spreading along the coast. Plus-fours and cavalry twills had been overtaken by jeans and bikinis, and a host of concrete parvenus had sprouted round the venerable Dome Hotel. The local fishermen and farmers loitered about the wharfs hiring out boats or serving drinks, as work-sore holidaymakers tried to relax and their blonde daughters flirted a little.

Only under the lee of the castle, where the Venetian walls rise eighty feet in sheer precipices, and bastions as huge as gas-drums roll from the palisades, did this holiday feeling chill. Through an entrance cut in many walls, where a faraway sunlight gleamed down sally-ports, the age and complexity of the place began to emerge. Each successive castle – Byzantine, Lusignan, Venetian – had been coated and thickened by the next. The older walls look shrunken now, tracing their towers delicately, while the Crusader battlements stay massive and sure; but the floor-beams have collapsed in the palace apartments, leaving them pierced by tiers of windows and doors hanging nonsensically in space. In dungeons whose cell windows show cruel slivers of sea, the Ibelin lords who revolted against Henry II mouldered away down bottle-shaped oubliettes. Peter I was himself imprisoned here by his father for a childish escapade, and his mistress Jeanne l'Aleman incarcerated by Eleanor of Aragon.

The castle was never stormed. It was starved out, or surrendered honourably. In 1374 the garrison withstood a fearful onslaught by the Genoese, hurling back rocks and Greek fire from trebuchets behind the walls, and overturning the siege-towers with sudden sallies. And after the capture of King Janus it was to Kyrenia that the king's regent took the royal children and treasure; the victorious Mamelukes saw the castle's strength and turned away.

Yet the Crusader fortress is little more than a coat of rough chain mail beneath the superb plate-armour of Venice. These girdling Venetian walls are cracked in their lower courses by the weight of stone above, but are hugely formidable still. Their bastions are honeycombed with passageways which emerge at dim, embrasured gun-ports to enfilade the ditches. Yet in September 1570, when the Turks sent a demand for surrender together with the heads of two Venetian commanders killed in the sack of Nicosia, the castle capitulated without a blow.

'The Turks still have us yoked,' said a custodian prophetically. He was gazing up at the darkening mountain-tops where a point of light had sprung. 'That's St Hilarion castle. They must read us like a map up there. One big gun aimed at Kyrenia and *Oof!* – where would we be?' He cast the town in fragments into the sky.

An hour later I made my way up the hillside towards this castle at dusk. Beneath me the lights were spreading through orchards filled with palm trees and the conqueror's minaret, and were thickening around the sea. I lay down in a carob grove, planning only to rest for a while and to walk on in the coolness of dark. A convoy of lorries groaned along the nearby road. A woman's laughter sounded. Then silence. The ground was soft under my back. I stretched out between the ploughed furrows and closed my eyes.

* * *

The life of St Hilarion is unknown. He was, it seems, not the Hilarion of St Jerome, but an obscure hermit who ended his days in a cell on the mountain, and around his grave a monastery and later a fortress was built, facing the Seljuk threat across the sea.

Even in ruin the castle is almost impregnable. Turkish Cypriots occupied it during the unrest of 1964, and beat off the Greek counter-attack with a garrison of boys. Now it was the stronghold of a Turkish enclave which straddled the Nicosia–Kyrenia road and refused passage to Greek traffic; and the next morning it was a Turkish police sergeant who prevented me walking.

'You're entering a military area. You must take a lift.'

I looked into a face as featureless as the Asian steppes from which it came. 'I've walked in other military areas.'

'This is a Very Military Area.'

'What if no car comes?'

'Something always comes.'

An hour later the driver of a petrol lorry stopped, and we clattered up through a drama of peaks turned dirty by our windscreen. We passed a platoon of soldiers stripped to the waist and marching at the double. A United Nations helicopter came nosing along a valley. Then the road entered a treeless clearing and above it, where a last upheaval of rock was cut by wind into sharp, brilliant shapes, hung the castle. It was insanely dramatic. Its walls fluttered up and down the precipice or sprouted from crags in a troubadour's dream. It is said that Walt Disney took it as his model for *Snow White and the Seven Dwarfs*; and this fairy quality – the garnishing of every peak with a wall or a wisp of towers

– seems not to belong to warfare at all, but to the fancies of an illuminated manuscript.

The local peasants say that a temple to Aphrodite stood here, and that demons clung to the mountain until the prayers of St Hilarion drove them away. They call the place 'The Hundred and One Rooms' of which the last can never be found, or 'The Houses of the Raegina', the mythic Queen who kept her treasure there. All the castles of the Kyrenia range share in these legends. And in each of them a wandering shepherd, entering a hidden doorway, finds himself in an enchanted garden, from which he awakes years later on a dewy morning.

The first recorded history comes with the renegade Emperor Isaac Comnenus, and with Richard Coeur-de-Lion who sent men to reduce the fortress, which the Crusaders called Dieudamour; 'and those who were shut up therein prepared to defend themselves, and for days on end hurled stones and darts at the besiegers, until they were commanded by the Emperor to surrender it; and in it the king placed the Emperor's daughter, lest she be recaptured'.*

During the wars between the Ibelin lords and the Imperialists of Frederick II, the castle often lay under siege, but like Kyrenia was never taken by storm. It was here that the warrior-poet Philippe de Novare fell wounded, and continued to taunt the besieged in verse from across the ravine. But for a century and a half of peace the castle served the Lusignan court as a summer residence, and a sense of leisure, almost of luxury, touches it.

---

* Geoffrey de Vinsauf, *Itinerary of Richard I.*

The lower ward held nothing but yellowed grass and ruin. Byzantine walls enclosed it, grey and unsafe. But beyond, through a vaulted tunnel, the Lusignan defences grew impregnably on shooting blades of mountain. The rock burst into their very chambers, as if they were light as dust above it, and through every window the views rushed dazzling in: white abysses and violent squares of sea.

Higher still are fortified apartments and the tower from which Prince John of Antioch, in a fit of suspicion, had his faithful Bulgarian mercenaries hurled to their deaths. Level with this a vulture dangled, gazing down three hundred feet with telescopic eyes. But in happier times – and they were longer than would seem – the Lusignans preened away their summers with pageants and tournaments in the glade below, while under the cool belvedere the officers and chamberlains, within sight of the hostile mountains over the sea, reclined on samite cushions and drank their sherbet and forgot the morrow.

CHAPTER ELEVEN

· · · · · · · · · · · · · ·

The Gothic Range

Bellapaix, nested in orchards and idleness, loveliest of Gothic abbeys, looms among lemon groves and hillside cottages. Lawrence Durrell's Mr Kollis, with the 'round, good-natured face of a Friar Tuck,' is still seated at the abbey entrance, but greyer now, and not so even-tempered. He abruptly stops any scantily-dressed woman from entering the grounds and obliges her to wear a dirty-looking, Victorian-length skirt which he keeps hanging on his wall for the purpose.

'I feel stumpy in the mornings nowadays, I don't know why. But the afternoon melts me. It's hard to be angry here. Look . . .' He nodded at the abbey gardens: massed roses and geraniums, the sea set in ruined walls. 'I've made these gardens myself over thirty-seven years. I'll die on the job. But the trouble is that the young don't care. Flowers! History! What can they do with those? And when I die . . .' He scratched at his white fuzz of hair, and suddenly twinkled: 'But now I've made the garden, perhaps they'll feel obliged to keep it up.'

We went through a gateway into the ruins. For a moment we were walking in a banked fragrance of flowers where the abbey overhung the hillside, and looking down a hundred feet on swallows crying faintly in the blue. Then all scent and colour had sobered to a cloister where grass and trees echoed old stone. In the centre of the courtyard four cypresses rose with a pencilled melancholy, and the mountains, close beyond, seemed to be pouring into its silence.

'The cypresses are giants already,' said Kollis. 'Yet I planted them myself only thirty years ago. There was only rubble here then.' He added quietly: 'But when we dug to plant them, we found skeletons.'

I almost jumped, the place was so peaceful. 'What skeletons?'

'Knights, monks, Turks – who can say? A few years underground and everybody turns the same.'

The cloister arches unfurled around us, the tracery clinging to them here and there in a remembrance of delicacy. Theirs was not the rusticity of Orthodox cloisters, but a harmonious order, filled with life. Over the huge refectory the vaults fanned with a breathtaking lightness. A trace of the dais for the abbot's table remained, and the stone pulpit from which the scriptures were read during meals. A rose window hung in its eastern wall, and the wind blew in from the sea.

Here and there, along the cloister, a moulding kept its fourteenth century richness with traces of heads carved on the corbels – faces which in the canon's chapter house had grown quaint, even lewd. Sirens wriggled from the stone, and dripped their hair seductively down towards the canon's bench. Two monsters hugged each other sleepily. A monkey and a cat peered through the foliage of a stone pear tree.

The white monks of Bellapaix were not exemplary. From the start they enjoyed royal patronage and wealth; Hugh III rebuilt the place handsomely and endowed its abbot with the privilege of mitre and sword; but throughout Lusignan years the monks quarrelled with the Archbishop of Nicosia and among themselves, until successive Popes were forced to intervene. By Venetian times they had even taken wives, as many as three each, and were accepting as novices only their own children. 'It is a great sin,' wrote the Venetian Proveditore to the senate, 'to see so great an abbey, such a miracle of architecture, falling into ruin.' But it is easy to understand. The heat, the orchard luxuriance, the very tenderness of stone might corrode the sternest ascetic iron. The spirit here feels more like a ripe fruit than a soldier of God. It sleeps in light and fragrance. The flamboyant style of the cloister, close to that of Sicily and Spain, belongs already to a mellifluous Mediterranean tradition, and even the abbey church is broader than its prototypes in northern France, deploying a space and stillness which is almost Romanesque.

This peace continued all through the village, through lanes where datura shrubs broke into cream-coloured bells, and up the mountain track behind. I followed the way drowsily, my pockets heavy with bread and fruit. It was a pleasant time to walk – late afternoon, and the earth giving up its heat. The coast emerged below, running eastward in withered promontries. I did not care where I would sleep, the nights were so warm. Besides, my map showed a village called Vouno on the farther side of the range, and already my track was slipping between the peaks of Trypa Vouno and Buffavento, and had flattened out.

Then the view was shut off. I passed a wayside shrine at the summit of the defile. And in one of those moments of astonished stillness which come upon a traveller unawares, I found myself at the edge of an upland valley where the sun touched the rocks with an ancient light, and the farmers had gone and the trees bowed in their tracks like old servants. At such moments a man feels as if he is breaking into a canvas. The path tapers whitely on, but nothing moves. And it seems as if he will linger on the brink of the masterpiece for ever, under the gold-touched peaks, the isolated trees, unable to enter it.

But then the mood passes – it was his own – and he walks on into the landscape. It fragments and dies. The road is solid underfoot. A wind sweeps the grass, and the clouds move again.

I came to Vouno. The apex of the range was behind me now, and I was descending. The slopes were bitterly bare. To the south I saw the spine of the Troodos resting on low clouds, while between the two ranges Nicosia was spreading into lights. I had no sooner arrived than a young man from the forestry department asked me to his home. At first sight Polyvios was rather suave. One noticed his heavy cuff-links and gleaming tie-pin, and he wore a newly-pressed suit. But behind his glasses the face was slow and friendly, and he lived in a destitute cottage with a bumptious dog and an old man who 'had nowhere else to go'.

'There isn't really any forest here at all,' he said, demolishing his own job in a fit of good humour. 'On the Kyrenia side of the mountains the sea air brings moisture, but here it's hopelessly dry. There's nothing wrong with the soil when it's there, but it's hardly ever there. Everything's eroded.'

I asked automatically: 'Goats?'

'Yes. And they don't just eat the tree shoots. They demolish the prickly ground-cover which people barely notice. When that goes there's nothing left to bind the soil.'

'What can you plant then?'

'The trees which nature shows can survive – cypresses.' His voice had taken on a faintly missionary fervour. 'Yes, in twenty years' time I hope these slopes will be covered with cypresses.'

A strange vision – it would touch all this part of the island with a Tuscan melancholy. Cypresses, of course, grew and were worshipped here long ago and perhaps took their name from that of the island. In classical times they were sacred to Pluto, emblems of grief and eternity, and they gave their dark, incorruptible wood to Phoenician ships and idols, and to the coffins of the pharaohs.

Yet they would not be planted for use, said Polyvios, but for beauty.

At midnight he lay down on the bare floor and told me to sleep in his bed; but I refused this last piece of hospitality, so he spread his dapper overcoat on the tiles and insisted I put my sleeping-bag on that. I slept uneasily, for behind my head was a food-safe raised on a pile of sardine tins, where mice scuttled all night.

We rose early, he to take his Landrover into the plains, I to traverse the mountains among scattered castles and monasteries. Near the village I hoped to find the place where the Dutch traveller Van Bruyn, at the end of the seventeenth century, had seen skeletons and giant teeth fossilized in the rock. Around them, he wrote, were scattered candle-ends, and it seemed that the place was held in veneration by the local people who believed that some of their saints were buried there.

But when I looked up the Greek for 'fossil', *apolithoma*, and enquired among the villagers, nobody understood. They thought that Fossil was either a person or a town. He no longer lived in the village, they said; or was situated on the other side of Nicosia; in any case, he was ill. Who this sick Fossil was I never discovered, although it was easy to picture him, and later I learnt that the place had been shorn away and its rock used for sand.

Much else has changed since the day Van Bruyn journeyed up to the monastery of St Chrysostom 'ruled by a Father-Guardian, who has under him three priests and eleven monks'. The monastery, dwindled to a single priest, had been turned into a military camp, and a heavy-booted soldier escorted me wherever I went. Of the two Byzantine churches, built side by side, little but the pavings survive, with splashes of fresco and some wooden doors whose panels are jointed without nails. Local tradition says that on the peaks above, in Buffavento castle, lived a princess cursed with leprosy; but her lap-dog also caught the disease and discovered a spring which cured both itself and its mistress. So she raised the monastery in thanksgiving, where the healing waters still tinkle into a pool, and for years her crown and sceptre were said to be kept here, while she herself was buried in the cloister between two slaves.

'There's always a nonsense attached to ruins,' said the

soldier, with the scorn of the newly educated. 'When people don't know anything they make something up.'

We were looking down on the husks of two chapels farther along the slope. I wanted to visit them.

'You can see them from here,' he said. 'Wrecks.'

But later I slipped away to inspect them and he set out too late to stop me, shouting and kicking stones as he came. While I approached the chapels I thought that he was right, and that there was nothing except decay. But then I saw that on a ruined wall, exposed to the sun and the southern wind, was a fresco – a twelfth century Lamentation over the dead Christ. Strangely perfect in survival, the Virgin pressed her face against the cheek of the Son, their black haloes overlapping, and caressed his body in a stooped, archaic grief. How many centuries of rain and wind have swept this mourning I could not tell, and the soldier had caught up with me by now and urged me away.

As if to emphasize the monastery's loneliness, clouds were thickening on the mountains and rolled from their gullies like cannon-smoke as I climbed towards Buffavento. Solitary and precipitous, three thousand feet above the sea, the castle was bitterly exposed. Only occasionally a bastion drifted from the cloud and faded back, as if on fire. Somewhere in the whiteness beneath me a party of tourists, arrived by donkey from Bellapaix, was trying to climb the path but turning back. Their shouting echoed and died in the stillness.

Buffavento has an evil history. The Lusignans used it as a political prison. Sir John Visconti, who reported the infidelity of Eleanor of Aragon to Peter I, was starved to death in its dungeons. It was never stormed. The Venetians, unable to garrison it, slighted the battlements and abandoned them. It became the refuge in folklore of the elusive Queen, and only a few travellers attempted the ascent, and wrote of emptied cisterns and rooms.

By now I was climbing through dense cloud. Once I realized that I was at the watershed of the northern slopes and could sense on other sides the desolation of many peaks and valleys. But I could see nothing, until close above me the southern towers stood out on the brink of the abyss.

'Freak weather,' said a voice from the gatehouse – a caretaker even in this eyrie – 'something strange is happening out there,' he pointed at the cloud. 'Nothing's the same any more. Not even summer.'

I walked through bare rooms. Scarcely a domestic feature was left. There were remains of cisterns, of vaults and pointed entrances. The wind ran through every chamber. On the summit stood a ruined chapel, its windows blown open on the sky. Of the stupendous view which reaches from coast to coast I could see nothing, only the boulders of the mountain under me flooding rough and armoured into nothing, as if the whole world was being poured away.

The man had been right about freak weather. At nightfall a cutting wind rose while I was still marching on the track which goes eastward along the mountains. My pullovers felt thin as paper, and the only shelter – I had wandered beyond the village of Koutsovendis – was a low building off the track which turned out to be a pig-shed divided into cubicles. I peered in on blackness and heard a rubbing of bristly bodies against walls. I went outside again into the freezing wind, but the hills showed no other cover, not so much as a tree. The entrances to the full pig-pens were blocked by tubs, but there were others which were empty, and spread with clean sawdust. I crept in like the Prodigal Son. Next door a boar was sleepily smacking its lips. In other compartments sows and piglets sucked and squealed; but they did not smell. So I spread my sleeping-bag on the sawdust, sat down gratefully in the warmth and apologetically opened my only tin of food, canned pork. Outside, along the lonely track, a lost goat clattered; soon after, I fell asleep.

'Help!' cried a voice.

'A foreigner!' shouted another.

At the end of my torchlight two white faces were staring at me in horror: boys looking for shelter. They took to their heels in the direction of Koutsovendis.

I tiredly returned my belongings to their rucksack. I knew that the villagers, with their curiosity and sense of humour, would not be able to resist coming out to see me. So I went back to the road – the wind was at last falling – climbed a short way up the slope and lay down on the ground, too tired to care.

An hour later I awoke to voices and saw lamps moving along the track. It looked as if the entire village had come out to witness the wonder of a foreigner in a pig-sty. Even the village cockerels were crowing derisively in the distance. I saw torches flickering among the cubicles, and heard the furious barging of the pigs against the tin tubs in the entrances.

'Where are you, Mr Tourist?' the voices called. But pride and cowardice kept me silent. I let the torch beams glide unanswered among the rocks. The steps of the men rang and clattered. 'Come on, Mr Tourist. You prefer to sleep with pigs?' But I only bunched tighter in my sleeping-bag, and was grateful for the shadow of the crevice, which covered me like a blanket. And one by one the lights and voices died away. The feet crunched on the track, faded. The grunting anger of the piggery subsided, and I was left alone under the stars.

Yet walking has its compensations. Because it shows trust, it is the surest way to reach a people's heart. In these remote villages the hiker is an almost unknown phenomenon, and his eccentricity momentarily places him on a level with the poorest, and excites a mingled curiosity and concern. And another, subtler factor is at work: so slowly does he travel that the country takes on larger proportions; a man walking among the ruins of the past finds himself knit to the ancient scale of time and distance.

Kythrea invited such an approach, for it was a place of ancient pilgrimage. In its watered softness, in the poetry of Virgil and in the rites of its sanctuaries, it belonged to Aphrodite; and as late as the last century its women were notoriously amorous and beautiful.

My track reached it from the north-west, skirting the gentler slope of mountains which on their farther side fell precipitously to the sea. I felt as if I was creeping along the back of stage scenery. But soon, where a metalled road wended between dead hills and valleys scattered with olive trees, I came out onto the plains. Behind me where the dawn light was hitting the mountain-tops, they sprang into resonance like struck gongs – Buffavento, Pentadactylos, Yaila – and for an hour my shadow was attenuated to a hunchback on stilts, wrinkling over the tarmac.

Between these hills from which all life had been wrung out, a spring of water rose and burst into the plain, and Kythrea stood in a lake of orchards. Its fertility is famous. Mulberries, olives, lemons, once cotton, have flourished, and the origins of the cauliflower have been traced back here – it was introduced into Europe from Kythrea in 1604. So abundant is the water that the Romans built an aqueduct whose ruins still exist, and guided the river thirty miles over the plain to Salamis; and the Byzantine emperors harnessed it to flour mills which ground the corn for all Nicosia.

'The sweetest bread is still made here,' an old miller told me. He unlocked the door of his mill where the troughs were warped and split. 'These stones don't burn the grain like modern machinery – but hardly anyone uses such places now, and only two or three are left.' In the darkness I could hear the water purling under the floor to glide away down bamboo-shaded channels.

'And what of cauliflowers?' I asked. I had come into the village with ideas of cauliflower cheese pie and white sauce, baked cauliflowers, pickled cauliflowers – only to find that it was Sunday and no vegetable shop was open. But even if I could not eat one, I wanted to hear the founder-cauliflower extolled.

'Cauliflowers?' the miller repeated. He looked blank.

'Yes,' I pleaded. '*Kunupithi*.'

'We don't have them. I've never heard of them. Perhaps you can get them in Nicosia.'

Later I stopped an old woman. 'Cauliflowers . . .' she said suspiciously. 'There aren't any. The Turks killed them.'

'But they aren't people . . .'

She said quickly: 'They were pulled down. Demolished.'

'They're *vegetables*,' I said firmly.

She wiped a dirty sleeve over her mouth as if to speak better, then answered with finality: 'The Turks ate them.'

So much for vegetable origins, I thought; and the village women looked neither beautiful nor amorous. The legends of Kythrea were fragmenting about me – no cauliflower-munching sirens at all (although later a priest told me that the cauliflowers were finished for that year, and that women should be kept indoors 'if they inflame').

Even the ancient city is elusive. A legend tells that it was founded in the twelfth century B.C. by the Athenian Chytros, a grandson of Akamas, and five centuries later it appears in the royal inscriptions of Nineveh. But a far earlier, Neolithic town is in ruins near the head of the river, and a Bronze Age temple filled with statues was found among the orchards. Out of these confused beginnings Kythrea emerged into the classical age as a city-kingdom, and seems to have been peaceful and affluent in a pastoral way.

But if nothing else were known of it, the statue of the soldier-emperor Septimius Severus, discovered here in 1928, would testify to its Roman prosperity. The virile grace of this figure – an over life-size bronze – dominates the Cyprus Museum, and marks it as one of the finest statues of its kind. The stance and the gesture of a hand suggest that the emperor is delivering one of those speeches which furthered his rise to the purple – where his example, says Gibbon, contributed more than any other to the decline of the Roman Empire. But on the svelte, almost Hellenistic body the face looks deeply troubled, as if echoing his despair that 'he had been all things, and all was of little value'.

I found the city strewn among harvest fields. Nothing could have been more desolate. Even the corn brushed poor and low against my feet among drifts of sherd, with scarcely a trace even of Roman walls. I came upon remains of a mediaeval building above a dry river, but it too was no more than ankle-high; the sun beat on its painted floors. In all that landscape the only coherent sign was an emptied sarcophagus, whose white marble shone in the corn.

By now I had strayed over some invisible boundary into a Turkish enclave and a policeman challenged me from an iron barrier. But in that heat and desolation he could muster no anger, and his eyes, behind their cracked glasses, held a diffident, almost scholastic look, which I have noticed among out-of-the-way communities in people gentler than their birth.

It was his father-in-law, he said, who had discovered the statue of Septimius Severus. While working in the fields the man's plough had broken off a bronze arm, and he had dragged it home not knowing what it was. 'But he talked about it in the coffee-shops,' the policeman added, 'and two sharper fellows – one of them was my uncle – dug up the rest of the figure and smashed open the stomach trying to find treasure; but they say they found none. I saw the statue myself as a boy.' A smile touched his face with a remembered delight. 'The earth still coated it then, but I thought it a beautiful thing . . . It must have been priceless. The Antiquities Department paid the two men twenty-five pounds for it, which was not bad in those days. But where the arm went, only my father-in-law knew. The one on the statue is a copy.' Then he lowered his voice, as if the dead of Kythrea, whispering in the corn, might overhear us. 'To tell the truth I believe he sold it to a sweetmeat pedlar – they used to deal in scrap iron, those fellows. All the same, he died poor as a mule.' He swung solemnly to and fro on the barrier, like a child. 'Our people were ignorant then.'

'It still happens,' I said, remembering the tomb-robber of Ghaziviran.

'But now there are some who'd stop it,' he answered. 'I would have done so myself if I had been more than a boy. In those days I spent my time bicycling to Nicosia and back.'

'Twenty miles a day?'

'That was what you had to do if you wanted any education.' He doodled in the dust with his boots. 'My father, you see, was poor. A shepherd. He could not write his name. But twice a year we would drive the sheep over the mountains and wash them in the sea.' He pointed over the range. 'And that was how I first saw my motherland. One day – a very clear day – as my father was herding the sheep into the water, he suddenly said "Look. Turkey." I looked up and there was my country – like a ship on the horizon. It appeared wonderful, but too far away. And to this day I've never been.'

'But you feel a Turk.'

'I am a Turk.'

I glanced at him again. His face might have been Greek or even Jewish – a reminder of that complexity of races which the Turks absorbed when they invaded Asia Minor, and of how unchartable is the ethnic result.

'I a Greek?' the policeman echoed. 'No.' He paused and repeated 'No, and there'll be no integration in Cyprus now.'

I mumbled that time could do anything.

But his face had deadened. 'Our young people don't speak Greek any more. And the young Greeks don't learn Turkish.' He hit the iron gate softly with his fist. 'The barrier has gone up.'

Towards evening I went back into the Kyrenia range, making at first for the heights of Pentadactylos, the 'Five-fingered', whose indented peaks, it is said, were left by the hand of Dighenis as he vaulted the mountains. Eastward, along a spine of rock so narrow that I could see the northern coast on one side, on the other the Nicosia plain, I passed the Armenian monastery of Sourp Magar, empty of monks, and slept at Halevka forestry station where the hills are famous for wildflowers. Even in this late May I saw the faded shapes of many delicate plants which I could not identify.

The owner of the forestry coffee-shop let me pass the night in its warmth. He had lost a leg while tree-felling and now lurched rumbustiously among his customers and a flock of daughters. At breakfast these eight girls, looking like different ages of the same person, all talked and giggled and moved in the same way. When one of them vanished into the kitchen and an older daughter emerged, I had the bewildering impression that the previous one had suddenly aged; then she would disappear and emerge a child again, or a teenager, as if some time machine was at work behind the walls.

'How many more children do you want?' I teased him.

Quick as a fox his wife answered from the kitchen: 'Another ten!'

'It's the pine air!' grinned the man. 'That's what does it. We go to bed once and – *yip!* – a baby!' He roared with barbarian laughter. 'We can be lying in separate beds, even, with a space between – and what? A baby! Oh, the pine air!'

'You should bottle it.'

'Yes, like wine or Moutoullas water.' He murmured: 'That might be a good business now . . .' Then his eyes narrowed and he said with sudden gravity 'Take my advice and don't have daughters. Stick to sons.' I was not sure how to answer this. 'Girls break your purse when you marry them off. Here a father has to build his daughter a house, and even give land or money with her.' His head slumped in his hands. 'Think of it. Eight houses! A whole village of daughters! I'll be ruined. And nowadays they must get married young or not at all. When I was young there were plenty of men about and the women could afford to wait – but not now, with fellows emigrating . . . My oldest is only fifteen, but at sixteen she can marry. We found her a decent fellow.'

'Does she like him?'

He wrinkled his nose. 'Well, she hasn't met him. But she'll like him all right. The girls here don't know about love. Most of them have never even kissed a man until they're engaged.' He grinned at me in collusion and said more softly, although no daughter was near: 'Their fiancé, you understand, is the first man to make love to them, so of course they fall for him like sparrows.'

While he prepared to leave on the lorry for Nicosia I asked him about the abandoned Antiphonitis monastery, where I was going.

'There's a story to that,' he said. 'Antiphonitis means "echo". You see, a rich man and a poor man met there, and the poor man asked him for money . . . One minute.' He lurched away to serve a customer, then returned. 'Where was I? . . . Yes, the poor man asked him for money. But the rich man said "Aha! But who will witness that I have lent you this money? Who will know?" And the poor man answered "God". And . . .' He got up again. 'One moment. I'll tell you in a second.' He vanished through a door while I waited, wondering what had been echoed. I waited five, ten minutes, but the man did not return. While he was away the lorry to Nicosia had come, he had caught it by a second and shouted to his wife to apologize. She was red with embarrassment, and the octave of daughters was shuffling its feet and trying to remember the end of the story, but could not.

The backbone of the mountains was deserted. As I went the sea rose between clefts, vanished, reappeared, vanished again. Above me the crags teetered at impermanent-looking angles, and poppies exploded over the hillsides among arbutus and thyme grumbling with bees. I had formed the habit of walking slowly and stopping often, so that I would cover less than ten miles in as many hours, the country unfurling with a sensuous slowness.

I wallowed along like this all day, following the mountain track. Once, five hundred feet above me, an Imperial eagle stooped from a crag. Without effort of his wings he lifted and circled three times like an augury, blown round and round, the sunlight flashing from his back whenever he tilted to turn. I glimpsed bee-eaters too – bluet-inted beauties which are more often seen dangling from the belts of hunters. And I noticed an abundance of camou-flaged insects – Cyprus is a paradise for them – rasping and clicking all day like the very sound of drought. Objects which appear to be dirt or pine needles will hop and crawl if touched, or whirr away with a clatter of muslin wings. There were black butterflies too, and fran-colin. And once a deadly snake flowed away in front of me, straight and calm over the cracked earth with a whistle of roughened scales.

Antiphonitis, whose legend I never discovered, is tucked in an alcove of the hills within sight of the sea. The Lusignans themselves were its patrons, and the Venetians, who gave Cyprus so little, added an elegant loggia to the church. The monastic buildings crumble round it, the frescoes are rustic and few and the place is an architectural mongrel; but its setting in that valley would turn a purist tender.

And now at last the marrow of the range was thinning.

It fell away at either side of the track, as from a parapet. I could lay my hand along its spine. The path zigzagged between views of the northern sea and of the grain-bearing Mesaoria plain – mile upon mile of dun and yellow rect-angles, with villages abstract as their dots on my map. Southward I could descry where the curve of Famagusta Bay began to pare the island to its tip – the finger which points at Syria. I had long passed the greatest width of the island. Now it was contracting about me, and I would never again be out of sight of the sea.

The Cypriots were not a great maritime power, as the Greeks or Phoenicians were, but the sea moulded them. It was the avenue which brought them commerce, ideas, invaders: all the stuff of civilization and discontent. Westward, early in the first millennium B.C., the horse-headed *hippi* of the Phoenicians came nosing round the Cilician straits, bringing their alphabet and their goddess. And already the Greek world was mingling its brilliant fragments with theirs. Ionian merchant ships with clipper bows and the new-fangled second sail kept a precarious commerce; and from time to time, when the Grecian motherland was roused, the sleek, predatory *trieres* cut their way south through the waters of the Great King, with banked oars and giant bronze catsheads for ramming.

If the sea could show tracks they would be as worn and old as the routes which cross these mountains between pass and pass. The wide-bottomed Roman merchantmen alone, *corbitae* stuffed with spices waddling from port to port, turned the island into an emporium. As for its own fleet, wrote Ammianus Marcellinus, 'so rich and various is the fertility of Cyprus that without the help of strangers it can build a cargo-boat from keel to truck from its own resources, and send it fully fitted with sails and gear to sea'.

At dusk I dipped to an inland village – a quiet, mud-brick place too high to partake of the wealth of the Mesaoria. Its people grew a few olive trees, and most of the young men left for the plains or for abroad, and came back decades later to sit under the vine trellises and die where they were born.

Meletios, an elderly olive farmer, bought me lemon juice and enquired about my journey. He had spare, aesthetic features, and I was distracted by his elaborate ears which looked as if they had been made for somebody else. He impulsively offered me the hospitality of his home, but a stout young man sitting by me whispered in my ear: 'I don't know where he is going to accommodate you. He has a lunatic son. In his house, it would be difficult . . .' And I saw now that the old man looked troubled. He kept bringing his empty coffee cup to his lips and sipping nervously on nothing. I did not know what to do, but left a flap of my rucksack open to show my sleeping-bag and that I was used to camping out.

But at nightfall Meletios got to his feet and ushered me away. He looked apprenhensive and once began 'Would you mind if . . . ?' but did not finish. We fumbled our way along clay walls. He unlocked a door, then lit a taper. I dimly saw an olive press whose great twin stones lay smooth and idle in their bowl. The candle's light set stray pieces of machinery glinting. In the corner was a bed. He looked at me anxiously. 'Could you . . . would you . . . ?'

I thanked him hard, but he was still embarrassed. He moved here and there putting things straight. He left. He came back again with a chair and some blankets. He brought me water. All this was done with a grave gentleness and concentration, until at last his face relaxed into calm.

A few minutes later I was in bed and he had gone. And after only a moment more, it seemed, he was shaking my shoulder and the dawn light was leaking through the slats of the shutters. He had brought me breakfast.

Had I slept well?

Yes, marvellously.

Was there anything I wanted?

Nothing. He turned away my thanks.

By the time I had left the village the bays of Larnaca and Famagusta, where I was going, stood clear of mist, and goatherds were driving their flocks over the dawn-softened hills. I passed the stout young man working in his orchards. He grinned and threw down his hoe.

'So you slept by the olive press? Fine. You see, this is a poor village. And Meletios has had a difficult life.'

'His son?'

'Yes, that. And he was a suspect during the war of liberation, although he'd done nothing. The British interned him in a prison camp for three years.'

Even to me, my voice sounded wan. 'But he knew that I was British?'

'Yes. But you didn't do it, did you?' He picked up his hoe again. 'The times make us mad.' He waved me on my way. 'Go to the good!'

All the land ahead seemed suddenly softer and fuller. By the pass of Mersiniki, where a main road links the coasts, I waited for a bus to Larnaca. I looked down on a headland where the ancient ruins of a city called Macaria 'the Blest' are forgotten, and far out over that haunted sea. I should have gone back and taken the old man in my arms.

CHAPTER TWELVE
∙∙∙∙∙∙∙∙∙∙∙∙∙∙∙
City of the Graves

At the beginning of the Dark Age of all the eastern Mediterranean, when the use of bronze was merging with that of iron, the decay of the older empires saw whole cities dwindle into obscurity. Around 1000 B.C. along with many others the metropolis of Kition, once an important harbour town, fell desolate. The *Chittim* of Isaiah and Daniel, with cyclopean defences and an outer road which still carries the ruts of chariot wheels, its excavations are so formless that I could scarcely tell whether they were ancient buildings resurrected or modern ones demolished. Colonized by Achaeans in the twelfth century B.C., sacked by the Sea Peoples, crippled by earthquake, Kition sunk out of history.

But it re-emerged as a Phoenician town, with Tyre as its mother city, and these oriental roots held strong. In the early struggles between the Greek and Persian factions in the island, Kition headed the Persian cause, and at the height of the classical age, strengthened by immigrants from Syria, it gobbled up the kingdoms of Tamassos and Idalion. The coins found here bear diluvian Semitic names: Baalmelek, Melekiathon, Pumiathon – priest-kings of the oriental kind.

It was Kition which broke the victorious progress of the

Athenian general Cimon when he attempted to liberate Cyprus from Persia in 449 B.C. He died outside its walls. The Greek forces, on his own orders, were not told of his death until the Persians had been defeated, and the citizens of Kition momentarily forgot their Phoenician bias and raised a monument to him outside their city, where he was honoured in times of famine. But Cimon's victory was transient and his troops were forced to sail back to Athens where Pausanias, six centuries later, saw their graves still honoured in the Academy beside those of Pericles and many heroes.

On the sea-front of Larnaca, which covers the site of the ancient town, the statue of Cimon shows a powerful, idealized head. But the statue of Zeno, Larnaca's other celebrity – born at Kition in about 333 B.C. and founder of the Stoic philosophy – was taken from life. The copy of a portrait bust discovered at Herculaneum, it stands in a backwater of the modern city, an incisive but thought-saddened face.

He was, perhaps, the most distinguished of all Cypriots – not a Greek, but a Phoenician, and his philosophy, which took its name from the Stoa Poikile in Athens where he came to teach, is tinged by the Orient. The happiness of man, he taught, was devotion to an inner but universal Spirit. Impalpable and fire-like, this Spirit was soul, God, reason, All, yet was in continual flux. Such a conception of man as a fragment in something changing but eternal made the accidents of his life trivial. Only his harmony with inner Spirit mattered, and of this nobody could deprive him, except himself. It demanded an austerely ethical life. His duty to his fellow men was rigorous and kindly – because all were one. But it was without passion. The passions were merely troubling dreams. Compared to the soul's harmony – pain, love, death itself was nothing.

In a fragmenting and uncertain world, this rock-like indifference to externals became increasingly attractive. Its moral precepts appealed to the more masculine and temperate Romans. They reflected the old Republican *pietas*. Cicero, Brutus, Epictetus, Marcus Aurelius embraced them.

It is strange that so austere a philosopher should have been a native of Cyprus. Although we hear that he was fond of eating figs and basking in the sun, he never returned to his country, and when he died the Athenians awarded him a golden wreath and a state tomb in their city.

His mind was cosmopolitan. Christianity, forced to define itself in the second century, found its defences already prepared by the Stoics – the concept of the Word was theirs – and gladly adapted and baptized what lay to hand. But compared to the full-blooded attitudes of fifth century Greece, the Stoic doctrine is defensive, almost hurt. Gone is the balanced, whole and powerful figure of the great age. And although it is dangerous to judge from such things, the bust of Zeno shows a face of mingled resolution and pain. Once, after all, he had been a Cynic, and his Stoicism, perhaps, was a hardening against grief, bringing not only the most sublime ethical system of its time, but its own repose, even gratitude. 'Observe, in short, how transient and trivial is all mortal life; yesterday a drop of semen, tomorrow a handful of spice or ashes. Spend, therefore, these fleeting moments on earth as Nature would have you spend them, and then go to your rest with a good grace, as an olive falls in its season, with a blessing for the earth that bore it and a thanksgiving to the tree that gave it life.'*

At the age of ninety-eight, Zeno died by his own hand.

Larnaca, which succeeded Kition, took its name from the ancient tombs and urns, the larnas, on which it was built. The very heart of the mediaeval city was a tomb – the traditional grave of Lazarus who was caught by the Jews after his resurrection in Bethany, so the tradition weakly runs, and placed in a leaky boat to Joppa. But instead of sinking, Lazarus sailed to Kition where he was consecrated bishop and lived for another thirty years before dying again. While his supposed body was taken to Constantinople in the ninth century, then stolen by the mediaeval French and shipped to Marseilles, the Church of St Lazarus was built above the empty grave and is lovely still for the patina of its stone.

Wandering under its walls I came upon a little Protestant cemetery with the graves of consuls, missionaries and members of the English Levant Company, who had mostly died too young in the unhealthy air. Larnaca had been a landing-stage for pilgrims as early as the Crusades, and under the Turks it revived as a colony of western merchants and above all as the seat of consuls. Here they kept a dusty and punctilious state, lapsing a little into oriental habits. Early in the nineteenth century the women still dressed *à la Turque* and wore the towering *calathos* head-dress copied from Phoenician idols. The British factor at the time, a

---

* Marcus Aurelius, *Meditations*. Trs. Maxwell Staniforth.

certain Mr Vondiziano, was so fastidious of etiquette that he even wore his huge cocked hat indoors.

'Our procession from the Consular residence to the Khoja-bashi's house was rather ludicrous,' wrote a visitor, 'but appeared to produce a very grand effect upon the minds of the good inhabitants of Larnaca, who all came out of doors, to stare at us. I could hardly retain my gravity on witnessing the awkward attempts made by an old Turk of the Consulate, in his long scarlet robes and grey beard, to stand up behind the rickety carriage of the Consul (*à la chasseur*) with a large truncheon in his hand, as an emblem of his office and dignity.'*

Nothing is left but the huddle of crested tombs with their worn inscriptions. 'Georgius Barton, Consul Britannicus . . .' '. . . Ye Body of Mr Robert Bate, merchant . . .' 'Augusta Jane, the infant daughter of Niven Kerr Esquire, Her Britannic Majesty's Consul for this island . . .'

The handsome houses are gone, and the town itself has fallen asleep. It is gentle and *déclassé*. Over an empty horizon the great bay swings low and undramatic, and a tideless sea laps on a promenade of palm trees. The deep-water harbour is smaller than those of Limassol or Famagusta, and the tourist traffic scanty.

Yet once a year, fifty days after Easter at the festival of Cataclysmos, Larnaca bursts into a vast and rather seedy funfair. After the solitude of the mountains I found myself drowned in noise. Even my room in a backstreet bordello was not private, but the procuress gave up bothering me

---

* Captain Colville Frankland, *Travels* (1831).

after her protegée, a girthy Lebanese, had been turned sleepily away. In fact the Cypriot taste, like the Arab and Turkish, is for such ample women that foreigners can generally sleep in bawdy hotels without serious distraction.

Outside, the promenade had vanished under a double rank of stalls, half a mile long, and for two days, all afternoon and evening, the people crowded into the waves and sprinkled each other with water. This enjoyment of the sea, and the half-remembered ritual of sprinkling, is bizarre and very old, and the festival is unique to Cyprus. The Church has consecrated it with the name of Cataclysmos in memory of Noah's salvation from the Flood, but the thin blessing barely camouflages a pagan festival, whose origins are lost. Whether, as most believe, it is Aphrodite's birth which is celebrated in the foam as it was in ancient times, or her ceremonial purification after union with Adonis – this is unknown. The Cypriots themselves have forgotten. They are simply happy to merge in a warm flood of humanity, gazing, processing and sucking sweet ice-cream and strips of jellified almonds – and the larger the crowd, the more ebullient they are.

The stocky men, with their slight moustaches, seem not to have changed in build from the dead of Khirokitia eighty centuries ago, while the warm-limbed girls, who yet are rarely beautiful, promenade in self-conscious shoals and are indefinably provocative: Aphrodite's children. In fact an almost female sensuality is the carnival's emanation – the physical self-assurance of the Mediterranean at its ripest. Lute and violin lilt under the stars. In their sashes and billowing sleeves the young men mount a wooden stage and tread out the dances of their trade – with sickles or churns – and the girls try some undemanding steps. Only once, I remember, the dance of a huge, violent-looking man broke the decorum, his eyes marbled over until he seemed to be glaring at something distant, and swung his arms with great thunderous claps under his booted legs.

Music and poetry competitions have been part of these celebrations since the ancient island festivals; and the favoured instrument is still the *aulos* of Arcadia and Phrygia which has piped its sadness over thirty centuries and more. A grizzled Turk stood up and played on the meanest sliver of bamboo – tunes which the shepherds compose from random sounds on the mountain, a rustle of wind which evokes a memory, and the memory a song – and he carried off the prize.

But the climax of the festival was the *chattismata*, the poetry battles. A vast crowd crammed round the wooden platform, while the two champions climbed up. One was quite blind. He leant forward with his stick, and although he was old the crowd saw a face as smooth as putty, as if sightlessness had spared him strain. Silence fell. He threw back his head. All the expression of his face seemed to be concentrated in the mouth, whose teeth showed irregular gaps. And suddenly he began to insult the other man in improvised iambics which brought explosions of laughter from the audience:

> *Aa'i – I've come to meet you*
> *This year, Mappoure,*
> *But first, may I ask you,*
> *Have you taken the Last Rites?*

His opponent answered promptly:

> *Aa'i – when I'm dead and after,*
>   *You'll have to make polite obituaries,*
> *So again you'll be my victim*
> *And will blush before my tomb.*

For long minutes this battle went on, weaving between irony and buffoonery and sometimes lapsing into near-senselessness, because the repartee had to be instant and the orchestra beat out a remorseless rhythm. Nothing, it seemed, had changed since the days of Aristophanes, who wrote of such a battle in his chorus from *The Frogs*:

> *Woe to the wretch, when the lord of the mighty phrase*
>   *His cavalry of speech arrays!*
> *Then the one rearing the crest of his shaggy mane,*
>   *bristling, horrid,*
> *Knitting together the brows of his terrible leonine*
>   *forehead,*
> *Volleying riveted words with their planks up-torn,*
>   *Will roar a Titan blast of scorn.* *

Now the blind poet, growing agitated, swore to hurl his opponent into a ditch and melt him in his hands like wax. The other replied that he would brain him with his own grave-slab. 'Aa'i' cried the blind man back, breaking the discipline of the iambic:

---

* Aristophanes, *The Frogs*. Trs. E. W. Huntingford.

> *. . . I'll grab you first*
> *When we come face to face,*
> *But I'll give you three minutes*
> *To tell your relatives*
> *To fetch a coffin and take*
> *Your corpse away.*
>
> *Aa'i – it is you who'll*
> *End up in the coffin,*
> *Phylacti, because you tell*
> *Me rubbish heard a hundred times before.*

And so long did their bucolic improvisation continue that they were both declared winners.

The salt lake of Larnaca and the Tekke of Umm Haram, one of the holiest of Moslem shrines, are a few miles to the west. People say that the lake was formed by Lazarus, who found vineyards there, and that when the owner refused him the gift of a few grapes, he laid down a thorough Hebrew curse and turned the whole valley to salt. A little below sea level, fed by winter rains and the percolation of water through the sand, it evaporates completely in August. Now it was almost June. Already the lake had shrunk to a grey opal, and I was walking into blinding wilderness. The gypsum ranges filled the horizon like mounds of dirty flour, but around their feet the salt shimmered as if a snowstorm had fallen freakishly between the hills.

Beyond the waters I saw the dome and minaret of the shrine of Umm Haram among its palms and cypresses. The lake is a haven of birds in winter, when flamingoes come with egrets and ibis and the storks which Herodotus saw twenty-five centuries ago, following their age-old highway between Scythia and the Nile. In Lusignan and Venetian times the salt was a commercial treasure. Slaves would dig it out with iron picks, and as many as seventy ships were loaded every year for Italy. But with the coming of the Turks the elaborate Venetian dams fell into disrepair, and by the seventeenth century a third of the valley had silted up.

I walked along the edge of the depression. Its surface was cracked and discoloured. No birds flew. Only butterflies – all white, as if they had contracted their colour from the lake – fidgeted along its shore. As I walked farther the glare became crueller and purer, and I began to sink through the crust. The heated air which rose from it gave it an appearance of liquefying.

I was approaching the silence of the oasis. My footsteps crackled like gunshot. Twice I was waved onto a track by Greek sentries, and barbed wire fences stood broken round about. I recognized this kind of quietness by now: the silence of Mansoura, of Koutraphas and many others. I reached the edge of the trees. The salt lapped them like the foam of some tideless sea. It was the dome of the shrine, hideously cracked, which told me for sure that the place had been deserted. The Turks, I learnt later, had fled during the troubles of 1963 and never returned. Their empty village came into view. The walls had crumbled like old biscuit, and abandoned dogs were barking miserably from the marshes. I passed a gutted dugout, and stopped to gaze.

Beyond the dead village stood the dead hills – a ravished, mineral pallor; a breeze came to flicker and dip the grass on the side of the grove and now, at noon, the rising of the air from the saline flats was like a smoke, as if the whole lake was flowing upward in the wind.

I peered over an enclosure into the village cemetery, where shrubs had burst through the graves, scattering slabs and bones. On the track a charabanc filled with Turkish pilgrims lumbered past me and vanished among the palm trees on its way to Umm Haram, and I followed a path into the sanctuary garden. I heard the sudden sound of water and walked under tended trees: pomegranates, lemons, medlars.

Even in so masculine a religion as Islam, the island is true to her nature and it is a woman, not a man, who is buried here. Her name was Umm Haram bint Milhan, 'the honoured mother', and her earliest biography – laudatory, charming and a little ridiculous – says that 'verily our Prophet (may the favour and blessing of God be upon him) gave leave to the honoured mother to search on his holy head for lice, for being his maternal aunt he might be intimate with her, for her ancestors were of his tribe'.*

While he slept with his head in her lap, Mahomet had a vision that Umm Haram would be the first of his people to cross the sea. But to most Arabs at this time the sea was weird and threatening. 'Describe to me the sea and its rider,' demanded the caliph in Mecca, and the bewildered answer came back:

* Anon. Turkish MS. Trs. C. D. Cobham, Journal of the Royal Asiatic Soc., Jan. 1897.

'Verily I saw a huge construction, upon which mounted diminutive creatures . . . Those inside it are like worms in a log. If it inclines to one side, they are drowned, if it escapes, they are confounded.'

'By Allah,' swore the caliph, 'I will not set a true believer upon it.'

Yet in the spring of A.D. 649 the governor of Syria launched a formidable Arab fleet, which invaded Cyprus, and Umm Haram accompanied it with her husband Umbada, 'the Pot-Bellied', governor of Palestine. But immediately upon landing 'the holy woman (may God be pleased with her) was set with all honour on a mule; and on arriving at the place where now her luminous tomb is seen, they were attacked by Genoese infidels, and falling from her beast she broke her pellucid neck, and yielded up her victorious soul, and in that fragrant spot was at once buried.'

Through the shrine's open door I saw a crowd of elderly women kneeling in silence. In the dusk shed by latticed windows their withered faces and hands looked of another century. Umm Haram is their special saint. Were it not for her intercession they would not dare to trouble God with their needs; for Allah is the supreme male, too awesome and too abstract to be approachable. But Umm Haram can be understood. At some time – a hundred, a thousand years ago – she walked the earth as they did. She was sacred and extraordinary, but human. Diaphanous in their white veils, they bowed and rose again: people who had lost their own voice.

Outside, ancient capitals and ashlars had been ranged

293

for stools around the ablutions fountain: relics of Roman Kition. The driver of the charabanc was sitting on one of them. Moslem women, he said, came on pilgrimage from all over Cyprus. Who could stop a woman praying?

The craving for a female intercessor, so potent in all the island, is naturally strongest among women. The blunt male saints, they feel, do not understand the complicated longings of their sex. They must speak to their own. Even the country Turks believe in Aphrodite and name her musically *Dünya Güzeli*, 'the Beauty of the World'. The yearning for a 'holy mother' could explain the very existence of the shrine. Umm Haram may have died and been buried according to the histories, but probably all that stood by the lake in the first centuries after her death was an immense dolmen – one of those monolithic graves which marked the resting-place of famous men. The landmark, I suspect, attracted reverence, and the reverence a history.

In the tomb chamber, by the light of my candle, I saw this trilithon towering above the grave: three vast, balanced stones – buttressed, I believe, by wood – such as might have inspired a numinous awe in anyone. The Turks explain them with a myth. On the eve of Umm Haram's burial, they say, the stones began to move from their place near Jerusalem, and were seen to walk through the sea to Umm Haram in Cyprus, where one of them set itself at her head, one at her feet, and the other suspended magically above her. Now the grave, covered by damasks, was piled with wax hands and legs and with the clothes of sick children left by the women.

The driver repeated the legend without a smile. 'The

stone was once hanging in the air, light as a cloud, but they joined it to the other stones because the people were afraid to come here to pray. They thought they'd be crushed.'

I went into the orchards where the women had settled with much smoothing of skirts and rearranging of veils. Their laughter flowed under the trees. In the deep and unexpected grass, overhung by fruit as in the Moslem paradise, they looked already as if their prayers had been answered. Certainty, truth, lay comfortably about them. Strong in the unquestioned, under the cracking dome and palm shadows, they talked and smiled pleasantly together. Galoshes, panniers and huge carrier bags appeared, spilling out picnics. The faces began to turn rosy. Their headscarves unwound to reveal grey wisps of hair or squashed, colourless curls, with here and there an expensive-looking hairnet.

One of the women, seated under a pomegranate tree, told me that she had made more than fifty pilgrimages, and some of them – with that easy interplay of belief among Moslem peasants – she had made to Christian shrines, to Apostolos Andreas and the Virgin of Kykko. What did it matter, she said? They were all touched by God. She gave me a pastry filled with spiced yoghourt. Did we not all believe in Abraham and Mary, and was not Christ the second among Moslem prophets? Another woman slipped chicken into my hand, and a third, with hennaed locks, pressed *dolma* on me – rice wrapped in vine leaves from which I covertly extracted several of her orange hairs.

The Turks of Larnaca, I remembered, venerate easily. They once acquired the tomb of an Orthodox bishop and worshipped him for years as an Islamic dervish. Another time, discovering a corpse strangely well preserved, they adopted it as a holy man without knowing its faith or sex. 'The old pasha at Nicosia,' wrote a traveller, 'is delighted that the event happened during his term of office, and hopes that it will be a special recommendation for him at Constantinople.'*

Late in the afternoon I ambled to the edge of the oasis. The wind had sunk. Nothing ruffled the dying lake. In the garden a few stately graves remained, their slabs pierced with holes for the pouring of water and the whispering of words, and for the dead to look on God.

When I returned I found that the women had thrown modesty to the winds. They had peeled off their stockings, rolled up their skirts and were squatting on the Roman capitals to wash their thighs at the fountain. One old lady had a bottle of brandy tucked at her side, so soon are Islamic precepts forgotten, and there I shall remember them, laughing and scrubbing round the pool on stones from an age which had once, like they, been certain of its gods.

For miles around the salt lakes the country used to be wilderness and its marshes so fever-stricken that travellers *en route* to Palestine would be afraid to disembark. Disease was spread by village wells, which were contaminated by being dug close to cemeteries, and plagues of locusts swept all the Mesaoria plain. 'The fields they have cropped were burnt as though by fire,' wrote Van Bruyn in 1683, 'my horse too at every step crushed ten or twelve.' In some years flocks of a mysterious plover-like bird would appear and

* Dr Ludwig Ross, *A Journey to Cyprus.*

dispel them, so the farmers thought, with their song and flight. In other years the swarms were blown out to sea. But as late as the last century the peasants might collect half a million pounds of locust eggs every summer, and bring them to the pasha in Nicosia who would pay them for their destruction.

Widespread farming – the turning of the soil and exposure of the eggs – has at last exterminated them, and the way westward to the village of Kiti now runs through fields of artichokes. But that year the price they fetched was barely equal to the cost of picking, so whole fields had been left to die in purple flower, their heads peering and drooping like a bored audience.

Nothing in this unhappy landscape, with its derelict hills and vanished cities, prepared me for the basilica at Kiti – the Panayia Angelikitisti, 'built by angels' – for in its jumble of chapels the island's finest mosaic has survived to glisten with an opulent beauty in the conch of the apse.

The Virgin Mary is attended by archangels. She stands on a jewelled footstool. Her crimson cloak sways outward to unite the composition – she inclines a little to her left – and her dress falls in deep folds to feet so slender that they barely touch the earth. In her left arm, almost like a detached image, she holds the Christ Child, whose robes reflect the glittering gold of the background heaven from which he came.

The effect of this composition, close to the imperial portraits of St Vitale at Ravenna, is one of extreme delicacy – the tesserae for the flesh are tiny – married to a hieratic directness which is not Greek but Syrian.

The conventions of the time, a period of waxing Hellenism, allowed the artist a freer hand with the archangels than with the Virgin. On either side of her they advance with orbs and wands. But while she is iconic and still, they are Hellenic heroes, charged with rhythm. Sandalled in gold and haloed in silver, they stoop towards her in protective reverence. Their eyes are immortally youthful, their fair hair bound in circlets. Wings of peacock feathers cascade from their shoulders, and in their hands the dark blue orbs are offered – magical and huge.

But these angels are not identical. Michael, the more damaged of the two, is blue-eyed, adolescent almost, like a handsome girl; Gabriel older, with red-tinted hair, heavier featured, darker outlined. His robes fly manfully about him, and the tinting of his face merges from pallor to a half perceptible flush.

The divergence in style between Mother and angels has confused scholars, and reflects, perhaps, the uncertainty of its time, the seventh century. The archangels, all intellect and human purpose, are fighting the rearguard action of the classical world. Their beauty is physical. They have become divine, one feels, under false pretences. But the Virgin poised between them keeps the frontal, absolute, but disengaged posture proper to a goddess. For all their ebullience the angels are less self-sufficient. They are flesh, while she, in her whole and exquisite calm, is spirit.

CHAPTER THIRTEEN
·················
Famagusta

Kyriakos owned a leaky fishing-boat and a limestone-pitted field where he grew tomatoes. Perhaps I was beginning to look ragged, for as I passed his cottage he offered me supper in a tone of real distress.

'*Kopiaste!* Sit down and eat! Where in the name of God have you come from? Nobody walks here.' He was a small man, bright and impulsive.

'I came from Larnaca.'

'Today? But that's ten miles.'

'Yes, three hours' walking.'

He contemplated this, idly dangling a bream's head before a disinterested cat, then asked with faint unease: 'Are you a soldier then?'

His wife, holding two small children against her, looked in, then stepped back shyly into another room.

'Not a soldier, no.' I realized that I must still be inside the boundaries of the British Sovereign Base of Dhekelia. Well-metalled roads, barracks, a feeling of Aldershot had hung about my way for the last five or six miles. But I thought that I had left it behind. Walking on tracks and paths, a person grows used to slipping over frontiers without noticing.

'Yes, we're still British here,' said Kyriakos. 'Me, I like the British. I always did, even in the war days.' He smiled candidly. His face was both jaunty and worn – the sort of face which only poor men have. 'EOKA even tried to kill me.'

'To kill *you*?' He seemed in his poverty, even in his goblin stature, too little to kill.

'Yes, me. They planted a bomb. By luck I was out of the house when it went off, but it blew my cat to bits. Not this cat,' he added unnecessarily. 'Another one.'

'Why?'

'Oh, people will do anything. Patriotism cloaked some odd business then, and still does. Old feuds . . .' As if remembering afresh, he burst out: 'May the Devil take them! Murderers!'

'The Devil probably has,' I said, trying to make him smile again. 'I expect they're civil servants now.'

He gave a flick of his stubbled head. 'No. They're the same as they ever were – gypsies, good-for-nothings. They weren't the real people, the patriots, but the hangers-on – may they go to the bad!' Some memory had snuffed the gaiety in him. 'Slogan, bombs – anathema on them.' He began to bang with his fists on the bare table in front. 'They might have killed my wife, or my children if they'd been born.'

'You were not married then?'

'I was just married. Living on nothing. It's a hard life, the sea. The shoals were thin that year. God knows, it's tough enough to keep yourself alive without . . . And even now, you know, those people make trouble – Grivas people.

Just because a family has a British passport.'

'You keep your British passport?'

'Certainly.' He dipped among a pile of papers and pulled it out; it was very worn, its gold blazon almost vanished. 'And I keep the British medals I won in the war, and . . .' Suddenly his voice froze. His lips parted and he stared in disbelief at his open passport. 'Holy Saints!' he cried. 'The photographs! Somebody's ripped them out!' He dashed his hands through his hair. His slight, dark face clenched into panic. 'Do you see that? Gone!' He went on glaring at the empty squares. 'Somebody must have . . . in the night . . .'

He shot glances all round the room, as if men might be hidden there. But the scrubbed table, the reed-bottomed stools, the bare innocence of the place seemed to calm him a little. He lowered his voice. He was thinking furiously. 'How in God's name did they manage to do that?' I could sense his mind reaching back over a hundred acquaintances, sifting, absolving, accusing: the faces passing behind his eyes like a strip of photographs.

After a minute, when his head was buried in his stilled hands, I asked: 'Who might have done it?'

He answered out of the back of his thoughts: 'There are people . . .' but his voice whispered to a standstill.

'Grivas people?'

'Yes.' He slipped the passport into his pocket. 'It's like I told you. Not politics, but jealousy. People will destroy what they can't get.' He added ominously: 'But I know who did it now. Yes. I know.' His voice rose again. 'They'll not get away with it. No, no!' His fingers clasped and unclasped in the air, as if closing round the handles of monstrous

301

weapons. 'How dare they break into my house!' He shouted for his wife: 'Electra!'

She came to the doorway, the children behind her.

'Look,' he said. 'Our passport. The photographs – ripped out!'

She peered with her head gently to one side – a head as classical as her name, the nose and forehead flowing together – then turned to the little girl behind her. 'Chloe, show me what you were hiding in your dress?'

The child's eyes became enormous with apprehension. 'Nothing . . .'

'Show me.'

Fumbling in the folds of her smock, the girl's fingers opened to show a pair of crumpled passport photographs.

'God preserve us!' moaned Kyriakos. He had turned quite pale. The fire had left his eyes. A thousand bloody revenges were receding and dying behind them in bewilderment and faint alarm at themselves. He was too stunned to be angry. 'Why did you . . . ?'

The child answered: 'I wanted pictures of you.'

Kyriakos said softly: 'May God forgive me.'

A minute after waving them away, and quietly at first, he began to laugh; it flowed out of him in enormous ripples of relief which shook his body and set his thin face on fire. 'The little she-cat! Wanting pictures . . . Holy Virgin! She'll be the death of us . . . or of somebody . . .'

At supper he talked about fishing, which of all Cypriot occupations is the least known. The old men went out to sea in pairs, he said, the young men alone. The job paid as poorly as any in the island. In winter, when the storms came, they would band together to work from larger boats. He himself would have to leave the house that night before dawn to pull in his nets. He was sorry that he would not be there to say good-bye to me; it was poor manners, but work was work.

I asked if I might go with him.

'Fishing?' He looked doubtful. 'It's dull . . .'

'Not the first time.'

He looked me up and down. 'Well, yes,' he said, brightening, 'why not?' He poured another glass of *ouzo* in confirmation. 'I'll wake you at three o'clock. You'll not get much sleep.'

Almost before I had slept at all, Kyriakos' lamp was at my door. His face, under a dirty straw hat, had regained its goblin brightness. 'Let's be off.'

The night held that quiet of early morning, the stillness before Creation. We came down to a rock-encircled harbour, where I could discern a few boats moored. A weak mist hung about us. Two other men had come first, were talking softly in the dark, and pulled up their anchor with a faint splash. The bottom of Kyriakos' skiff was strewn with floats made of gourds and pieces of driftwood tied together. He slotted the rudder in place and set up buckets in the stern.

Soon a faint, diffused light was spreading over the sea, and the stars were being brushed away; the dawn mist lay over a surface so colourless that air and water were one.

'We can't see ten yards,' Kyriakos said. 'You watch for rocks.'

He switched on the spotlight at the prow, but it shone into nothing. Our passage was no more than a ruffling of grey silk, the sea closing after us without a sigh. He sat in the stern: a cigarette tip under a straw hat, nursing the tiller and guessing our position. The boat which had gone before us momentarily loomed to starboard. It was the same colour as the water, but the men who stood in it were darker, like two figures standing on glass. We veered away, then were alone in the mist again. Our boat, our useless light, ourselves, were all that existed in the world. It was infinitely restful.

'There!' Kyriakos switched off the motor. His floats came bobbing against the prow and I glimpsed the net curled far down in a white line over the sea bed. We could see farther beneath the surface than we could to either side of us, and now, with a long, methodical rhythm, unhurrying, Kyriakos began to haul in the nets while the fish flashed in them, caught singly far down.

'We should catch *menoula* tonight,' he said. 'Blotched pickerel. I've laid three light nets and a heavy one – been following them for days.'

Now the fish were coming up into our hands: grey mullet with mother-of-pearl faces. Kyriakos left them in the net on the floor of the boat, where their dislocated-looking eyes clouded. Then the indigo pickerel appeared, with a fish he called *salema* and sea-bream in silver armour. They came beautiful from the dull, grey sea, which did not look as if it could contain anything solid at all.

'Painted comber,' said Kyriakos, throwing it into the nets. 'Good for soup. Ah! And here's a red mullet. That brings in two pounds an oke.' In the cold light their bodies' iridescence dimmed. Among the piled nets the mound of fins and scales stared out through eyes which had never seemed alive, and obscurely died. It was hard to care about them.

The first net was up and we moved on towards the second. Over that plastic sea nothing yet showed but our own wake, a ripple on the world's brow. Once a tiny, long-beaked bird alighted on the craft, and flew away into mist.

'The sun will clear this before we start back,' said Kyriakos blithely, 'otherwise we'll hit Cape Kiti.'

We splashed anchor again, Kyriakos mumbling sea jargon to himself as if to a crew. I could pick out pieces of the Italian maritime vocabulary, inherited by all the Mediterranean from seafaring Venetians. He straddled the prow, tirelessly hauling, while I peered over the side in child-like fascination. Already the rainbow pile of fish could have filled an aquarium, and now he pulled up a swollen-cheeked mouse-fish, with sting-rays, barracuda and the dark-plated scorpion-fish whose eyes seemed to bulge in amazement at its capture. He gave a running commentary on their worth and character.

'The comber's stupid. It'll nibble at your toes it's such a fool. If you want trouble, call a fellow a comber . . . And you see the *sparos* there?' He pointed to an annular bream. 'That always stays the same size. If you tell somebody he's a *sparos*, it means he's out of work, he'll never get any fatter . . . The sea bream fetches a pound and a half an oke. That's good . . . cuttlefish only half a pound . . . crayfish you eat in *mezze* with *ouzo* . . . and *ho-ho*! Watch out for this one. A dragon-fish.' Keeping his fingers clear of the spiny back and splayed wings he held out the net to show a little weever. 'Those spikes can kill you.'

From time to time he would catch an octopus. He killed

the smaller ones by biting them in the back of the neck, then threw them into buckets with cuttlefish whose shell-like backs quivered round their edges in a hem of living flesh. Each cuttlefish, newly caught, let out a pneumatic squeak as it was thrown into the pail, and squirmed for long minutes until its head sank down among the rest. None of them was worth much, said Kyriakos, and their price was still dropping. But he caught more of them than anything else, until the buckets were overflowing with their slime, and the octopuses, already killed but overlapping the buckets' lip, went writhing and slobbering along the planks.

By now the sun had risen in mist like a city on fire far away. The heavy net brought up a catch of pickerel, and Kyriakos was humming to himself, his hat balanced over one ear, while I took a turn at the nets. Thousands of sea-centipedes had attached themselves to the pickerel. Even before we hauled them in, half the fish had been killed by them. They squirmed inside the gills, where they hung in tomato-coloured clusters, or burrowed through the eyes which they would riddle in a few minutes, leaving a clean hole from socket to socket.

A few minutes later the mist was gone and the sunlight lay on the sea. A desolate shore appeared on our right. Kyriakos sang hoarsely, pulling in the last nets, and the fish came up flashing in the light.

'*Po-po-po!*' he cried, as he tugged in two cuttlefish mating. 'That's the way to go!' he threw them in the bucket where they continued to grapple one another, and went on with his monologue. 'Look there—' he dropped a grumpy-looking fish onto the planks. 'That's a star-gazer. It never dies. It goes on breathing for hours.' Lighting a cigarette, he set it in the downturned mouth. 'See, it smokes.' And sure enough, the sad-faced fish, by its odd, heavy breathing, exhaled the smoke in miniature puffs. A minute later he caught a sea-horse. The equine head looked more unlikely than a unicorn. I returned it hurriedly to the water, where it blew bubbles through its flared snout and floated away on its back as if sunbathing, but already dead.

Kyriakos, meanwhile, had almost pulled in the last net, but for a full minute he had brought up nothing but the skeletons of eaten fish. He kept saying 'It must be a big one' and craned harder over the bows. Then: 'There he is, the culprit!'

Far down, a creature like a pink star released the fish which it had been eating. Kyriakos took a three-pronged spear from its socket in the prow, and pulled the net close; gritting his teeth, he jabbed down and heaved up a giant red octopus. It was twice the size of any we had caught before, and in a single movement he had seized a knife and sliced into its head until the brains oozed out. I had never thought to pity an octopus, but the creature shut its eyes in agony and pursed a blue-tinted mouth. Then, in a revolting simulacrum of prayer, it wrapped its tentacles imploringly round Kyriakos' boots, and long after he had flailed it again and again on the boards it seemed to live, dropping its arms into the buckets to feel the other fish.

Even Kyriakos looked unnerved. 'That octopus will fetch nearly a pound,' he said. Which was the highest praise an octopus could elicit.

* * *

307

All morning I sauntered along the coast, and succumbed at noon to a little bay of pale, fine sand. By now I was only ten miles south of Famagusta, but the shore was uninhabited. I stripped and bathed in the luxury of its silence. To the east the heel of Cape Greco was clearly visible, and beyond it the whole of Cyprus contracted dramatically in a smooth gulf where Famagusta and Salamis lay, before straightening to the Karpas peninsula.

The hamlets of this area are called the 'Red Villages' from the colour of their soil, and are rich in potatoes. Numberless pumps, turning in the wind, drag up the water which lies close underground. As I passed, the crop was being gathered by women, of whom the stoutest, invulnerable in their plainness, shouted innocent coquetries. This region, I remembered, was one of the last strongholds of the Linobambaki, that sect of furtive Christians who paid lipservice to Islam, but I could see no sign left of their practices, and the afternoon brought nothing but some ancient tombs carved by an inlet – the necropolis of a lost town. At twilight I reached the empty Venetian monastery of Ayia Napa.

Settled by the shore at dusk, I cooked one of Kyriakos' mullets on driftwood. The night was stifling. I decided to sleep on the beach, which was a poor choice because it was riddled with sandflies, and no wind rose. Hour after hour I lay awake, pouring sweat and maddened by mosquitoes. Sleep, even when it came, was tense with dreams; the sea made noises on the headland like cries. Long before day I shouldered my pack and left, covered with bites and swearing to complete my journey by taxi as soon as I reached

Famagusta; but this mood, softened by a cool *livas* blowing from the sea, did not survive the dawn.

All the same, the approach to Famagusta was unpleasant. Past the half-Roman aqueduct which still carries water by Ayia Napa, a road climbed to Paralimni, where in autumn thousands of migrating warblers, the *beccaficos* prized by Crusaders, land on cunningly limed trees and end up pickled in vinegar.

A few miles farther, Varosha began, and it was alarming to realize that this had once been a suburb of Famagusta, for it is now many times the size of the old city and has covered four miles of beaches in blocks of flats and tinsel hotels. A rather snobby town, and sensitive of Nicosia, a tourist centre with the finest harbour in the island, it was soon to be evacuated wholesale before the Turkish invaders of 1974.

For a long, depressing hour I walked north through the mass of the city, which still looked like a suburb to nowhere, and came at last to its formidable and perfect heart. More complete than Istanbul or Antioch, stronger than Fez, Jerusalem and even Avila, this prince of walled cities dominates the port and on its landward sides, where the bastions go muscling into the moat, its ramparts lift more than fifty feet from the living rock.

The rise of Famagusta was spectacular. Before the loss of Acre in 1291 and the expulsion of the last Crusaders, it had been a useful but undistinguished port called Ammochostos, 'Buried in the Sand'. But with the Moslem triumph the merchants and bankers of the Italian maritime republics, who only a year before had been scattered in a dozen ports along the coasts of Syria, converged on the one safe and deep harbour left to Christendom in the Levant. Within a generation Famagusta became rich. It received all the trades of the East and diffused them to the West. Its people, engaged in cosmopolitan luxury, were said to be the wealthiest in the world, and every language from Norse to Tamil might be heard in its marts.

'A citizen once betrothed his daughter,' wrote a German priest, 'and the jewels of her head-dress were valued by the French knights who came with us as more precious than all the ornaments of the Queen of France.'* The Lachas brothers, richest of all, flaunted their wealth with such parvenu vulgarity that one of them pounded up a jewel to sprinkle as a spice on his food; when they entertained Peter I and his court, they burnt aloes wood instead of logs, and poured out coins and precious stones in different corners of the room, to which the more impoverished knights eagerly helped themselves.

The courtesans were as opulent as the merchants – 'I dare not speak of their riches,' shuddered the priest – and St Bridget of Sweden, preaching in front of the Cathedral of St Nicholas, called down fire and brimstone on the city for its immorality. Yet by the middle of the fourteenth century it was filled with churches – three hundred and sixty-five, it was said, one for each day of the year. Merchants bribed their patron saints by promising to build them basilicas if cargoes came home safe, and the prostitutes quieted their consciences in the same way.

* L. von Sudheim, (1350) *Excerpta Cypria* Trs. C. D. Cobham.

But in 1372 there occurred an apparently trivial incident which brought about the decline not only of Famagusta, but of all Cyprus. It had been the custom for the Lusignan monarchs to be crowned kings of Jerusalem in St Nicholas Cathedral, because Famagusta was the Christian city closest to the Holy Land; and on either side of the king as he rode to his coronation, the envoys of Venice and Genoa would hold his horse's reins. But at the crowning of Peter II, as the parade began, the Venetian representative grabbed at the right-hand reins, which had always been a Genoese privilege, and bloody riots ensued.

In a furious revenge the Genoese invaded the island and sacked the larger cities. Famagusta, which remained in Genoese hands until 1464, never recovered. More than twenty years after the sack a traveller reported a third of the city in ruins, and one of the sons of the Lachas family – 'a poor little fellow,' says Makhairas – was seen peddling sweetmeats through the alleys for a living.

Now, immured beyond the ramparts and the rub of Greek traffic, I found that the Turkish community had taken refuge in the old town. Under an entrance which tunnelled through the battlements near the harbour, policemen and soldiers were vetting passports. The gateway shed an instant's darkness between new and old, between modern Varosha and the Lusignan town; the change took place almost in the silence between one step and another. The cacophany of the harbour faded, and I entered a city of ruins.

It was as if time itself had been embalmed under that desolate rectangle of sky. The churches stood in fields of yellowing grass. Some were still almost complete, but many others had turned to delicate husks. Palm trees grew in their aisles, and their vaults rose only into the thick sheafs of the Gothic roof when it is broken, revealing the strength behind the airborne illusion.

Turkish houses straggled in and out of this decay, sometimes built from the ruins, sometimes leaning against them. Gothic arches gave onto coffee shops; a mediaeval lintel, its blazon worn away, served as headstone for an Islamic holy man. But most of the ground lay barren. The whole town had shrunk within its ramparts, like a corpse withered in its armour. I walked among endless churches: churches whose names and even whose faith were sometimes unknown; churches turned to mosques and then to rubble; while high above, improbably vast and fastidious, rose the Cathedral of St Nicholas. In several of these churches refugee families had settled. Children giggled in their darkness. Beds were laid in the apses or along the chancels, where the people slept under the dim, frescoed stare of unidentifiable apostles. 'See!' cried a woman to me, pointing. 'Angels.'

The Church of SS Peter and Paul is said to have been built by the Lachas brothers with the profits of a single voyage. Its huge façade still stands, and is suddenly delicate in a doorway whose capitals show kneeling angels. Inside, where for centuries the Christian loaf and chalice were blessed and transfigured, some children had set up a theatre for their school play; as I peered in, a simian boy, holding a wooden sword, was proclaiming war on Habsburg Austria.

Even in ruin the town bears witness to a miasma of sects. I passed Orthodox, Armenian and Nestorian basilicas, the twin chapels of the Knights Templar and Hospitaller nested fondly together as their orders never were in life; and a shrine of Franciscans built by the epileptic monk-king, Henry II. The slender walls of St George of the Latins, whose roof was blown clean off during the Turkish siege, had kept their fragile windows intact, like a brown-skinned memory of the Saint-Chapelle, together with a curious capital formed as a cluster of bats, which seemed to gossip evilly together.

Nothing could be stranger for a lover of architecture than to walk through so many mediaeval ages together. One moment he is lost in the High Gothic of northern France, the next in the Champagne or among the intimate, jewelled churches of the Midi; an instant later an opulent Provençal style has appeared, a North Italian or a Syrian influence, or the ubiquitous Byzantine.

Of all the marriages between Gothic and Byzantine, the Orthodox cathedral of Famagusta – St George of the Greeks – must be the most ambitious and imposing. The Greek community built it to emulate the Latin cathedral of St Nicholas, and the two buildings continue to stand side by side – the hybrid and the pure – like a belated lesson in integrity. The Greek cathedral was left in ruins by the Turkish bombardment of 1571, but its heavy magnificence can still be felt. Six columns lumber down its aisles. Byzantine are the domed apses, the murals and the fallen cupola which overhung the nave – everything which gives the building space and stillness. Gothic is the long triple

313

aisle which creates a Western tension, and Gothic the mural tombs, the sacristries and the careful working of stone.

The two traditions have not blended. The blundering vaults and wall-shafts are the work of strangers to Europe; the mural tombs were set so deep in the walls as to undermine the fabric, and the Greek dome, placed somewhere along the thrust of the nave, must have looked isolated and trite. By the fourteenth century both the Byzantine and the Gothic, like middle-aged men, were too set in their ways to modify.

But independently their ways continued vigorous, and the neighbouring Latin cathedral, modelled on the purity of Rheims, still rises with a miraculous intricacy from the waste. The window of six lights, the counterpoint of gable and flying buttress and traceried tower, are like a lucid and perfect dialectic. Even inside, through doors whose statues have been hacked away, with the tombstones torn up and the furniture of a mosque superimposed, the ascent of Gothic stone is scarcely troubled, and all this air-invading delicacy has somehow been carved from a porous and inferior rock.

The High Gothic splendour mesmerized the Orthodox. The meanest village masons copied its carving, introduced pointed arches, wall-sepulchres, rib vaults and even window tracery. All over the island many small churches with rectangular naves remain as witness to the alien spell, yet are untouched by its heart. The Greeks juggled with the motifs and design, but they did not share the Gothic spirit. This strained and aspiring architecture differed too much from the spatial calm of their own. It was the cry of men cut off from God. The Orthodox found the Latin mind tortured and legalistic, viewing the soul too much in the colours of darkness and damnation. To the Greeks the cycle of sin, confession and forgiveness was rather exhausting, and already their Church had become more an instrument of praise than a theatre for human guilt and redemption.

Besides, the Latin dominance was on the wane. With their kingdom drowning in an Islamic sea, the Lusignans gave up persecuting their fellow-Christians, and as early as the fourteenth century the resilient Greek faith began in-sidiously to absorb them. The women were the first to succumb. They began to attend Orthodox services. And after the Council of Florence in 1439, which declared Orthodox and Roman to be brothers in Christ, the distinction between the two faiths started to fade. Greek churches became barnacled with Latin chapels. A single family might be split almost casually between the Latin and Orthodox faiths, and many people attended whichever liturgy appealed to them.

This ease, one suspects, was less a sign of mutual under-standing than of lethargy. As in art, so in life, the Greek and Latin union was generally a pallid one. The Latin priests, when they went over to Orthodoxy, usually did so in order to marry (if they had not already done so in secret) and the standard of morality was a scandal. 'Of the bishops and clergy, both secular and regular,' wrote the monk Felix Fabri, 'I cannot speak but with bitterness of heart, and if I would speak I could not, unless I whisper it into the ear of Heaven.'

After the Turks had overrun the island, and the Orthodox

Church was once more in the ascendant, Roman Catholicism vanished almost overnight. It became clear that its influence had merely been a surface one, like the gorgeous Italian dresses which clothed the Virgin in contemporary icons.

I awoke to the sound of music in the darkness outside. Other men in the hostel dormitory had woken too, and were craning out of the windows, half naked, but with their worker's caps squashed over their heads. From here, by an optical illusion, the sea appeared to reach unbroken to the top of the ramparts, as if at any moment it must pour through their crenellations and the ships come sailing in. Somewhere near the Sea Gate the noise of drums came up to us.

'They're celebrating Ataturk's proclamation of the Republic,' a man volunteered in English – a heavy, crisp-haired man, called Kemal. 'I thought of waking you. But you looked like a corpse lying there, tired out.' I had slept away the late afternoon, and now the dusk was almost here. 'It's good to have something to celebrate. It keeps a people together.' The man's fists were banging on the window-ledge in time to the music. Under his arm I saw a copy of Arnold Toynbee's *War and Civilization*. 'We're giving ourselves confidence.'

I pulled on some clothes and we went down to the cathedral square; but it was empty. A Turkish moon hung in the sky. Whereever the torchlight procession had passed, discarded brands were burning in the gutters.

'They'll come back,' said Kemal.

The parvis of the cathedral shone pale under the street

lamps. Two Venetian columns, once crowned by emblems of St Mark and St Theodore, stood empty. All I could remember of the place was sadness. Here the titular kings of Jerusalem knelt before the porch to be crowned sovereigns of a city they would never possess. 'I will uphold the Christian population of the realm in their rights and justice,' they swore, 'as a Christian king should.' But the last two monarchs, husband and son to Catherine Cornaro, were laid to rest still young in the cathedral, and a century later the Turks tore up their bones and threw them into the sea.

Last of the royal line, but herself a Venetian, Catherine Cornaro was wedded to the Lusignan James II by the design of her mother-city, which hoped to acquire the island by a dynastic stratagem. Titian painted her, fashionably gold-haired, and with magnificent eyes, and her buxom beauty inspired such enthusiasm that the Cypriots hailed her as Aphrodite returned to their island. But when her husband died at the age of thirty-three, and her only child in infancy, her position became precarious. For fifteen years she continued to reign, but at last the Venetians undermined her power, persecuted her supporters and secretly bullied her into subjection. Here, on the parvis of St Nicholas, after Mass, with her maids dressed in black satin around her, she abdicated in favour of her homeland, and with elaborate cynicism the Doge sent his own *Bucentaur* in state to collect 'our most serene and beloved daughter'. The same year she was settled in the Venetian hill-town of Asolo, where she kept a smaller and happier court, and patronized the arts and scholars of the Renaissance. Up to her death the Republic insisted on her sham royalty, and when her funeral

317

cortège crossed the Grand Canal on a stormy night in 1510, her bier was seen to be topped by the crown of Cyprus. But it belonged to no recognizable queen. Gentile Bellini, a little before, had painted her tired and fat, and inside the coffin her corpse was dressed in the rough habit of St Francis.

Ambling with Kemal around the cathedral square I listened to him castigating the Venetians as if they had left only yesterday. They were crude imperialists, he said, bourgeois, godless and cunning. Why they had produced artists he could not understand. It must have been a fluke (you never knew with Italians). They had fought bravely, of course, but then they had something to fight for.

'What was that?'

'Greed,' he said, circling his arms in depiction of plenty. 'Empire.'

In the case of Cyprus it is true. The eighty-two-year Venetian rule was scarcely more than a military occupation – the Serenissima guarding her trade routes. Everything – commerce, agriculture, the population itself – declined, and although she proved more lenient to the Greek peasantry than the Lusignans had been, her imperial attitude promised nothing more. 'If the gentlemen of these colonies do tyrannize over the villages of their dominions, the best way is not to seem to see it, that there may be no kindness between them and their subjects . . .'

But to the career of the island goddess, filled with metamorphoses, the Venetians added a curious footnote. The Greek gods, as is well known, shared the infirmities and loves of men, and paid the same penalties. One of these was death. The grave of Zeus was shown in Crete, the tomb of Hermes at Hermopolis, that of Ares in Thrace. Dionysus was buried in Delphi by the golden statue of Apollo. Even the gods of Egypt were mortal, and while their bodies lay mummified in cities along the Nile, their souls shone as stars in the sky.

Aphrodite died in Cyprus. We hear of her end under the precipice of Curium, and of her grave at Paphos. Here the Venetians, always proud of their scholarship, dug up a handsome Roman sepulchre, and since it was accepted that Aphrodite had been a real person (wife of King Adonis, mother of Prince Cupid) who had ruled over the island in some remote age, they assumed the sarcophagus to be hers. So the 'Tomb of Venus' was brought in triumph to Famagusta, the capital, and laid reverently in front of the cathedral. There it remained until 1878, when the British Commissioner in Famagusta died. Less sentimental than the Venetians, the British commandeered the sarcophagus for their dead civil servant, and set it where it now stands, in the Orthodox cemetery of Varosha.

The Venetian proveditor's palace still faces the cathedral across the square – a façade of heavy, Renaissance splendour, whose Doric columns were pilfered from Salamis. Classical, grave, its very balance is strangely appalling. Alone in this city of ruined Gothic churches, which ascend like broken prayers, its earthy weight denies any presence but its own. Walking over the small flagstones picked out in grass, Kemal and I saw nothing beyond it but gutted apartments whose doors and windows, all resolutely square and framed in bossed stones, carried the same self-assurance.

'They must have collapsed at the time of the siege.' Kemal

319

kicked a fallen lintel. 'It's said we fired a hundred and fifty thousand cannon-balls into the city.'

This may be no exaggeration. At that time the Turkish sappers and artillery had proved the most formidable in the world, and their invading army, under the infamous Lala Mustapha, was huge. By late September 1570, Nicosia had fallen, Kyrenia surrendered, and the rest of the island had given itself into Turkish hands. But Famagusta was imaginatively defended by a small garrison of Venetian and Greek troops under Marcantonio Bragadino, and for ten months, through a series of assaults and counterattacks, they held their own. The Turks wormed their way towards the bastions in a maze of trenches which zigzagged for miles over the plains – networks which were so extensive that they could absorb the whole army, and so deep that little but the lance-tips of advancing cavalry showed above them.

The defences were slowly ground down by mines and the terrible artillery, and at last the Turks blew up the great ravelin of the Land Gate at the south-west angle of the walls, and swarmed to the attack. But for six hours the garrison repulsed them; even the women crowded to the ramparts to shower down missiles and boiling water; until the enemy became dispirited and fell back. For a few days all was quiet. Then, on July 7th, the Turks assaulted not only the ravelin but the whole of the south curtain wall; again the Land Gate saw the fiercest fighting.

'This third attack,' wrote a Venetian historian, 'continued for five hours, and was most bravely met. But the soldiers who were set to defend the ravelin at the Limisso gate were thrown into disorder by the enemy's fireworks, and were unable to manoeuvre in the small space they could command, so that when at the other points assailed by the enemy the battle was well nigh done, they were still engaged, and suffering very severe losses. They gave way at last, and allowed the Turks to scale the ravelin . . .'*

Now, in desperation, the commanders detonated a huge mine which had been laid beneath the ravelin. A thousand Turks and a hundred Venetians were buried in the debris. Again the attack faltered. For days longer the besieged huddled behind palisades of casks and sandbags, weakened with plague and so famished that they were reduced to eating dogs and cats. The last three days of July saw ferocious fighting. The attackers were desperate and no longer disciplined. Their losses were appalling. But inside the city three quarters of the garrison were dead, and on August 1st Bragadino negotiated a truce by which they might be allowed to leave for Crete on Turkish ships, and the townspeople stay unmolested.

'But as soon as our men got beyond the trenches . . . they were staggered at the prodigious number of the force they saw in the Turkish camp. For over three miles from the city it stretched over a vast circuit, and was everywhere so full of troops that the turbans, which on every side showed white above the trenches, covered the ground like snowflakes. The Turks, on the other hand, when they saw the defending force so small in numbers, the emaciated bodies and pale faces of our soldiers, who seemed as though they

---

* Paolo Paruta, *History of the War of Cyprus* Trs. C. D. Cobham, *Excerpta Cypria*.

could hardly stand, much less offer so long and gallant a resistance to a foe, marvelled at their courage, and felt some trace of shame.'

Perhaps it was this humiliation which caused Lala Mustapha to go back on his word, or perhaps the fifty thousand Turkish slain. But he took both soldiers and citizens prisoner, and hacked the commanders to pieces before the eyes of Bragadino. For the general himself he prepared an end of calculated humiliation. Three times Mustapha made him stretch out his neck as if for execution, before his ears and nose were cut off. Then Bragadino was forced to carry earth up and down the redoubts of the city, to kiss the ground before Mustapha every time he passed, and was finally flayed alive in front of the cathedral. 'His saintly soul,' wrote Calepio, 'bore all with great firmness, patience, and faith, never losing heart, but ever with the sternest constancy reproaching them for their broken faith.'

Even after his death the Turks could not leave the corpse alone. The skin was stuffed with straw and paraded through the streets astride a cow under a scarlet parasol, then slung from the yard-arm of a galley and sailed up and down the Syrian coast. But eventually, said Calepio, it was sent with the heads of the other generals to the sultan in Constantinople, 'who caused them to be put in his prison, and I who was a captive chained in that prison as spy of the Pope, on my liberation tried to steal that skin, but could not.' Years later it was bought at a great price by the brothers and sons of Bragadino, who laid it where it remains in an urn in the Church of SS Giovanni e Paolo in Venice.

But by now the cathedral square of Famagusta, ghastly

in memory, was starting to fill with people. The sound of drums drew nearer. Kemal and I were sitting on the fallen lintel of the Proveditor's palace, staring through its gaping façade and arguing about the siege. Kemal showed the terribleness of the Turk when aroused. At any mention of Ottoman atrocity his burly hands ground fiercely at his knees and his face darkened with patriotism so that one forgot the intellectual forehead and noticed instead his belligerent mouth and nostrils. It was Bragadino, he said, not Mustapha, who had broken his word. 'He killed Turkish captives. Mustapha accused him personally. The diaries of those present are still kept in Istanbul. I have read them.'

'The Venetian historians say the accusation was a lie.'

'The Turks do not lie,' said Kemal.

'So you think Mustapha acted well?'

He frowned and muttered: 'They were hard times.'

'But even in those hard times,' I said relentlessly, 'our historians wrote that Mustapha was "much blamed even by his own people".'

'Did they? Yes . . . I suppose so,' he grumbled. 'You shouldn't flay people.'

The procession was stamping up the streets beneath us. Behind the band marched troops of soldiers carrying torches. The flames glinted among the ruins and threw out a cascade of sparks. A marching-song of chilling archaism floated up to us. Its quick drumbeat reverberated from the walls; it seemed to mimic the kettledrums of the Janissaries. The flames burst and died among the blackness of the wrecked churches.

The band was led by a huge, hirsute man, the kind of

warrior who planted the horsehair standards on enemy ramparts, and was buried with honour where he fell. But when the other soldiers passed close I saw that their torches were only tins of paraffin-soaked cloth held on sticks – tins for motor oil and luncheon meat – and that they marched in a carnival spirit.

'Mine are a good people,' said Kemal as we followed the crowd into the streets, 'and Cyprus is ours by right. We are conquerors, warriors. The Greeks are only merchants.'

'This is an age of merchants.'

'You in the West,' he growled, 'you think too much of the Greeks. You exaggerate. Don't forget, civilization came from the East.' His thatch of black hair flopped morosely on his forehead with each stride. 'In any case, these Cypriots – are they Greeks? No!' He stamped in time to the music. 'No! No! No! They're a mongrel lot. Arabs, Arameans, Phoenicians. Slave peoples! All this about ENOSIS – why should they want to be united to Greece? It's a charade, a trick. There's no drop of Greek in them . . .'

'But more Mycenaean remains have been found in Cyprus than . . .'

'Pottery!' he boomed. 'What does pottery prove? One day archaeologists will find the remains of German cars here. Will that mean there were German colonies?'

'The earliest histories tell of Greeks in Cyprus.'

'Propaganda.'

'Then why do the people speak Greek?'

'They've lost their own identity,' he half shouted. He was growing angry. 'Whoever they were, they've even lost their language!'

I thought it wiser to be silent. Now the procession was tramping over wasteland, its music echoing among distant walls, as if another army was moving abreast of it through the ruins. Then it re-entered the streets where the churches stood. They rose around us in a traceried blackness. They seemed to be holding their breath. Kemal embarked on a loud monologue. The Turks were by nature fine, he repeated – the best on earth. They had always been provoked. If Greeks had suffered at their hands, it was because of double-dealing. As for the Armenian massacres, they were the fault of British diplomacy. 'And the atrocities of Famagusta,' he ended, as if annoyed by my silence, 'were the fault of the Venetians. Bragadino was a hypocrite.'

The churches cried out not to be betrayed. 'Lala Mustapha was a monster.'

Kemal was not listening. '. . . and the Greeks are no better . . .'

'But the Turks have Greek blood,' I said in irritation. The very faces around me, accentuated in that cruel light, were less those of Mongols than of old, miasmic races absorbed by the Turkish bands which had penetrated Anatolia a thousand years ago – Phrygians and Lydians, Jews and Greeks, Hittites and Celts and that earlier people, some of whom had crossed the sea to become the first Cypriots – and even in Cyprus Greek and Turk had intermarried.

But the noise of the procession drowned my heresy. We were squeezing down the narrowest streets. The whole lost city was crowding round us, lit by our flares. The band stamped and crashed. Marble Venetian lions looked down from niches in the citadel, whimpered in the dark of the Proveditor's palace. The church of St George of the Latins sent up a flutter of bats.

'Let's stop.' Kemal suddenly sat down on a broken wall and motioned me to join him. He was agitated and breathless. The dwindling torchlight picked out prickles of sweat along his forehead. He hadn't meant to be aggressive, he said, laying a hand on my shoulder, but he badly wanted the world to understand his country. Not only his country, but his whole people. For the Turkish heartland, he said, was not Asia Minor but southern Russia. The steppes were the core of the world. Out of them had come all civilization. That was where the Sumerians, even, had got their horses.

'Horses aren't civilization,' I said softly.

But Kemal dreamt of all Turkish peoples united, their home spread across central Asia to the China Sea. Bulgars, Finns, Hungarians, Esthonians were racially their cousins, and there were forty million more in the Soviet Union and China. He spoke of them with a mystical longing and brotherhood – the Turkmen of Russia and the eastern Elburz, the Khazaks and the mountain-loving Khirgiz, the tribes of western China and the northern Mongols who (he said) were fair and blue-eyed as Swedes. Their lands and cities dropped from his lips with the sound of gongs: Kokand, Tashkent, Samarkand, Bokhara, the Aral Sea, and the Altai Mountains which enclose the Turkish paradise. Their names rang with a vast, landlocked desolation and romance. They drugged his mind. Like so many Turks, he was a Slavophobe. All races, even the Greeks, had their good points, but the Slavs were dangerous, a cesspit of incendiary ideas. He envisaged a Soviet Union splintered up, and all its nomad-haunted lands and peoples returned, until the Turkish state would become as it had been in the seventh century – bald plains and horse-high grasslands stretching to the Great Wall of China, an empire poor to industrialists but rich to the soul.

By now the procession had vanished. Its last flames scattered in the cathedral square. The cymbals died away with a noise like tiny waterfalls, and the city sank again into its maimed quiet.

The difference between Greek and Turk, said Kemal, stemmed from his people belonging to a vaster and older land. 'Listen. I will tell you the respective qualities of ourselves and the Greeks. These are simple, obvious.' He left a moment's silence to emphasize the importance of his thoughts. Below, the masts of ships, lit up in the harbour, were moving and winking over the crenellations; above us the shell of St George of the Greeks reared on the stars.

'First,' said Kemal, 'while the Greeks are fun-loving, the Turks are terrible' – by this *terribilita* he meant something awesome and formidable – 'and where the Greeks are materialists and lovers of luxury, we are simple and moral.'

In a sense I could agree with this, but it was clear to what conclusions his arguments were tending, and already a ghostly dissenting Greek had arisen in my mind.

'This austerity explains why we live as we do.' He pointed to some poor houses nearby. 'Now the Greeks mistake that for poverty. But I myself live in a house no larger in Nicosia, and I've never wanted for anything. And I'm a typical Turk.

327

Yes . . .' He relished the thought with a romanticism which betrayed its falseness. 'I am the Turk-in-the-street.'

I mumbled: 'You're not typical.'

'I am,' he repeated. 'And why not? Let the ant keep to its size. I represent my people.'

'I've found your people vary.'

He ignored this, but buttonholed me with his gaze. 'Now the Greeks are crafty. They prostitute themselves . . .' *Adaptable and intelligent*, answered the ghostly Greek in me. '. . . While the Turks are more solemn.' *Stupid*, said the soundless voice, growing bigoted.

'Simplicity, morality, dignity.' Kemal clasped his big hands together. 'So you see, the first Greek characteristic is *Slave*! The first Turkish one is *Ruler*!'

But the simple, the moral and the dignified, whispered my phantom Greek, no longer rule.

Next morning I walked round the city walls, tramping along the dry fosse cut in its solid rock. A few palm trees leant dusty and small against the fifty-foot ramparts. Within the city the earth sloped up to the parapets in grass-covered mounds. Only at the embrasures did the thickness of the defences become apparent, where the line of bastions, with stubbled walls and sonorous names, dropped sheer to the moat and its dwarfish trees.

Their loneliness filled my mind with the siege. I sat down by the crenellated scarp, unnerved by their memorial solitude. Under my hands, deep in the stone, Christian symbols had been carved by the garrison as prayers or talismans, to no avail. I entered the Land Gate, where the terrible ravelin bulged into the moat. Although altered by the Turks, its strength and complexity survived in a nest of parapets and gun-chambers, knit from dressed stone and virgin rock, and its ramp still plunged under it to debouch into the fosse. But such ravelins, ironically, were soon antiquated. 'This defence,' wrote a Venetian military engineer only a few years after Famagusta's fall, 'has been found in our times to be not only imperfect but highly dangerous to the garrison. The ditch around the ravelin is difficult to enfilade and becomes a cover for the enemy . . .'*

Yet compared to these Venetian works the older Citadel in the sea walls looks mellow and feudal. The windows are slit for arrows and its ramparts capped with toy crenellations. Its curious name, 'Othello's Tower', derives from Shakespeare's tragedy, which is laid in 'a seaport in Cyprus', probably Famagusta. The true source of Shakespeare's story, based on a trivial novella by the Italian Cintio, is uncertain, but the archives of Venice record that in 1545 an Italian soldier, nicknamed *Il Moro* for his dark skin, was condemned to banishment by the Council of Ten, and with him two others, the counterparts in rank of Iago and Cassio. Yet the inscrutable Council, although it published its sentences, was always silent as to the charges, and a rival theory claims that the true Othello was Christoforo Moro, a governor of Cyprus whose wife died while they were returning to Venice.

Of 'the importancy of Cyprus to the Turk', as Shakespeare wrote, there can be no question. The island pointed at the heart of the Ottoman empire. The Turks allotted only a

---

* Lorini, *Della Fortificatione* (Venice, 1609).

small corps of soldiers to its defence, but twenty thousand settlers, mostly veterans of Mustapha's army, were quickly established there. As for the conquered, a profound gulf – more political than religious – still separated Greek and Latin. In some parts of the country the Turkish invaders were innocently welcomed by the Greeks while the Latins, disinherited, fled overseas or into remote regions of the island. The Orthodox faith was restored to its old supremacy and the Greeks, in an explosion of hatred, tore down many of the Gothic churches, while the rest were turned into mosques or stables. Afterwards, since the Ottomans liked to hedge the power of their own officials, they permitted the Orthodox archbishop to be spokesman and governor of his flock: President Makarios was the last in a line of authority stretching back to 1670.

But now, with the discovery of the seaway round Africa, the flow of commerce was changing its bed, and the whole balance of the civilized world was tipping from the Levant to the western rim of Europe – Portugal, Spain, Britain, France, and to the Americas. Under the corrupt and death-like hand of the Ottomans, Cyprus became a backwater. Even its own modest prosperity fell away. Cotton and silk were the chief products, with a little wool and wine. 'So much only remains to the wretched creatures from the fruits of the earth,' wrote a traveller as early as 1599, 'as allows them to sustain life, to provide bare necessities and sow their fields anew.'* Most peaceful of the Ottoman domains, its peace was a dazed stagnation. The harbours silted up

---

* Ioannes Cotovicus, *Itinerarium*. Trs. C. D. Cobham.

and the land parched. Within seventy years of Turkish rule the population had dwindled to a quarter.

Famagusta became a barracks and a political prison. Christians were forbidden to live there, and foreigners, however distinguished, were forced to dismount at its gates. To the Turks themselves it was a limbo of exiles and dead-end soldiers, its air so unhealthy that it coated the lungs in salt, and distempered iron. By the mid-nineteenth century, with the construction of the Suez Canal, whole churches were pulled down and their stone shipped away to build the quays and hotels of Port Said.

But when the Canal was opened in 1869, the eastern Mediterranean drowsily awoke. The area became a cause of sharpened concern. Disraeli, wary of Russian encroachments, signed a pact with the Sultan after the Russo–Turkish war of 1877, by which the British were to occupy Cyprus and safeguard the creaking Ottoman Empire. 'If the Sultan does not consent to the above arrangement,' Lord Salisbury telegraphed his ambassador to the Porte, 'it will not be in the power of England to pursue these negotiations any further, and the capture of Constantinople and the partition of the Empire will be the immediate result.'

So in June 1878 Lord John Hay, admiral of the Channel Squadron, landed two mules laden with newly minted sixpences to pay off the Sultan's soldiers and officials. Sir Garnet Wolseley, the first High Commissioner, reached the island a few days later and was met by Archbishop Sophronius who, in an elegant speech, looked forward to a new life for his people.

CHAPTER FOURTEEN
· · · · · · · · · · · · · · · · ·
The Greek Heart

The Lusignan Age, sometimes called the Great Age of Cyprus, bequeathed nothing durable. It was impermeably alien, and died exotically in a soil which could not nourish it. The ages which expressed and developed the island were more obscure, but both of them were Greek – the formative Mycenaean centuries which saw her Hellenized, and the Byzantine which turned her Christian. The stronghold of Byzantium, of course, was the Troodos Mountains; but the more shadowy Mycenaean era, a time which laid the very cornerstone of Cypriot culture, was cradled in the flat littoral of Famagusta bay. Nothing but this calm sweep marks out the land. The soil is sandy and almost waterless. Here and there it creases into the bed of a lost marsh or river, then flattens again into plains blotched with mimosa and pine.

In the fourteenth century B.C., towards the end of the Bronze Age, this area was infiltrated from the west by Mycenaeans, a dark-haired people, warriors and pirates as well as artists, who sailed along a corridor of islands from their heartland in the Peloponnese. There had been settlers in Cyprus before, from Anatolia and perhaps from Syria, but this was the first true colonization, and the greatest.

The vestiges of Mycenae are most impressive in the city called Enkomi-Alassia, whose real name is uncertain. Perhaps the Alassia which the Hittites and Egyptians knew – its acres of excavated ruin lie in a dipping plain where the harvest was already ripe. Its streets ran straight and symmetric through ruins never taller than a man, but were mostly so narrow that two people could have scarcely walked abreast. In its rooms and alleys I found nobody, not even an archaeologist. The only moving thing was an immense toad flopping along the streets in a military camouflage of yellow and green. Yet as I walked, the confusion began to reassemble, and patterns emerged. In the rubble shone walls whose stones had been cut with the care and pride which a man might give to a statue. Here and there a grander threshold or a more generous court showed where some two-storeyed mansion had housed a noble or a merchant; while the poor lined the streets in terraced squalor. I came with surprise upon a double rank of cyclopean stones – the base of the city walls and towers; they seemed too huge for men, such stones as in a later and poorer age might give rise to legends of giants.

Yet within them had grown up one of the richest city-kingdoms of its day – a metropolis of some fifteen thousand inhabitants, copper merchants and metal-workers whose public buildings were superb and whose graves yielded handsome jewellery, ivories and faience, with gold and silver bowls. We hear of the king of Alassia shipping copper to Akhenaton of Egypt, who sent back horses and perfumed oils, a prize bull and a gilded bed. And all this time, although it was adapting its art to the more opulent tastes of Cyprus and the orient, the Mycenaean influence was intensifying. Soon pottery began to show chariots, and bulls with decorated bodies. They gallop among flowers. Elegant women appear, a memory of Minoan times, and figurines abound – female fertility idols and centaurs whose double-heads stare at each other in amazement.

As to their gods, the conquerors brought with them a horned divinity, a primitive Apollo perhaps, which was dug up in one of the fine houses of Alassia; the hand which he stretches out, palm downward as if in soothing, is perfectly human, but under ebullient horns his face has not yet arrived at an expression, and above the knee his legs bend backward in a suggestion of goat-like thighs, as if he were still dogged by an anthropomorphic past. With this mysterious deity came the Great Mother of the Aegean, a primitive Aphrodite who added her strength and complex symbolism – the dove, the lion, the snake – to that of the island goddess.

Meanwhile, on the Greek mainland, the Mycenaeans had been overrun. Brown-haired Achaeans, tribal lords and charioteers, came with iron from the north and ruled the cities which they had no skill to create. The Mycenaean work in Cyprus – more plentiful than anywhere else – may be the fruit of craftsmen fleeing overseas. But the Achaeans followed them. As on the mainland, so in Cyprus, they settled and dominated, adding a new impetus to Hellenism. Their cemeteries at Alassia have never been discovered, but beneath the palace of an Achaean chief were found the bodies of two unusually tall men, heavily armoured and buried with the weighty, slashing swords of northern Europe. Theirs was the Greece of the Trojan wars, and they the Greeks of whom Homer wrote with awe in *The Iliad*, prodigious in arms.

But in the eleventh century Alassia was overthrown by some unknown catastrophe, perhaps earthquake. You may still see where the courts and rooms of its heyday were divided into rubble partitions by the poor remnant of its people who returned. Nothing could be more eloquent of decay. And a few years later, it seems, the whole site was abandoned in favour of Salamis, which became the backbone of the Greek cause in its day.

So, about 1050 B.C., after the ravages of the Sea Peoples had maimed the sun-softened cultures of the Levant, Cyprus slipped into the Dark Age of the eastern Mediterranean. The era of Bronze came to an end. To the north the Hittite Empire disintegrated; Babylon fell in the east; southward, Egypt was waning under indolent rulers. And while the Dorians were flooding into Greece, Cyprus remained the last refuge of the old Mycenaean–Achaean civilization, which was to change her for ever. Isolated, her earlier population was overtaken by this Hellenic language and culture, and little by little it remoulded them. Two hundred years later she emerged from the darkness as a Greek land.

Between Alassia and Salamis I followed a road which ran straight over the plain, but by now the sun was falling, turning the red soil redder still, and I stopped at St Barnabas Monastery in the hope of a bed for the night. Seated outside in the last sunlight were three patriarchal monks. They did not smile or speak, only looked at me with an assortment of stern or indifferent eyes.

Chariton, Barnabas and Stephanos were brothers, all in their late seventies or eighties, and held sway in the monastery over a troop of weathered hermits. Their white beards exploded over their cassocks, and their hair fought loose from buns and pigtails to fly around pairs of huge, shell-like ears. 'Are they alike?' echoed a young monk when I said I could not distinguish one from the next. 'When one sneezes, the other two sneeze!'

At meals they occupied the head of the refectory table, seated in high-backed chairs like a triumvirate of wintry kings. They loved their food. The silence was lacerated by the smacking of their lips and the sucking of their fingers. Fish, dolma, tomatoes, raw artichokes vanished into their mouths or beards. And that evening a deacon climbed into the belfry and strangled some young pigeons, which were gobbled in a few seconds with a crackling of bones.

In daytime, between liturgies and meals, the brothers painted icons. One would sketch an outline, another fill in the broad colours, another complete the details. This easy-going manufacture, far from those artists whose icons were eked out in prayer and vision, brought the brothers a modest revenue, together with the sale of honey and medallions of St Barnabas.

The St Barnabas pilgrimage is still popular among the islanders. He is the country's special saint and patron of its Church. Ever since the fifth century a basilica or a monastery has stood here above his reputed tomb. 'And Joses, who by the apostles was surnamed Barnabas, (which is, being interpreted, The son of consolation,) a Levite, and of the country of Cyprus, having land, sold it and brought the money, and laid it at the apostles' feet.'* So the Bible introduces him, and he became the co-worker with St Paul on his missionary journeys to Cyprus and Asia Minor; but later the two men fell out, and St Barnabas sailed with his kinsman John Mark to Cyprus. Here he vanishes under a cloud of apocryphal stories, which recount that he was stoned to death by Jews in the hippo-drome of Salamis, and that Mark buried him secretly in a cave on the city outskirts.

Four hundred years later, when the Church of Cyprus was threatened with absorption into the Apostolic See of Antioch, St Barnabas appeared in a timely vision to the Cypriot archbishop and revealed his burial place. A huge procession wended to where the monastery now stands, and after digging as the saint had directed, uncovered a sepulchre in which the body lay as Mark had interred it, with a copy of St Matthew's Gospel on its chest. The arch-bishop sailed at once to Constantinople and laid his case before the Emperor Zeno, claiming that the Cypriot Church, founded by St Barnabas, was as apostolic as that of Antioch, and therefore its equal. So successful was he that the emperor confirmed the island Church's independ-ence, and granted its archbishops the right to wear a purple cloak of office, carry a sceptre and sign their names in scarlet ink – privileges which only the emperor had known, but which Archbishop Makarios keeps to this day.

But when I visited the tomb, venerated for fifteen cen-turies, I saw a sepulchre older than the time of Barnabas.

* *Acts*, iv. 36–37.

Even in the monastery it was not truth which seemed to matter, but belief, continuity, repose; they hung in the trees like incense. From my cell window I could look down the long road to Salamis, past the tombs and tumuli of Iron Age kings to where the classical city mounded against the horizon. I did not leave for three days. Instead I wandered in the garden of olive and fig trees, lilies and snapdragons, and adopted its peace. I found where the earliest church traced itself through grass in a pavement of tessellated marble, broken. My feet and body repaired themselves after overwalking. The only sounds were the sharp, sweet birdsong, and semantra clinking on a carob tree.

Father Barnabas sat at his easel, touching up the face of St Heracleides. He looked up and addressed me for the first time: 'You Germans always camp.'

'I'm English.'

'It makes no difference.' He frowned at St Heracleides. 'Do not camp where graves are, or among the Turks or in St Catherine's grove.'

I said that I liked the Turks and had grown used to the dead (I had once passed a night in a cemetery in Vietnam). But what was wrong with the grove? It stood near the monastery: a copse of *spina christi*, whose thorns in legend crowned the head of Christ.

'It's haunted,' he said. 'If a man cuts down any part of it with his plough, he will die. Even a fellow who took branches for firewood was struck blind the same day.'

'You saw this?'

'It was before our time.' The hair of St Heracleides grew golden under his brush, but the flesh remained dead, mere paint. 'The man's son told me of it. Such things come of flouting God and His saints. Camp by the sea. The sea is everyone's.'

At seventy-five Father Barnabas was the youngest of the brothers. They called him 'little boy'.

Father Chariton was the oldest, and half blind. He often talked into space. During meals he would cross himself incessantly and stumble away before grace was over.

Father Stephanos was now the abbot, and presided over baptisms on Sunday mornings. Every year scores of families drove out from Famagusta with their babies. I found him in the church, pouring water into a portable font. He was in his element. His face shone above its beard like an aged cherub peering over a cloud. Three monks were chanting conversationally behind, while a lace-wrapped tyrant of a baby was being humoured by twittering relatives. Grandmother joggled him; father gurgled. A host of aunts undressed him, fussing like guinea-fowl. But Father Stephanos rolled up his sleeves to the elbow and said remorselessly: 'Ready'.

The boy was stretched out naked, while his hands and body were anointed, then the abbot lifted him high in his arms and lowered him to the font. The small hands clutched the edge, slipped, and the head vanished suddenly; but from the water rose a terrible howl and a moment later the outraged face reappeared, black eyes and mouth wide open and puckered with rebellion. 'The servant of God, Vassos, is baptized into the Name of the Father, Amen . . .' The abbot raised him high and glistening for everyone to see, plunged him inexorably down again – 'And of the Son,

Amen . . .' pouring water over his head, lifted him once more to desperate wails, immersed him again '. . . And of the Holy Spirit, Amen.' Finally he scissored off three locks of the damp hair and handed the baby back to his godmother, whose face clearly said '. . . and he'd been so good up till now.'

At once, in accordance with Orthodox tradition, the infant was confirmed and the long-suffering body anointed on forehead, eyes, nostrils, mouth, ears, chest, hands, feet, while Father Stephanos murmured 'The seal of the gift of the Holy Spirit.' Then the grandmother buttoned the child's head in an Elizabethan bonnet, so that he looked like a watery Holbein, his father took him in his arms, and the family paraded round the font, while a flock of tiny sisters held up candles and a little boy stumbled under a processional cross.

All morning this went on: baptism, confirmation, howls and silences, bodies plucked from the water and plummeted down again. Original sin evaporated in cries and blubberings. There were terrified babies and Stoic babies, and a fighting baby who locked her fingers round everything she could find – candles, crosses, beards. But the adults uniformly smiled and were happy, and at last the infant would be carried away in triumph: two inky eyes in a lace whiteness, astonished at this sudden madness.

'Anointing is a symbol of kingship,' said a voice at my ear, 'because we are called to be brothers in Christ, the King.' I turned to see a priest, some forty-five years old, a cruelly ravaged face. 'Water signifies death to sin. The three Immersions are the three days of Our Lord in the tomb.'

The crowds had filtered from the church. I noticed how bare it was, its walls spotted with ancient capitals placed at random like nuts in a cake. My gaze returned to the priest, to a pair of beautiful, ambivalent eyes, set wide apart – but the face was feverish and weak. 'After the third immersion the Holy Spirit descends. If the child dies immediately after, he will become an angel.'

'What is the difference in heaven between an angel and a soul?'

'An angel is pure,' he answered. 'A soul is only forgiven.'

We walked out into the cloister. Its garden blazed with cannas and geraniums.

'A soul cannot of itself be pure.' He winced at the bright flowers, and put on his dark glasses. For some reason he made me shudder. 'How can we conceal our sins? Satan exposes us before the face of God.' To my mounting amazement, he breathed: 'That is what is happening to me.' He turned by the door of his cell and stared at me. 'I mean Damnation.'

His expression was lost behind the black discs of the glasses. He bowed his head. The placid sun and the bright flowers seemed to mock him.

I echoed feebly 'Damnation?'

Then the words poured out of him. How many others had heard them, or whether I, as a stranger, could be vouchsafed secrets denied to his own people, I do not know. He closed the door of his cell behind us and sat down trembling in a chair. 'Yes, Damnation.' He could scarcely control his movements. 'When you die, as the angels are carrying away the soul, the Devil presents them with a history of your sins. He remembers what you yourself have forgotten, everything you've omitted in confession . . .'

I half smiled, but he saw and flashed out: 'The Devil writes in his book, I tell you! Don't you know this? And you an educated man!'

My smile vanished. The man's face, his whole appearance, were too pitiful. His fingers twisted round a little filigreed cross. His voice lifted in a theatrical cry: 'O my God, how terrible it is – the sweetness of sin! The eyes of the young!' He gazed at me with an emasculated look which made me uncomfortable. 'Isn't sin sweet really? Isn't there a terrible loveliness about this awful thing? That is how Satan buys us. Lying in bed in the dark, if I only think I touch a woman's arm – *Anathema!* In the day, you see, the eye is like a camera. It focuses things. But in the night they are developed – by the mind first, then by the heart!' He jerked himself up and looked outside the door, shuddered, closed it. His eyes flickered to the window.

'There's nobody there.'

He leant back and sighed, his hands in his lap. I noticed their long, elaborate fingers, the hands of an El Greco saint. 'For us, even to imagine women is mortal sin. Yes, even to think, let alone to touch. That is the doctrine of our Church.' Narcissistic in its self-contempt, his voice trembled between sensuality and disgust. Neither he nor I could tell which god he was embracing. 'You see we priest-monks are so cloistered, so enclosed . . . Things inflame us. If I so much as glimpse a young girl, the Devil . . .' He stopped and lifted his eyes to the ceiling. 'Then I cry "O my Christ! O Saviour! Help me!" And He comes to my aid and gives me peace.' The heavy lips curled. '*But in the night the Devil returns her to me.*'

'You can't help what happens when you're asleep.'

'But I must wake up and pray, wake up and pray.' He clutched at his thighs. 'If I can fall asleep with a prayer on my lips, then I am absolved. If it happens then, it is only the Devil trying to abuse me.'

I felt as if I could no more help him than I could have reached some mediaeval penitent, or an inmate of those frescoed Byzantine hells. Eras separated us. Every day he leapt up to his God, and was pulled down.

But I heard myself say absurdly, in an almost parental tone: 'I haven't seen you at refectory meals. Have you been eating?'

He grimaced with that Levantine mixture of fierceness and effeminacy. 'I saw the deacon killing a chicken yesterday. Ugh! I don't want to eat it, or anything. Not for days.'

He had been almost twenty years in Italy and the United States, he said, living as a monk. Now he had come back, and had been promised a small parish near Larnaca. That was what he wanted. Somewhere to rest and die. 'The morality abroad is disgusting. I cannot tell you . . . the filth . . .' He loathed his own sin in others. They held a mirror to him and he wanted to smash it. There was no good man in the world. Priests were either hypocrites or fools. Even his cross, he said, fondling it, had once been inlaid with precious stones of which he had been cheated. His voice had turned quiet. He looked exhausted. 'In America I was corrupted. I have done such terrible things. I paid with a nervous breakdown.' He touched the cross to his lips. 'But now, thank Christ, I am back here. For ever.'

His cell was filled with possessions: a tape-recorder, gramophone and all sorts of expensive electrical equipment which he had bought in Los Angeles and which was now heaped in a corner, unwanted. Over his bed were icons which he had painted himself. He said: 'I find comfort in our predecessors who have triumphed.' His gaze devoured them. They stared grimly back. 'Our faith, you see, is like a family of which each generation has left treasures in the house. Saints, teachings, traditions. And we are the inheritors.' But he sank his head in his hands, unable to bear the stare of the icons – he had painted them savage. 'I am fallen too far, too far. Even God's patience must have a limit.'

'The Bible says not.'

'But the demons claim some men even on earth.' Now the fever had returned to his eyes. His hands stretched taut over his ribs; his voice had risen. 'When I pray I can feel snakes clutching at me. I swear it. They catch me in the back. They suffocate me when I try to pray.'

'No . . .'

'You think I'm mad?' he blazed. 'I feel them, I tell you. Haven't you noticed that sometimes I put my hands around my shoulders, touching my back?'

Yes, I had noticed.

'At night the pain is excruciating. By God, I tell you, I'm mortally afraid.'

He began to weep. The tears sidled from the corners of his eyes and one by one rolled down behind the dark glasses which he kept between himself and other eyes. 'I often weep.' Sorrow and astonishment touched me, and a revulsion which I could not break. I remained fixed in my chair. I wanted to tell him that it was his penitence, not his sin, which was disquieting. He had probably done no more than the next man. But he did not seem to be asking for help. He was already doomed. I recalled paintings of the Orthodox hell in mountain churches, and there rose in my memory frescoes of the damned twined by spotted snakes, which bit them.

He whispered on: 'I'm scared to death. Surely the time will come when God will spit me out? I am only alive by His grace.'

'You waste yourself on introspection,' I said curtly. 'That's an abuse of God's gifts.'

'You're right, you're right.' He clutched at any straw. 'God is sweet, so sweet to me. I tell you, when I have prayed and my prayer is answered, this cross gives out a perfume. It scents the whole room.' Out of his haunted world, he actually smiled. His lips still glistened with tears at their corners, in a beard turning grey. Then again I saw that look as if he was half in love with sin, half with God. He spat violently on the floor. 'But am I any better than that spittle?' he groaned. 'I've committed horrors ... I've shaken the heavens. God is the ocean of sweetness. *But I go back to sin as a dog to its vomit.*'

I started down the long, straight road to Salamis and to those tombs and tumuli, the city's royal necropolis, which had pervaded the horizon for days. They go back seven and eight centuries before Christ to a time when the Dark Age had lifted to reveal Alassia in ruins and Salamis the first city of Cyprus. In legend its founder was the Greek hero Teucer, brother of Ajax and son of Telamon, king of the isle of Salamis who brought Achaean hosts to the siege of Troy; and archaeology has confirmed the tradition by uncovering here remains from the Heroic Age.

The necropolis lay outside the western gates. I entered its tumulus down an avenue of baked brick and dressed stone, which still showed the marks of the pyre on which the body of its unknown king had been cremated two and a half millennia before. But in the burial chamber at its core the grandeur of the avenue and the towering hillock dwindled to a film of dust and some cubic feet of darkness. On its blocks, and on the stone plug heaved from its entranceway, the chisel marks showed fresh and white. Buried as a sacrifice in the earth filling of the ramp, lay one of the small, swift chariots shown in contemporary vase-painting, with the bones of its two horses still clamped in harness. Nearby was the impress of a rotted spear in the ground, some seven feet long, a round shield and one of the silver-riveted swords of which Homer sang. Lying near the traces of the hearse, with the iron bits still in their teeth and blinkers over their eye-sockets, were the skeletons of other horses, together with standards shaped like nine-petalled flowers, bronze horse-armour, pendants and bells.

Could anything, I wondered, more perfectly evoke the Homeric age – Patroclus, the beloved of Achilles, laid on the funeral pyre at the close of *The Iliad*? His corpse, in the great epic, was smeared with animal fat, sheep and cattle slaughtered round him and piled with jars of honey and oil such as were found in this very tumulus. And Achilles 'cast on the pyre four high-necked horses, groaning aloud as he did so'* and drenched the earth with wine. Then the bones were gathered in a golden vase and a mound raised over the tomb. 'They designed his barrow,' says Homer, 'by laying down a ring of stone revetments round the pyre. Then they fetched earth and piled it up inside.'

All through the royal necropolis the giant-stoned tomb-chambers were mostly rifled centuries ago, but in a few were still found the cremated remains of the dead wrapped in cloth like those of the Homeric heroes, their ashes mingled with jewellery and placed in cauldrons, or the bodies inhumed. The great ramps which sloped down to them have preserved the same warrior's sacrifices: the decayed chariots with metal trappings scattered enigmatically, the skeletons of the horses half fossilized, their ribs collapsed and their legs and necks – delicate, for the breed was small – outstretched to one another in a heraldic dance. But they were killed incompetently, still yoked in the entranceways. The necks of some were broken as they twisted in panic, and one of a pair of hearse-drawing asses, on seeing its companion killed, seems to have torn loose from its harness and was stoned and suffocated in the earth fillings.

In several ramps the bones of men were uncovered, prob-ably of servants who accompanied their masters in death. Achilles had sacrificed on the pyre of Patroclus twelve of the high-born youths of Troy, and at Salamis too the victims had not all gone willingly; the feet and wrists of one man were tied.

In another grave, the richest found in Cyprus,

* Homer, *The Iliad*. Trs. E. V. Rieu.

347

the breastplates of the horses were covered in Assyrian ornament. Amongst the funerary furniture was an ivory and silver throne, like the chair of Penelope, Ulysses' queen, and a wide, ivory bed, whose headpiece showed a frieze of gods kneeling in the graceful Egyptian way. The feel of the East – Assyria, Phoenicia, Egypt – is never far. The half-barbarian monarchs lay on couches and sat at tables whose delicacy was not theirs. Almost everything luxurious and refined was attributed by Homer to the Phoenicians in his day, like the silver mixing-bowl which Achilles offered in the funeral games and whose equal was found in these tombs: 'the loveliest thing in the world, for Sidonian craftsmen wrought it cunningly, and Phoenician traders sailed it over the misty sea . . .'

Homer probably lived in the eighth century, precisely when these first sepulchres were built. Yet with their long ramps and their sacrifice of horses and slaves in honour of the dead, they were typical of the Achaean heyday at the fall of Troy four hundred years before – everything except the custom of cremation, which arrived with Cycladic Greeks early in the eighth century. Of all lands Cyprus preserved the Achaean culture most purely, and its people, like many others, claimed Homer as a fellow-countryman, citing an archaic prophecy of his birth:

> In sea-eaten Cyprus will be a great singer
> Themisto will bear him in the fields, a godlike
>   woman,
> glorious far from the riches of Salamis:
> he will leave Cyprus sea-drenched, wave-lifted:

alone and first to chant the troubles of wide Greece:
*he shall not die or grow old for everlasting ages.**

It was as if the whole necropolis belonged to that twilight where legend and history mingle, and the memory of the gods is still fresh among men.

Since mediaeval times the last tomb on the road to Salamis has done service as a Christian chapel called the 'Prison of St Catherine' from a belief that the saint was interned there for her faith. But it had nothing to do with this controversial lady; it was a sepulchre like the rest, its ramp hidden under the ground, and for centuries the devout walked into it unknowing over the horses of Iron Age kings keeping their sacrifice under the entrance. Yet the Christian belief lingered, and peering into the burial chamber I saw on one side a Swedish student of archaeology making notes about *dromoi*, while on the other a peasant woman was striking her head softly on the stone, and crying on the saint.

I emerged into sunlight again. To my left the Roman aqueduct from Kythrea went limping over the plain, while in front of me two miles of ramparts had once locked Salamis against the sea. Their walls, buried and soft with trees, showed no more than a sandy bank where I walked, and even the square Byzantine towers, built inside the older bastions when they fell, stood shoulder-high in grass. Beyond, the city was so barren and enormous that tourists were motoring about it on tarmac roads.

---

* Pausanias, *Guide to Greece*. Trs. Peter Levi.

Already rich when her early kings were wheeled to their tombs, the city by the fifth century B.C. was so powerful that she headed the first rebellion of the island states against Persia. Onesilus it was – his head was soon to hang on the walls of Amathus – who closed the gates of Salamis against his brother, the Persophile king. But the Persian strength was too much for him, and in the battle on the plains of Salamis, which saw the treachery of Curium and the valour of Soli, he and his cause were both destroyed.

But by the end of the fifth century the city had again bred a remarkable man. Evagoras claimed descent from the royal dynasty of Teucer, and set himself the task of freeing and uniting all Cyprus. With a handful of friends he returned to Salamis from exile and overthrew the Phoenician puppet-ruler in a palace *coup*. Yet he convinced the Persians of his loyalty, and paid his tribute while he grew stronger. Athens was his ally all through his life, and Athenian refugees swelled his court and armies. When one by one the Cypriot towns fell to him – even Kition and Amathus, the bastions of Persia – he turned them steadily towards Greece and replaced the cumbersome Cypriot syllabary with the Greek alphabet. As for Salamis, she was called the most Hellenic city of her day, and her constitution was more democratic than any in Greece.

The writings which preserve Evagoras are as much panegyric as history, but by his achievements alone he must have been a remarkable man. He did not remain idle while Persia prepared her attack, but crossed to Cilicia and rallied all its cities to his cause, with the rulers of Caria, Lycia and Pisidia; then, entering into alliance with the King of the

Arabs, he invaded Phoenicia, seized Tyre and deprived the Persians of any port from which to launch an assault on his country.

This was his zenith – dazzling but too precarious. The huge Persian force which subdued Cilicia and ferried across the straits to the Karpas peninsula found his strength hollow. His allies were little use and the core of his army a mere six thousand hoplites. Brilliantly he prolonged his fate. He attacked the Persian fleet and created such discord by diplomacy that the invaders, faced with mutiny in their forces, entered into treaty with him. So Evagoras remained king of Salamis, but of no more, and paid his Persian tribute as a king to a king, dying by assassination six years later in a sordid domestic plot.

The city recovered from its wounds and remained the champion of Hellenism. When Alexander was besieging Tyre the king of Salamis sailed to his aid and was rewarded with the copper-town of Tamassos; and eight years later the king's sons were commanding Macedonian warships on the Indus. But in the divided world of Alexander's successors, the greatness of Salamis waned. It continued the island's largest city, but the Ptolemies built a rival to its harbour, and took the capital to Paphos. The last king, Nicocreon, fell out with Ptolemy I and slew himself rather than fall into the hands of his enemy. Not one of his relatives survived him. His queen, Axiothea, killed their daughters and committed suicide with all his female relatives, while his brothers set fire to the palace and fell on their swords. When his cenotaph was uncovered in the royal necropolis, it was found to contain no bodies (for these were immolated under the palace ruins) but portrait statues of the dead. Moulded around wooden frames for the fleeting ceremonial of the pyre, they had baked hard in the flames, and had been preserved under the tumulus which was raised to quiet the dead souls and to honour the last of the great kings.

All afternoon and evening I walked over the smothered city. Sometimes through groves of eucalyptus and bitter little pines, sometimes where the sea winds had spread sand, I trod hour after hour over the sinews of a man-made land. Here and there hewn stones broke the surface or pottery clinked underfoot; but more often only the blurred geometry of mounds surrounded me with its disquiet and with a half-pleasurable melancholy under the tired trees. Once, in an excavated clearing, a tessellated pavement told me that I was standing in an early church; once I came upon the granite columns of a forum, all toppled; and beyond, as I waded through a field of barley, my feet scraped on Roman mosaic.

In the theatre the tiers of seats rose unbroken, their steep stairways all in place. Lower down they even kept their limestone facing and concave lips, and the plinths of statues were carved with inscriptions to the late emperors. I stood there bemused. It was as if the audience had only just left, the city councillors risen from their marble seats. But a moment later I realized that the upper rows were restored and that above them, resting on a huge network of radiating buttresses, other tiers had once doubled the auditorium's height, seating fifteen thousand.

The baths, with their vents and pools and hypocausts elaborately intact, opened onto a gymnasium whose forty marble columns surrounded it in glistening porticoes. High in the eastern colonnade these fluted titans, carved all of a piece, showed the sureness of Rome which cut its stones in the measure of its empire, to last for ever. Their veins rippled like water. At their end statues stood round a pool, their heads lopped off by Christian bigotry, leaving only jagged necks and the drip of marble robes.

It was in Christian years, after terrible earthquakes, that these columns were set up again – often in the wrong places and crowned with too-small capitals. The baths were re-developed and the latrines prudishly walled across. Figures of Zeus and Apollo, half pardoned, continued to stand along the corridors, decapitated, but the naked Aphrodites and Hermaphrodites were hurled into the drains. The great gymnasium square was no longer a symbol of physical achievement, the glory of the body, but an annex to cleansing baths in a time obsessed with guilt and purification.

A long way to the south I found the main forum, probably the largest in the world, and coarse in its dereliction. Up its avenue the drums of pillars tilted in half-excavated trenches. In their day no doubt, stuccoed and painted, and restored by Augustus, they had seemed grand enough, and at their end a ruined temple to Olympian Zeus shone with marble steps which I mounted into nothing.

These Roman years were not peaceful. During the revolt of the Jews in A.D. 116 – their colony had been large even when St Paul preached – massacres depopulated much of the city. For centuries afterwards no Jew was allowed to set foot on the island and even shipwrecked Hebrew sailors were slaughtered by the vindictive peasants.

But in A.D. 350 the Byzantines christened the city Constantia and once more it became the capital. The pillars of this period suddenly lose their classical dignity and sicken into sugar-white capitals, the veined floors are beautiful with another beauty, and the colonettes which prop the sky are no longer Rome's, but are a trifle effeminate. In these basilicas Byzantium has not found its voice. It is still, architecturally, picking the bones of the classical world. And soon the Arab invasions ground Constantia to ruin, the harbour silted up and the sand eased over it.

I reached the harbour after sunset, and spread out my sleeping-bag on the shore. The sea glistened dully. Near the shore a swarm of minnows gnawed at a dead fish which was shedding its scales over the waves. I fell asleep quickly, but woke again after a few hours. A three-quarter moon was bulging from the sky. I sat bolt upright, scratching sand-flies out of my hair and forgetting where I was. Then I saw the dunes bright with moonlight, and the trees crawling over them, their trunks shining flesh-white and all laid westward by the winter wind. I struggled out of my sleeping-bag and stepped down to the sea's edge. There was no other sound. The fish's backbone, picked clean, glinted in the shallows. I waded in, parting liquid moonlight, and swam. It was colder than I had thought, and so still was the water that the moon dropped its light unbroken into the deep. Here, where the first quinqueremes had sailed, I saw far beneath my feet the breakwater of the ancient harbour curving into darkness out to sea, then broken and scattered.

CHAPTER FIFTEEN
············
The Karpas

The ancients likened the shape of Cyprus to a deerskin spread on the sea, tapering to a long tail at the Karpas peninsula which is carried towards Lebanon by the last thrust of the Kyrenia mountains. In recent centuries the isolation of Karpasia saved it from Turkish troubles, but the coasts were exposed instead to Maltese privateers who laid waste whole tracts. The inhabitants are still sparse; they grow tobacco, carob and a little corn, and are grazers of flocks. Their solitude has preserved them in old customs. A few of the women keep the laced bodices and white Syrian trousers of a century ago, and some fairness of skin or hair, with a greater beauty, betray Venetian blood, or that of immigrants from Asia Minor. In the last century these people were a law to themselves; they cut the throats of stray travellers, and their sexual morals were rumoured light.

The first and last man to penetrate the area in depth – the scholar David Hogarth – travelled here on horseback in 1888 and mapped out its fallen cities. Since then a road has been built for fifty miles up the peninsula, but the coasts remain empty and their ruins unknown; so I determined on walking along its length.

But now the summer heat had become ferocious; it shook and dazzled the whole sky. All morning like the strokes of a giant hammer, the sun clanged on the earth. Already the trees had the passive, colourless look of drought, and the birds were dazed to silence in their branches. The turned fields could almost be heard to crumble, the ground cracking apart. Only the corn moved faintly at my passage, then stood all day under the sky's fire with blackening ears.

Towards noon I crept into Trikomo, the home town of General Grivas. Slogans for ENOSIS blazed on every wall, and I noticed that the engraved initials of the British sovereign had been hacked from the concrete freshwater fountains which were installed all over the island. I sheltered in the jewel-like church of Ayios Yakovos, which so bewitched Queen Marie of Roumania that she copied it for her private chapel on the Black Sea, and emerged into the cooling day to wander round the coast towards the cape where Hogarth had seen the ruins of Cnidus.* And there they were still, but more formless than even he had seen, with the fields half ploughed over them.

The promontory of Gastria beyond, where the Templars had erected a castle, held nothing but rock-hewn foundations and cisterns filled with stones. In the Lusignan wars against Frederick II its harbour was used by Jean d'Ibelin crossing from Beirut to rescue the royal family, and years later Henry II, defeated by his brother and by the Templars, sailed away to exile beneath the hostile fortress. But he did not forget the place, and on his restoration destroyed it so

---

* Not the famous Cnidus, in Caria.

thoroughly that I could find no wall by which to shelter. On its summit at dusk I watched the Karpas mountains blacken, and in the dark I slid down to the harbour where the vessels of troubled rulers had come and gone, and slept peacefully.

In the hour's coolness before sunrise, the towers of Kantara castle showed on a dawn sky.

But within an hour of daybreak, haze had turned the mountains unreal. The world was plunged back into furnace. Dazed under its brightness, I followed a little road instead of finding my own track. Along it the villages had been deserted by their young; only the old sat under the trellises of the eternal coffee-house, slouched in clothes gone to seed, eyes half closed under straw hats. These were curious hamlets, even in architecture. Gothic arches appeared in the house arcades; the Lusignan lion (or was it the Venetian or the Mameluke?) had been carved pop-eyed on gates and consoles; and other walls were hung with amphorae – whole museums of village pottery, in which pigeons were kept for their manure.

It was in one of these hamlets that I met an old man who had spent his youth as a waiter in London. He was sitting at the entrance to the village store with a look of deferential abstraction. When I asked the storekeeper for bread and was told that there was none – the baker came from a village miles away – this man rose with a faint bow. He was dressed in frayed, pin-stripe trousers, and a black waistcoat flapping open, too tight for him now. 'I will find you bread, sir. Certainly.'

'You speak fine English.'

He bowed again. 'I was a waiter, sir, at the Piccadilly Hotel.'

I bowed back.

'But you would not remember the hotel as I knew it. It was bombed during the Second War. A great tragedy.' He shook his silvered head. His fingers strayed over his chest where the waistcoat buttons had once met. 'I don't know how it is now, but then it was a first-rate hotel, if I may say so. Top notch.'

I wondered if he had actually said that. 'I'm sorry?'

'Top notch,' he repeated more slowly. 'You must please excuse me . . . Your bread . . .'

Now he was up and walking in a responsible, delicate way along the street, weaving a little as if between tables. I stared down at my trousers and made a surreptitious gesture at dusting them, half imagining myself in a foyer. But in three minutes he was back.

'I have put a little cheese with it, sir. I think you'll find that satisfactory.' He had brought the bread from his own home, and I had scarcely thanked him before he was gone.

I picked my way across wheat fields all afternoon towards Kantara. And all afternoon the castle receded before me. Birds sang with a lonely clarity from nowhere I could discern. Even the cistus flowers had died, leaving their seeds in tight-leaved chalices, and the maquis was a ghost underfoot, coated with the webs of dead spiders. It was evening before I stood astride the mountain ridge and from that stillness looked down two thousand feet onto the north coast, whose pygmy estuaries and capes carved out the sea in blue. On either side the wooded ranges ran into infinity, while before me, a fanfare of towers, Kantara rode its peak high and alone in the sun.

I knew as much of its history as is common to all these eyries: built by Byzantines, rebuilt by Crusaders, never stormed. Yet Kantara looked less like a fortress in history than a castle from German folk-tale, where the green hand of an ogre turns the dungeon key, or clouds enfold a pure-hearted king. Those towers, I thought as I climbed sweating on, could never come closer. They were the towers of a dreaming child. And I approached almost delicately, as if something must be damaged, or something untrue.

Then, slowly, I saw the ruin of its crenellations, how the sky pierced a window, shrubs scaled the parapets. The king was poor. Or the princess slept. A wall was cracked, an entrance gaped open; soon black breaches appeared, as if scooped away. Yet the castle was still formidable. It hung out its bastions on the strength of the rock; the horseshoe towers of the barbican stood above its winding access, and a curtain wall loomed behind.

As I reached it the sun, as if to complete the Piranesi landscape, was setting over the sea. It became an ellipse, a gory skull, until the tide was turned to blood, and sky and water mingled. I climbed through the barbican and up under the waiting walls. But the entrance was locked. Almost in darkness, I crawled under its spiked iron gate and settled in a turret of the ward. I fell asleep while still eating the old man's bread and cheese.

Kantara, wrote Hogarth, 'looks out over the two seas of the Carpas, and who built it and why, no one had been able to say.' But it seems that it was raised in the tenth century to keep a watch on the Seljuks, and in Lusignan times the faction of Frederick II was besieged by the Royalists who shattered the outer works with shots from a giant catapult. We hear too of the Prince of Antioch escaping to the castle from Genoese captivity with the help of his cook, who dressed him as a scullion, covering him with smuts, 'And he put a copper pot on his head and a little copper pot in his hand . . . and took him to Kantara.'[*]

The sun, shining through the slit window, woke me. Two crows were standing on the sill. The early light showed up nothing inside the bastions but steps which circled and disintegrated among pines, yet the towers themselves enclosed chambers which were complete even to their passageways, and on the summit was a ruined chapel. Its single window enclosed a map-like view. Along the range to either side of me the crags lifted in Gothic pinnacles of rock. Like an exile or a hawk I could look down on the near shores, where a frayed sea rubbed round cities decayed in their harbours: Pergamon with its tombs and monoliths; the cape of Acheon Acte; Aphroditessa. Southward the terraced hills bulged and rippled into the Mesaoria, whose yellow was not of barrenness but of corn. On brilliant days you may see half the Karamanian Taurus banked over the sea, and eastward, more than a hundred miles away, the snows of Lebanon shining in the sky.

But at Kantara all Cyprus narrows to the fifty-mile pencil of the Karpas. From coast to coast it nowhere measures

---

[*] Leontios Makhairas, *Recital concerning Cyprus*. Trs. R. M. Dawkins.

more than eight miles across. Tramping along its backbone, I felt as if I was walking along a parapet in space, so thin was it, as though the ridge must soon snap off into air. Butterflies flew over its maquis – green and yellow, black barred with cream, pale orange.

But now at last the great mountain range, which had started far west of Kyrenia, was breaking up. The Jurassic peaks no longer burst along its spine, and all at once it foundered into separated hills, and the whole earth from sea to sea was filled with a pale flame of corn. Swathed and booted women were reaping with sickles on the knolls. They turned to stare at me. The hills stood isolated in a golden lake.

The driver of an old tractor, lumbering behind me, motioned enthusiastically to the trailer, so I hoisted myself up and sat down on its boards. In the corner opposite, fast asleep with her crinkled hands folded on her stomach, lay his mother. She was so small that she had slipped neatly into the softness between two sacks, and the lines of her face ran together at a tiny, dry-looking mouth which seemed to be smiling. Although what had she to smile about, I wondered, breaking her ancient body in the fields?

The corn passed on either side of us; the dogs which basked against the stooks were no longer English hounds but the yellow half-wolves of Syria. It was another sign of the Karpas isolation.

'Holy Virgin!' squeaked a voice. 'Where have you come from?'

The old lady slapped her cheeks and adjusted a pair of spectacles, which were tied round her headscarf with a piece of dirty string.

'I've come from Kantara.'

'*Él!*' she cried. 'From the Houses of the Queen!'

At Kantara, she said, the Queen had sat on a throne and gazed on the lands below; but nobody had heard of her since before the time of grandfathers. She was probably dead, or just disappeared like most of *ta pagana*, 'the pagan ones'. You didn't see them so much any more.

She settled down to polishing her spectacles on her skirt. 'When I was a girl,' she went on, 'the old people had all seen the pagan ones, or at least heard them. Any night after Christmas, if you didn't keep indoors, you might end up in the mud. The *kallikantzari* would tweak and trip you.' She laughed creakily. 'I remember years when it wasn't safe to leave the shutters open or they'd slip in and smash things.'

These *kallikantzari* are ancient survivors. In their most common, blackskinned form they stand no taller than a ten-year-old boy, but beneath the waistline their bodies suddenly grow shaggy and blend into the legs of a goat. They are, in fact, satyrs, left high and dry in remote regions of the Greek world by the ebbing tide of paganism. Unruly, malformed and lecherous, their period of activity – the twelve nights between Christmas and Epiphany – is mercifully short, but at this time they run amok in village streets and fields, trampling on latecomers or whirling them into dance. Then it is prudent to leave offerings of pork or dough on the roofs and doorsteps, although wine is their favourite, and to stay at home. Even so, the *kallikantzari* may urinate down the chimney in the hope of putting out the fire and dropping into the room, or barge through the doors and gorge themselves on whatever lies to hand, smashing crockery and furniture, and fouling the water jars.

But fortunately they are thick-headed. They are absurdly gullible, and terrified of fire. In Greece the swiftest way to deal with a *kallikantzaros* is to ask it to count the holes in a sieve; since it cannot count above two, this will occupy it until dawn. On the twelfth night the village priest hunts them from each house with incense, in exchange for an offertory – censing the *kallikantzari* is one of his regular sources of income – and the brutes are banished for another year.

By now our tractor-drawn cart was lurching over a path so rutted that the old woman had stood up to grip the sides with little simian hands and cry Holy Virgin. 'It's old people like me,' she said, 'who have to look out for *kallikantzari*. They're a rough crowd and they get you from behind.'

'Don't you ever see one?'

'Not now.' She rubbed her pale eyes. 'And before only once – as a young woman.'

'What was it up to?'

Her forehead wrinkled with remembering. She seemed surprised by my curiosity. 'Up to? He wasn't up to anything. Just sitting on a heap of manure.' She added crossly: 'That's the sort of thing they do. Dirty as Arabs. So I asked "What are you doing here?" and he said "I'm just a *kallikantzaros*" and dashed off.'

The cart hit a bump. It jerked her clean off her feet, for her eyes and her mouth, still talking, came momentarily level with mine. Then she landed, her hands clutched the rail again and with no more than a routine *Panayia* she went on: 'This *kallikantzaros* was about three feet high with tufts of brown hair, and he had blood on him. They eat the blood of pork in the roads.'

'And what about his head?' I curled my hands.

'Big horns? No. He was quite a young one.' She put her fingers to her brow in a pair of pubescent feelers bent acutely forward. 'Don't you have *kallikantzari* in England?'

'No.'

'*Ehé!*' she cried in disbelief.

'I've never seen one,' I corrected.

She said philosophically: 'Too many cities, I expect. They don't like cities . . .'

By now the cart was jolting so violently that she went back to canvassing the saints while I stopped talking altogether and sat down on the boards. Long after the tractor had dropped me, and the woman's fluttering hand had lost its farewell among the corn, I lay under an olive tree feeling sleepy and faintly sick, while heavy-mailed insects droned and buzzed.

Evening brought me to the ruins of Kanakaria, whose monastery has left behind a misshapen church. Inside, piers and arches stood independently of walls built at later times, supporting nothing. But over the conch of the apse spread a mosaic of the Virgin and Child even older than the mosaic of Kiti, and three quarters effaced. The bust of one angel still spurted a gold-blue wing, but of the other only the open hand survived in amputated adoration, and the Virgin showed little but a silhouette. The tesserae were larger than those of Kiti, coarser; the villagers used to chip them off in the belief that they cured skin disease. Alone in his preservation, throned on the lap of an obliterated Mother, the Christ Child shone above me with the look of a boy-emperor, and dangled a gold-shod foot as if he might descend.

'Have you eaten?' The ginger-bearded priest looked at me worriedly. I had slumped down in the coffee-shop of a neighbouring village, after walking through the twilight from Kanakaria He handed me some vegetables (how thin was I looking, I wondered?) and a loaf stamped with a roundel which announced 'Jesus conquers.' It was Communion bread; but none of the semi-circle of stupendously whiskered old men who surrounded me looked surprised.

'Should I be eating this?' I asked nobody in particular.

'Yes! Eat!' bellowed a red-faced ancient – a Father Christmas out of season. 'They bake it on Saturdays and if there is any left over the priest gives it away. Take advantage!'

He handed me a penknife. I tried to dig it into the crust, but it slid off; the loaf was like a circle of varnished wood. Baked on Saturday; today was Thursday. Smiling weakly at the priest, I pulled out my own penknife which was very sharp, excavated a hole in the crust and worked my teeth into it. The pantheon of old men watched my progress and punctuated my mouthfuls with questions. Why was I walking? Where had I come from? Why was I alone? Where was I going?

I answered through bread-clogged teeth that tomorrow I was going to see the great cave-tomb near Ayios Symeon.

'Tomb?' cried Father Christmas at once. 'That's not a tomb. That's the summer palace of the Queen. Her army retreated there in the off-season.'

A shiver of assent passed along the fountains of white moustaches. And I suddenly wanted to get to the root of this Queen of whom they talked so matter-of-factly.

Extracting my teeth from the bread, I asked: 'How long ago did she live there?'

Nobody knew; but a frail-voiced man said: 'It was before my time. My father used to talk of her, though.' He rested back in his chair, sighing. 'Yes, he might have seen her.'

'But she never stayed in one place,' added another. 'She had castles all over the island. Kantara, St Hilarion, Buffavento. You had to have a pass to get into them . . .'

'You mustn't believe that,' said the frail man in his weak, confiding whisper. Their heads all leant forward conspiratorially. 'There were, you see, many Queens. One at Kantara, one at Vouni, one at Ayios Symeon . . .'

'No! No!' He was shouted down.

'Was she Aphrodite?' I asked in exasperation.

Father Christmas plucked the cigarette from his mouth. 'Certainly not,' he said severely. 'Aphrodite lived at Paphos. This Queen lived everywhere.' He stubbed the cigarette on his boot. 'Although why the goddess chose such a hole as Paphos I don't know. And as far as the palace at Ayios Symeon is concerned, you can't get in. Its doorway is forty feet off the ground. Sheer.'

'I thought there was a ledge.'

'There is,' said the frail man. 'When I was a boy a tree grew near that ledge and once I climbed up it and crawled in.'

'You've been in?' The others stared at him with new respect. Under his papery skin the bones looked delicate as glass; so fragile was he, that the time when he had climbed a tree seemed unimaginably remote.

'Oh, yes. When I was a boy several of us got in.' The whisper of his voice hushed them all. 'It's a big palace, very dark. At the back there's a kind of well. Two criminals once ran away down that well and they found a passage and an enormous church. Yes, down there in the blackness under the mountain. On Sundays, they say, the incense used to come up thick as smoke. You could hear chanting . . .' He leant forward into the stillness of his listeners – their heads almost knocked together – and barely audibly, as if percolating from the deeps of the earth, a ghostly anthem rose from him:

And what is in the cup, the precious blood of Christ,
Transfigured by Thy Holy Spirit. Amen. Amen. Amen.

He drew out the last Amen to a silvery sigh, which died in total silence.

It is strange how these tales reproduce themselves. All over the Levant streams regurgitate lost garments or silverware in other lands; passageways re-emerge beyond distant hills or seas; cathedrals and mosques burgeon under the ground.

The frail man said: 'One thing's for certain. The Queen

367

was guarded by some curious animals. Did you know that? They sat at the entrance to the castles, and you showed them your pass. This is known, because one of them was found at Ayia Varvara near here.'

'That's true,' said another man. 'Get Giorgios.'

'Yes!' The snowy heads wagged in concord. 'Get Giorgios!'

A moment later a young man was pulled bleary-eyed into the coffee-shop. His hair was still tousled from sleep and his clothes crumpled. He stood bewildered and oddly clean-shaven among the rest, like a hunter surrounded by Arctic walruses.

'Giorgios' father found the animal,' they said.

The man looked at me emptily, as if this were all part of an idiotic dream, which in a way it was.

'Yes,' he blurted. 'About forty years ago. They took it to Nicosia.'

This was perfectly true. I had seen it in the Cyprus Museum – a crowned sphinx of the first century B.C., winged as the Ionian, but not the Egyptian sphinxes are.

'It had the body of a lioness,' Giorgios went on, 'but a woman's head and breasts.'

'I remember it too!' cried Father Christmas suddenly. 'A beautiful creature. And its breasts, I must tell you, were magnificent. Very round and high, like pomegranates . . .'

'How could it be beautiful,' carped the priest, 'with the body of a lioness?'

'It was,' he insisted. 'A face to dream of. And – who knows? – perhaps the lioness' body was beautiful to a lion. Yes, apart from the human torso I believe a lion would be similarly enticed . . .'

A storm of laughter shook the circle, even the priest and the sleepy Giorgios.

The frail man said: 'Perhaps it was a portrait of the Queen.'

'Certainly!' shouted Father Christmas, who was quite carried away. 'After all, in those days it was nothing to couple with a lion, or even a bull. Think of the Minotaur . . .'

An hour later, thinking of the Minotaur but anxious to walk for an hour in coolness, I wandered on in the direction of Ayios Symeon. Night had fallen. The air was still, and I loitered on my way, listening to the owls which echoed one another over the fields. Suddenly two torches shone on me together. I stopped stupidly in their light. They shone in silence, inspecting me, like the twin eyes of some fabulous but hesitant monster. In the end I walked up against them to find a pair of Turkish soldiers with their rifles unslung, staring at me quizzically. One of them – a heavy man with the wide, smooth-jowled look of the Mongol, said in English: 'Are you alone?'

'Yes.'

'Why?'

I faltered and tried: 'Nobody would come with me.'

'No wonder.' He looked through my papers, which were in order, and there began the slow transformation between official suspicion and natural friendliness. At last he smiled. 'Did you realize you were entering a Turkish area?'

'I'd forgotten.'

He laughed and shouldered his rifle. 'You're obviously not a Greek.'

'I was looking for a place to camp.'

He said at once: 'Stay in my house. There are snakes round here.' And he walked on with me to the half-lit village. 'I was four years in England,' he said, 'in a canning factory at Newton Abbot, twisting a knob day after day – twist, twist, twist. In the end I got fed up and came back home. What sort of life is that for a man – twist, twist, twist?'

We reached his house. He had a strangely negroid daughter who stood in the doorway in a nightdress, sucking her fingers. Two of the four rooms were occupied by goats, which poked their noses through holes in the walls, and threatened to break out. Hogarth considered these Moslem villages to be not Turkish at all, but Greeks forcibly converted to Islam. They are 'almost ignorant of Turkish,' he wrote, and the 'women rarely veil, but stare at or speak to western strangers in presence of the men.' But in such areas, cut off from the Turkish mainstream, three centuries can go far towards assimilating a minority; and the negro girl was a sign of Turkish blood, for the Turks, not the Greeks, took Africans as slaves. But the loss of their language is strange, for the Moslems of Cyprus speak an old-fashioned Turkish, which they have kept pure, while the Greek dialect is rustic and slurred; (as early as classical times a Greek traveller answered his friend, who complained of the solecisms in his letter, that when he reached Cyprus he would send them by the bushel.)

The soldier's wife was a big woman whose mouthful of superb teeth stretched in an animal smile. She commanded me to eat beans and goat's meat, and stood over me with arms akimbo so that every time I stopped she shouted 'Eat! Eat!', as the Arabs do, and her red, round face looked as if it would burst at the wrinkles with pleasure. The stoop of her sunken breasts was enormous – she had had thirteen children, and nine of them, all boys, had died in infancy.

'But why?' I asked.

'God knows. God knows best. They were not strong.'

'Just that?'

'Yes. Just that. A person must be strong to live.'

She brought me tea in which cinnamon wood floated. The English liked tea; she remembered that. I was placed in the second room for the night, in a bed under one of those immense, baroque mirrors which the Ottomans, defenceless against nineteenth century French taste, loved and copied all over their empire.

I remembered what it was like to sleep in a Turkish village again. The Moslem will not kill animals unless he must. He lets them die. Even the fatally diseased dogs had not all been exterminated, and barks and howls filled the night from end to end – hundreds, there seemed – repeating one another on far hills. Early in the morning an old *hajji* in a white-turbaned fez stooped in the mosque porch and let out his immemorial bidding.

> *Up to prayer,*
> *Up to salvation,*
> *Prayer is better than sleep.*

But the village slept on.

North-east of Ayios Symeon the hills disperse around a corridor of tobacco-filled valleys where settlers from Asia

Minor filtered in remote ages. From far away I saw the cave-tomb hanging alone in a barren cliffside, apparently inaccessible. Hogarth, on a blazing July day, had tethered his horse under its height and scaled the five hundred-foot ascent, 'a foretaste of purgatory.' Nothing had changed, as I climbed in his steps. The very thorns might have been immortal, and the scar of winter rivers in the stone. High up, a crumbling shelf ran beneath the tomb entrance like a natural fault all along the cliff. I reached it by unsure footholds, and started to wriggle along flat on my stomach under the overhanging rock. Disintegrated sandstone littered the ledge in soft hunks like cake. The feet of birds had left twig-like patterns in its dust. I looked below, and froze. Across the valley the hills seemed tiny. By now the shelf had almost crumbled away, leaving a width of six inches. The cliff fell forty feet to rock. I stopped looking down. A few yards farther, sweating with more than the heat, I twisted my head round and realized that the entrance was directly above me.

I walked with amazement into aisles of sepulchral chambers. The footprints of birds were numberless over the floor. On all sides black entrances showed other chambers carved in the tender rock and rank with bats' urine. Through these the dead had lain under niches, corridor by corridor, sleeping in the filtered light of the mass sepulchre in a primitive peace.

A wealthy or royal family, I thought, must have hewn it in a secure time; but either robbers or fugitives used it later, and sliced out tunnels and windows near the entrance. At the back I found the well of which the frail man had spoken. Its sides were incised with slots as if some framework had been mounted in its mouth. I shone my torch down, but its beam, although powerful, reached nothing. I dropped a stone, but never heard it fall. 'I had neither the means nor the will to descend the shaft,' wrote Hogarth, 'more especially as persuasion and threats had alike failed to induce my servant to follow me up the cliff.' I too had no rope. But haunted by the tale of incense and the ghostly Amen, I put a match to a large sheet of paper and dropped it in. Knocking the walls, it descended the smooth, white gland of rock as if for ever, floating down until it became a star which died on the pit bottom, showing no cathedral, no subterranean river, but bare earth at a depth impossible to measure.

By the time I had wormed back along the ledge to safety, it was mid-morning. I followed the Lucha river, brash with oleanders, to the sea, and disturbed some twenty-five storks which lifted from the shore in alarm. Slowly they mounted and flew eastward, filling the sky with the leisurely beat of their going, led strangely by four seagulls which appeared to be guiding their flight; and within an hour they must have accomplished the journey to the headland which was to cost me five days to complete.

These days took me through a country of lunar wilderness. The inland fertility of wheat and tobacco was gone. And the furnace had intensified. Even the sea shone with a dead, too-bright glitter, and made no sound. The ranges gleamed like platinum, sank their flanks in powdery plains, crawled under the waves. Among their boulders little survived but the tough membrane of plants which the

Greeks call *phrygana*; all other shrubs – lentisk, terebinth, broom – had faded to a hetacomb of spikes. Towards midmorning, twisting round sandy headlands and bays, I would find my feet dragging in stupor, until I set my rucksack crunching down, peeled off my clothes and flopped into the sea.

Then, sheltering under some blackened tree, I would pass the midday hours too dazed to eat or think, and waited for the flailing sun to cross its meridian.

> *Grant we meet not the Dryads nor Dian face to face*
> *Nor Faunus, when at noon he walks abroad.*

Thus Ovid, on the 'Weirdness of Noonday', the hush and pause of nature feared by the ancients, and by remote peasants still. Then Pan walks abroad, and the nereids grow harmful. Even the cicadas cease to drill their dry, insistent nothingness. Time stops. The day is a held breath.

But at night mosquitoes and sandflies drove me from the coast to sleep on hillocks – a hundred feet higher was enough to escape them – with views of a moon-whitened sea or cold, star-filled skies. For three days I scarcely saw a soul. Centuries of piracy had emptied the shores. Once I came upon a shepherd washing his flock in the sea, and once upon an army lookout post, whose soldiers shared their lunch and sent me away with a warning not to tell their whereabouts. Loitering among rocks, the garrison of bored National Servicemen was successor to a long tradition; Persian, Seleucid, Roman sentries had all sweated out their exile on that bony strand, and watched the same sea for an enemy prow.

The peninsula is resonant with ruin. Destruction hit it time and again. It was a natural foothold for northern invaders. Somewhere near Aphrodisium is the legendary landing-place of Teucer and his Achaeans; and twice the Persian armies ferried over from Cilicia and carried their destruction through the hills towards Salamis. In 306 B.C. the Seleucid general Poliorcetes sacked the cities of Urania and Karpasia, and for centuries all the towns in the peninsula were tormented by Arab and Maltese raiders.

Formless, sometimes nameless – only Strabo described the region in antiquity – their melancholy heaps litter the shores on either side. A dusting of pottery, a mound of blocks, a ruined apse – and here some community flourished in classical or Byzantine years, or, precariously, later still. Rambling across them, I no longer wondered to what civilization they belonged. The scene was too desolate for analysis. I was overwhelmed more simply by a sense of *vanitas* and the might of Time, by entire populations who farmed and traded and cut their rooms and graves carefully in the stone, and died unheard. The whole littoral, rocked in its silted quays and harbours, was like a chapter from Jeremiah.

Near the tortoise-shaped rocks of Khelones I found the Roman launching-slip which Hogarth had discovered, lying a few feet under the sea. From here a road cuts inland for Rizokarpaso, the last town of the peninsula. Some of its people show evidence of the vaunted Crusader or Venetian blood. Their pale skin or brown hair could be German or North Italian, and it is true that the women are more handsome than most. The heavy, sensuous look, which keeps its beauty too briefly, is gone; and for all one knows the blood of Nores and Nevill runs in their veins.

A few miles away, on the north coast, I swam round the harbour of ancient Karpasia. Within its different inlets the colour of the sea changes startlingly, here indigo, there ultramarine; and its eastern mole, whose hewn blocks were once clamped with iron, stretches for 370 feet. But sand has drifted over the remains of the city – founded by Pygmalion, bishopric of St Philo – which was smashed by the Arabs in A.D. 802. Sometimes its shards turn up in the furrows of the tobacco fields, with a few pillars battered to anonymity.

Five miles beyond, mediaeval churches showed the peninsular love of dressed stone and marked the site of Aphendrika. Hogarth identified earlier remains – graves, a quay, a citadel – with ancient Urania, but this is not sure. The only inhabitant left was a goatherd who had commandeered the vestigial gates and chambers of the citadel for his flock. Half a mile north-east, while climbing steeply inland, I discovered under scrub the remains of a battlement which I traced through thicket for forty yards. Six feet wide and built of heavy stones, it was, perhaps, a fragment of the city wall which Poliorcetes took by assault in 306 B.C.

By nightfall I was again over the spine of the Karpas – very low now – and descending to the southern shore, above whose darkness, like some enchanted symbol, a full moon hung. This was the last night of my journey, and was spent on so abrupt a hillside that at dawn, turning in my sleep, I rolled down chuckling with laughter into a clump of sage.

A road, even in this remote region, continues to the monastery of Apostolos Andreas on the cape. After so many days' quietness I was bewildered to find it streaming with traffic. Families from Famagusta – businessmen, coiffured daughters, black-swathed grandmothers – were driving to the monastery for their Sunday outing. Yet along the beach, and out of sight, the coastline was as solitary as before, its sands starred with campanula, and filled with teal and duck by freshwater pools.

But the monastery of Apostolos Andreas was crowded by a carnival of pilgrims. A giant square of beach-huts, as they seemed to be, accommodated visitors by hundreds. For St Andreas is a great miracle-worker, and this is the Lourdes of Cyprus. As early as A.D. 1191 a fortified abbey occupied the site, where Isaac Comnenus was brought to bay by the Coeur-de-Lion, and fell at his feet pleading not to be put in irons. Nothing is left of this abbey; but a fifteenth century chapel covers the healing wells, which in legend sprang beneath the feet of St Andrew as he landed on the shore.

The monastery would have remained obscure were it not for the well-attested miracle of a Greek woman, Maria Georgiou, a native of Cilicia. Her child was captured by Turkish bandits in 1895 and she despaired of recovering him. But seventeen years later St Andrew, she said, ordered her in a dream to petition him for her son's return at the monastery on the cape. While she was crossing in a boatload of travellers, she happened to tell her story to a dervish. He grew increasingly excited as she spoke, and finally asked her what distinguishing marks her child's body had borne. As soon as she told him, he threw back his robe to reveal on his chest and shoulder the birthmarks of her son – sold in Istanbul, educated as a Moslem – and fell into her arms.

After this the monastery of Apostolos Andreas received a torrent of pilgrims which swelled every year with rumours of healing miracles. Blindness, epilepsy, dumbness, limping – the saint is sovereign against them all. The monastery has grown hugely wealthy and philanthropic. In the narthex of its church I saw baptisms being carried forward with the drive of an industry; the font was equipped with hot and cold water taps and a shower; baby-admiration parties spilt into the aisle with christening cakes and candles.

Trailing round the walls and the iconostasis, suave businessmen, hoary peasants, sighing women, even a few Moslems – all kissed the icons or smeared their faces in lamp-oil for a blessing. They lifted up children clutching balloons and waterwings to kiss the paintings too, and even pressed the lips of the newly baptized there. Votive images in wax were piled about the windows – one of a pregnant woman, another of a cow left by someone who depended on milk, together with vast candles calculated to weigh twice as much as their donors – such figures and plinths as have represented the Cypriot worshipper before his god since a remote age.

'Old customs,' a deacon agreed. 'Traditional people.'

I asked him if he had seen anybody healed. 'I have,' he answered. 'Last year a paralysed girl came. She could barely walk or even unclench her hands. But she had dreamt that St Andreas had asked her to sleep a night in his house. Her parents took her to hospitals in Athens and London instead, but nothing could be done for her. So at last they brought her here, and I took her to the old chapel. It was quite late, already dark. Her parents had gone to rooms near the main building. She asked for an icon to be put on her breast, and that I should lay her on the floor near the altar – a complete cripple. But she was flushed, and convinced she would recover. I put the icon on her, feeling sad. She held it against her with her closed fists. Then I left.' The deacon paused and put a hand over his eyes, as if himself perplexed or cynical at what happened next. 'An hour later I heard a cry. I looked out and saw the girl walking fast up the path from the chapel. Her hands held the icon. A moment later she was running among the rooms of her relatives crying "I'm healed! I'm healed!" She was going like an animal, not quite upright, but almost. This I saw with my own eyes.'

Four miles beyond the monastery, at the tip of Cape Dinaretum, Cyprus ends. Walking above chalk cliffs, I sensed that the sea was closing in and that I was moving along a passage between its twin waters. In ancient times a temple to Aphrodite crowned the promontary. Goddess of the sea and protectress of sailors, she overlooked one of the most feared headlands of antiquity, and was worshipped here as a progenitress, although women were not allowed within sight of the temple.

Almost on the headland I reached the place where her acropolis rose – a greyed butte, emptied of divinity, and found nothing but two drums of column beneath it. Here, where the shores joined at the feet of the vanished goddess, the northern coast lay gentle and windless, and had left at the foot of the bluff a bay of beautiful, sulphurous blue. At the cape's tip dark slugs of rock were scattered eastward over the waves. These, called the Keys of Cyprus, wrecked many early mariners: men whom Aphrodite did not protect.

In Christian times she still haunted the cape, but cruelly. 'From the southern seaboard of Cilicia,' wrote Leonardo da Vinci on his journeys, 'may be seen to the south the beautiful island of Cyprus, which was the realm of the goddess Venus; and many there have been who, impelled by her loveliness, have had their ships and rigging broken upon the rocks that lie among the seething waves.'

The complexity of this goddess – mother, protectress, slayer, standing midway between Asia and Europe, instinct and order – is the complexity of Cyprus herself. The flux and blending of peoples, gods, ideas, tempers her every facet. Yet out of the confusion a quality emerges – a kind of battered Hellenism, pulled like a damaged statue from the earth of civilizations, its outlines softened by the East and dulled through distance from the motherland. But perfectly recognizable. For the spirit which most deeply formed the island was the triumph, however partial, of Greece.

The acropolis, as I climbed it, showed nothing but lavender and a summit filmed with bluish, wind-bitten stones. From here you may sometimes glimpse other lands – Turkey, Syria, Lebanon – but today, as on most days, the shrine of Aphrodite marked the end of the world.

Bibliography

Alastos, Doros. *Cyprus Guerrilla: Grivas, Makarios and the British*. (Heinemann, 1960).

Alastos, Doros. *Cyprus in History*. (Zeno, 1955).

Baker, Sir Samuel. *Cyprus as I saw it in 1879*. (Macmillan, 1879).

Balfour, Patrick. *The Orphaned Realm*. (Marshall, 1951).

Bannerman, David. *Handbook of the Birds of Cyprus and Migrants*. (Oliver & Boyd, 1958).

Brassey, Mrs. *Sunshine and Storm in the East*. (Longman, 1880).

Casson, Stanley. *Ancient Cyprus: its Art and Archaeology*. (Methuen, 1937).

Cesnola, Louis Palma di. *Cyprus: its Ancient Cities, Tombs and Temples*. (John Murray, 1877).

Cesnola, Louis Palma di. *Cypriot Antiquities in the Metropolitan Museum of Art, New York*. (Met. Museum Art, N.Y., 1903).

Chapman, Olive Murray. *Across Cyprus*. (The Bodley Head, 1937).

Cobham, Claude Delaval. *An Attempt at a Bibliography of Cyprus*. (Nicosia, 1929).

Cobham, Claude Delaval. *Excerpta Cypria*. (Clarke, Nicosia, 1895).

Cobham, Claude Delaval. *The Story of Umm Harám*. (Journal of the Royal Asiatic Soc., 1897).

Davidson, J. Thain. *Cyprus: its place in bible history*. (Hodder & Stoughton, 1878).

Delehaye, H. *Saints de Chypre*. (Imprimerie Joseph Polleunis, Brussels, 1907).

Desborough, V. R. d'A. *The Last Mycenaeans and their Successors*. (Clarendon, 1964).

Dikaios, P. *Khirokitia*. (O.U.P., 1953).

Dikaios, P. & Stewart, J. R. *The Swedish Cyprus Expedition*. (The Swedish Cyprus Expedition, Lund, 1962).

Dixon, W. Hepworth. *British Cyprus*. (Chapman & Hall, 1879).

Durrell, Lawrence. *Bitter Lemons*. (Faber, 1957).

Enlart, C. *L'Art Gothique et la Renaissance en Chypre*. 2 vols. (Ernest Leroux, Paris, 1899).

Enlart, C. *Les Monuments des Croisés dans le Royaume de Jérusalem*. (Librairie Orientaliste Paul Geuthner, Paris, 1925).

Enlart, C. *Villes Mortes du Moyen Age*. (Boccard, Paris, 1920).

Esin, E. *Turkish Art in Cyprus*. (Ankara, 1969).

Foglietta, Umberto. *The Sieges of Nicosia and Famagusta in Cyprus*. (Waterlow, 1903).

Foley, Charles. *Legacy of Strife: Cyprus from rebellion to Civil War*. (Penguin, 1964).

Forwood, William. *Cyprus Invitation*. (Garnstone, 1971).

Gjerstad, Einar; Lindros, John; Sjoqvist, Erik; Westholm, Alfred. *The Swedish Cyprus Expedition, 1927–1931*. 8 vols. (Swedish Cyprus Expedition, 1934–1956).

Hackett, J. *A History of the Orthodox Church of Cyprus*. (Methuen, 1901).

Haggard, H. Rider. *A Winter Pilgrimage in Palestine, Italy and Cyprus*. (Longman, 1901).

Harbottle, Michael. *The Impartial Soldier*. (O.U.P., 1970).

Hasselquist, Frederick. *Voyages and Travels in the Levant*. (Davis & Reymers, 1766).

Hill, Sir George F. *A History of Cyprus*. 3 vols. (C.U.P., 1940–52).

Hogarth, D. G. *Devia Cypria: Notes of an Archaeological Journey in Cyprus in 1888*. (Henry Frowde, 1889).

Hogarth, D. G. *A Wandering Scholar in the Levant*. (John Murray, 1896).

Home, Gordon. *Cyprus then and now*. (Dent, 1960).

Jeffrey, George. *Cyprus under an English King*. (W. J. Archer, Nicosia, 1926).

Jeffrey, George. *A Description of the Historic Monuments of Cyprus*. (W. J. Archer, Nicosia, 1918).

Jones, A. H. M. *The Cities of the Eastern Roman Provinces*. (Clarendon, 1937).

Karageorghis, Vassos. *The Ancient Civilisation of Cyprus*. (Barrie & Jenkins, 1970).

Karageorghis, Vassos. *Chronique des Fouilles de Découvertes Archéologiques à Chypre en 1968*. (Bulletin de Correspondance Hellénique. XCIII, 1969).

Karageorghis, Vassos. *Fouilles de Kition 1959*. (Bulletin de Correspondance Hellénique LXXXIV, 1960).

Karageorghis, Vassos. *Mycenaean Art from Cyprus*. (Department of Antiquities, Cyprus, 1968).

Karageorghis, Vassos. *Salamis in Cyprus*. (Thames & Hudson, 1969).

Lancaster, Osbert. *Sailing to Byzantium*. (John Murray, 1969).

Latrie, M. L. de Mas. *Histoire de l'Ile de Chypre sous le Règne des Princes de la Maison de Lusignan*. (L'Imprimerie Impériale, Paris, 1861).

Lewis, Mrs. *A Lady's Impressions of Cyprus*. (Remington, 1894).

Luke, Sir Harry. *Cypriote Shrines*. (Faith Press, 1920).

Luke, Sir Harry. *Cyprus: a Portrait and an Appreciation*. (Harrap, 1957).

Luke, Sir Harry. *Cyprus under the Turks 1571–1878*. (O.U.P., 1921).

Maier, F. G. *Excavations at Kouklia (Palaepathos), 1970*. (Report of Dept. of Antiquities, Nicosia, Cyprus, 1971).

Makhairas, Leontios. *Recital concerning the Sweet Land of Cyprus*. Ed. & trs. R. M. Dawkins. (Clarendon, 1932).

Mariti, Giovanni. *Travels in the Island of Cyprus*. Trs. C. D. Cobham. (Herbert E. Clarke, Nicosia, 1895).

Matthews, Ann. *Lilies of the Field. A Book of Cyprus Wildflowers*. (Zeno, Limassol, 1968).

Meyer, A. J. *The Economy of Cyprus*. (Harvard Univ. Press, 1962).

Mitford, T. B. and Iliffe, J. H. *Excavations at Kouklia (Old Paphos) Cyprus, 1950*. (Antiquaries Journal, Vol XXXI, 1 & 2, 1951).

Mogabgab, Theophilus A. H. *Supplementary Excerpts on Cyprus*. 3 parts. (The Pusey Press, The Zavalli Press, Nicosia, 1941).

Nicolaou, K. *Excavations at Nea Pathos. The House of Dionysos*. (Report of Dept. of Antiquities, Nicosia, Cyprus, 1967).

Ohnefalsch-Richter, Max. *Ancient Places of Worship in Kypros*. (H. S. Hermann, Berlin, 1891).

Ohnefalsch-Richter, Max. *Kypros, the Bible and Homer*. 2 vols. (Asher, 1893).

Papageorghiou, A. *Masterpieces of the Byzantine Art of Cyprus*. (Department of Antiquities, Cyprus, 1965).

Perrot, Georges & Chipiez, Charles. *History of Art in Phoenicia and its Dependencies.* Trs. & ed. Walter Armstrong. (Chapman & Hall, 1885).

Peto, Gladys. *Malta and Cyprus*. (Dent, 1928).

Pococke, Richard. *A Description of the East*. (W. Bowyer, 1745).

Purcell, H. D. *Cyprus*. (Benn, 1969).

Ravenstein, E. G. *Cyprus: its resources and capabilities*. (George Philip, 1878).

Riley-Smith, Jonathan. *The Knights of St John in Jerusalem and Cyprus, 1050–1310*. (Macmillan, 1967).

Rice, D. Talbot; Gunnis, Rupert; Rice, Tamara Talbot. *The Icons of Cyprus*. (Allen & Unwin, 1937).

Ross, Dr Ludwig. *A Journey to Cyprus*. Trs. C. D. Cobham. (Nicosia, 1910).

Sacopoulo, Marina. *Chypre d'Aujourd'hui*. (G.–P. Maisonneuve et Larose, Paris, 1966).

Schaeffer, Claude, F. A. *Enkomi-Alasia, Nouvelles Missions en Chypre, 1946–1950*. (Librairie C. Klincksieck, Paris, 1952).

Schaeffer, Claude F. A. *Missions en Chypre 1932–1935*. (Librairie Orientaliste Paul Geuthner, Paris, 1936).

Sitas, Amaranth. *Kopiaste: Cyprus Customs and Cuisine*. (Zeno, Limassol, 1968).

Storrs, Sir Ronald & O'Brien, B. J. *The Handbook of Cyprus*. (London, 1930).

Stylianou, Demetrios. *The Inner Life of Cyprus*. (Apollo Press, Nicosia, 1931).

Stylianou, Andreas & Judith. *Byzantine Cyprus as reflected in art*. (Nicosia, 1948).

Stylianou, Andreas & Judith. *The Painted Churches of Cyprus*. (The Research Centre, Cyprus, 1964).

Ussishkin, David. *Observations on the Architecture of the 'Royal' Tombs in Salamis*. (Palestine Exploration Quarterly, July–December, 1971).

Westholm, Alfred. *The Temples of Soli*. (Swedish Cyprus Expedition, Stockholm, 1936).

INDEX

COLIN THUBRON

To a Mountain in Tibet

'I would rather read Colin Thubron than any other
travel writer alive'
John Simpson

Mount Kailas is the most sacred of the world's mountains – holy
to one fifth of humanity. Isolated beyond the central Himalayas,
its summit has never been scaled, but for centuries the mountain
has been ritually circled by Hindu and Buddhist pilgrims. Colin
Thubron joins these pilgrims, after an arduous trek from Nepal,
through the high passes of Tibet, to the magical lakes beneath
the slopes of Kailas itself. He talks to secluded villagers and to
monks in their decaying monasteries; he tells the stories of exiles
and of eccentric explorers from the West. Yet he is also walking
on a pilgrimage of his own. Having recently witnessed the death
of the last of his family, his trek around the great mountain
awakes an inner landscape of love and grief, restoring precious
fragments of his own past.

'A master class in travel writing'
Sunday Times

'Exquisitely written... A heartfelt hosanna to the travails of
walking'
Irish Times

'This is a bold and brave journey, an elegiac book by a master
of prose at the height of his powers'
Evening Standard

VINTAGE BOOKS
London

COLIN THUBRON

The Hills of Adonis

A Quest in Lebanon

'An unforgettable experience'
Irish Times

For four months and five hundred miles Colin Thubron walked
the mountains of Lebanon, following tracks and rivers. His
journey was not only a survey of a remarkable country, but a
quest for the gods and divinities who held the secrets of death
and rebirth in the land's ancient cults. He visited almost every
place of cultural importance, and lived with the people along
his way, recording a country of outstanding natural scenery,
rich with a unique medley of races and religions. *The Hills of
Adonis* is both a travel book and a personal journal; for the
quest is a search for meaning, a reflection on faith and reason
and a poem on the joy and complexity of living.

'Adventurous, observant, modest, poetical, Mr Thubron is a
traveller after one's own heart'
Sunday Times

'He has the mind of a scholar, uses language like a poet and
has written a lovely mosaic of a book'
Daily Telegraph

VINTAGE BOOKS
London

www.vintage-books.co.uk